Lawyers before the Warren Court

University of Illinois Press *Urbana Chicago London*

Lawyers before the Warren Court

CIVIL LIBERTIES AND CIVIL RIGHTS, 1957–66

Jonathan D. Casper

© 1972 by The Board of Trustees of the University of Illinois
Manufactured in the United States of America
Library of Congress Catalog Card No. 74–186342
ISBN 0–252–00244–X

For my mother and father

Contents

Preface

This is a book about lawyers who argued civil liberties and civil rights cases before the Supreme Court of the United States, 1957–66. The decisions of the Court during the past 15 years, especially in the area of political and civil rights, have become the subject for intense national debate. Issues like racial discrimination, reapportionment, religion in the public schools, and law and order have deeply divided our society, and the Court has been one of the major institutional arenas in which these issues have been fought. There is a tendency, both in public debate and in legal scholarship, to focus upon the Court itself: to debate the merits of its decisions, to examine why the Court might decide cases one way or another, to talk about its decisions as though they were the products of the Court acting on its own. Clearly the Court is at the apex of the American legal system, and in some sense it is natural to focus attention upon it. Equally clearly, though, the Court does not act on its own. It is part of a *system* whose members include, among others, law enforcement officials, lower courts, and the legal profession generally.

Thus to talk about and understand the process by which the Court participates in national politics and policy-making, we must go beyond the justices themselves. This book looks at one group that participates in judicial policy-making: lawyers in private practice who argue before the Court. How they become involved in litigation, what goals and interests they are pursuing,[1] why they take cases up to the Court and provide it the opportunity to make important national policy—these are among the questions examined.

The material presented here is addressed to two related issues. (1) Given the fact that important and controversial decisions in wide areas of social and political concern emerge from the Supreme Court, what can examination of the lawyers who argued these cases tell us about the ways in which the cases reached the Court? (2) In addition to this essentially descriptive material, how can discussion of the behavior of the attorneys assist us in understanding more fully and in refining models of the judicial policy-making process? I attempt here both to provide information and insight into the characteristics of recent civil liberties litigation and to extract from this material some suggestions about judicial policy-making in general.

As in all such exploratory studies, to some extent many of the most important issues discussed are the furthest removed from the data at hand. Thus, for example, I will talk about trends developing in the process by which civil liberties and rights are argued at the appeals level. Moreover, this discussion will lead to consideration of the potential impact of these trends upon the general nature of litigation and the role of the Court in the broader society. These are extremely important questions, and I hope that the discussion of them is provocative even if it does not convince all who read it. But it must be kept in mind that much of what is asserted should be taken as suggestions and sometimes even speculations, not hard and fast empirical propositions established with the rigor many wish to attain in the social sciences. This tentative quality of some of the discussion may on the one hand be a weakness of the study; from another perspective, though, it represents the strength of exploratory re-

1. In discussing the goals and interests of attorneys who argue before the Supreme Court, some special terminology is developed, and some of the terms are the focus for much of this book. The definitions of the terms used are discussed in detail in Chapter 3. In addition, short definitions of some of the key terms can be found in the Glossary.

search, for it suggests new questions and ways in which they might fruitfully be the subject of further scrutiny.

If the reader takes nothing else from this study, I hope that it does convey the complexity of the judicial decision-making process, the limitations of exclusive focus upon the Supreme Court, and the importance of lawyers and the legal profession in judicial policy-making.

I am indebted to many for their help in conducting this research. The lawyers who are the subject of the study must accept my thanks anonymously and collectively. Their willingness to give up both their time and their privacy made my research possible. The personal kindnesses that many of them extended to me are also gratefully acknowledged.

I also wish to thank the American Bar Foundation and the National Lawyers' Guild for helping me to obtain the cooperation of many of the lawyers with whom I had contact. The National Science Foundation, the Brookings Institution, and Yale University provided the financial assistance necessary to carry out the research.

Many individuals provided me with valuable advice in analyzing my data and attempting to present my results in a coherent fashion. Special thanks are due Barry Casper, Douglas W. Rae, and Clement Vose. Finally, I am deeply indebted to David J. Danelski for his advice and encouragement, from the beginning of the enterprise to its end.

1. *Introduction*

As Tocqueville observed nearly 150 years ago, "Scarcely any political question arises in the United States that is not resolved sooner or later, into a judicial question." The controversy surrounding the work of the Warren Court[1] suggests that Tocqueville's point is still quite apposite, for both the praise and the vilification heaped upon the Court stem in large part from its attempts to help shape national policy in areas of intense social and political concern.[2] If one considers the issues that have torn our society in recent years—racial equality, the limits of dissent, law and order, regulation of public morality, the war in Viet Nam—only in the last did the Court fail to play an important role in focusing the issues and attempting to resolve them.

There can be little question that the legal system and especially its most prominent institution—the Supreme Court of the United States—plays an important role in public policy-making. Yet courts and judges differ from other political institutions and

1. Earl Warren became chief justice on 2 October 1953 and retired on 23 June 1969.

2. Critics of the Warren Court have dwelt upon its alleged overemphasis upon the rights of minorities at the expense of the wishes of the majority, its interference with the activities of coordinate branches of the federal government and with so-called "states' rights," and its general lines of social and political policy. For philosophical and legal criticism of the work of the Court, see Alexander Bickel, *The Supreme Court and the Idea of Progress* (New York: Harper & Row, 1970), and Philip Kurland, *Politics, the Constitution and the Warren Court* (Chicago: University of Chicago Press, 1970).

from those who participate in them in a variety of ways: the process by which members are selected, the criteria that influence the choices that are made, the ways in which issues are framed for decision, the forms of interaction with the public at large, the way in which decisions are translated into changes in behavior in the broader society. One characteristic of courts is of special significance: more than other political institutions, like legislatures, bureaucracies, or executives, courts are passive. They do not, traditionally, possess the power to place an issue upon their own agendas. Rather, they must wait for others to bring disputes and issues to them before they can attempt to participate in the process of resolving them. Thus courts must wait for "occasions for decision,"[3] provided by and often under the control of individuals and institutions who are not themselves members of the legal system.

Thus, to say that most or all significant political disputes in our society eventually come before the courts encompasses a complex series of activities worthy of attention. Granted that the Supreme Court makes important public policy decisions, how do such issues manage to make their way into the legal system in the first place and then through the long, arduous, and expensive winnowing process that eventually results in decision by the Court?[4] This book examines the activity of one group of participants in this process: lawyers in private practice who argued civil liberties and civil rights cases decided with opinion by the

3. This phrase is suggested by the approach of Richard S. Wells and Joel B. Grossman, "The Concept of Judicial Policy-Making: A Critique," *Journal of Public Law* 15 (1966): 286–310.

4. As a result of the Judiciary Act of 1925, the Supreme Court has almost complete discretion over its docket and hence can refuse to decide cases that it does not wish to hear. The Court's own Rule 19 states, "A review on writ of certiorari is not a matter of right, but of sound judicial discretion and will be granted only where there are special and important reasons therefor" 398 U.S. 1030 (1970). Since the bulk of cases that come to the Court for review come via the writ of *certiorari*, the Court can and does duck issues that it does not wish to hear and choose those cases that it wants to decide. For a discussion of the types of cases the Court is likely to hear, see Joseph Tanenhaus et al., "The Supreme Court's Certiorari Jurisdiction: Cue Theory," in Glendon Schubert, ed., *Judicial Decision-Making* (Glencoe, Ill.: Free Press, 1963), pp. 55–78. For a discussion of the activities of the justices of the Supreme Court, see Henry M. Hart, "Foreword: The Time Chart of the Justices," *Harvard Law Review* 73 (1959): 84–125.

Supreme Court during the years 1957–66. How did these lawyers become involved in their litigation? What motivations led them to pursue their cases to the Supreme Court? What kinds of goals were they pursuing in their cases? What does the comparison of the goals of the attorneys with the outcomes in their cases suggest about the nature of judicial policy-making? What trends appear to be developing in the characteristics and goals of lawyers who are involved in civil liberties litigation?

Initial impressions about the answers to some of these questions—how lawyers become involved in cases, why they carry them through the appeals process, what they are trying to accomplish—occur quickly. Lawyers are retained by clients (or appointed by courts to defend indigents), appeal cases because they have lost at the lower level, and are trying to vindicate the interests of their clients. All of us have these images of lawyers. All who have had any contact with lawyers realize that these traditional images don't go very far in capturing the complex motivations that surround the activities of lawyers. They are men, like the rest of us, not automatons programmed to perform a service. One of the things this study will do is to explore more closely how the lawyers under consideration actually did behave, what kinds of preferences and goals motivated them.

Permitting a few of the lawyers to speak briefly for themselves will give a bit of the flavor of the complexity surrounding what appears on the surface to be a simple process—serving a client.[5]

To be blunt about it, the real reason why . . . was because I wanted to win. I wanted to score because this is just an emotional thing with me—I can't stand to get beat. It drives me crazy. I not only wanted to win, I wanted to be noticed, and the desire to win and the desire to be noticed as a good attorney who has done something outstanding was the basis for the whole thing. Which doesn't mean it was incorrect or ill-founded. And sure there was some altruism in it, but altruism is not what makes the world go round. And it didn't make anything happen in the "Smith" case. [52]

5. Because of assurances of anonymity given to the lawyers interviewed, the attorneys quoted are not identified by name. The number in brackets following each quote is an identification number assigned to each attorney.

I was very worried about it and I prayed. I prayed the Lord would give me wisdom. And all that kept coming back in my mind was, "jurisdiction, jurisdiction."

Why did I do it? Well, the Lord told me to do it. I just definitely felt it was the Lord's will. It was the Lord's will and though it didn't turn out as I had expected [the defendant committed suicide after his release from prison], I had prayer with him out there at Alcatraz. [62]

You know, when you get down to writing deeds and mortgages and contracts about the sale of a tamale stand—you know, what the hell—there's no excitement in that for me. And I think a lot of lawyers, a lot of ACLU lawyers are not motivated entirely by just a pure love of wanting to do right. A lot of them take these cases because the general practice of law bores the hell out of them. [7]

We shall see that different recruitment patterns predominated in different areas of litigation. For example, interest groups were important in the provision of counsel in civil rights and some loyalty-security cases; court appointment provided attorneys for many of the criminal justice cases that eventually reached the Court; ideology and friendship relations provided important ties between lawyer and client in many loyalty-security and reapportionment cases.

Lawyers with quite different goals and perceptions of the importance of their cases participated in the litigation discussed here. Some lawyers (to be called *Advocates*) were simply interested in winning their cases, regardless of the potential social or political ramifications that might be implicit in their cases. Another group of lawyers (to be called *Group Advocates*) viewed their cases as representing the interests not simply of individual clients but of groups (e.g., racial, political) with whom they felt long-term personal or ideological ties. Finally, many of the cases were argued by lawyers (to be called *Civil Libertarians*) who were interested in using their cases as vehicles by which broad democratic principles might be vindicated, not in the interest of an individual or group, but for all of society. These types of attorneys predominated in different areas of litigation. Most criminal cases were argued by Advocates; the civil rights, reapportionment, and early loyalty-security cases were argued by Group Advocates; the loyalty-oath and some criminal justice cases were argued by Civil Libertarians.

Litigation in all of these areas produced decisions with important social and political consequences. Examination of the contrasting goals of the attorneys and the outcomes suggests that different models of judicial policy-making apply to different areas of litigation.[6] In the criminal cases many of the important decisions were the unintended by-product of the activities of attorneys who provided the Court with occasions to make policy but who were themselves relatively uninterested in policy. The reapportionment and loyalty-oath cases resemble more closely our image of the "test" case: the attorneys initiated and pursued the cases with particular goals in mind and were largely successful in vindicating these principles in the Supreme Court. Many of the loyalty-security and sit-in cases were pursued by lawyers with broad policy goals but produced decisions of limited application.

Thus to understand the process of judicial policy-making, we must not only look at the Court itself—at the goals of the justices—and at the implementation process.[7] The recruitment and goals of the lawyers who provide the Court with the opportunity to decide these issues are also important aspects of judicial policy-making. It is important to place these lawyers in the broader context of the judicial policy-making process. In any particular case a vast number of individuals—private citizens, public officials, members of interest groups—play important roles in the policy-making process.

Any court case, whether it eventually reaches the Supreme Court of the United States or ends with an out-of-court settle-

6. For an introduction to differing views of the judicial policy-making process, see Herbert Jacob, *Justice in America* (Boston: Little, Brown, 1965); Glendon Schubert, *Judicial Policy-Making* (Glenview, Ill.: Scott, Foresman, 1965); and Wells and Grossman, "Concept of Judicial Policy-Making."

7. The question of what happens after the Court decides a case is treated in a growing body of literature dealing with the "impact" of Supreme Court decisions. For examples and reviews of this literature, see Theodore L. Becker, ed., *The Impact of Supreme Court Decisions* (New York: Oxford University Press, 1969), and Stephen L. Wasby, *The Impact of the United States Supreme Court: Some Perspectives* (Homewood, Ill.: Dorsey Press, 1970).

ment before it even goes to trial in the lowest court, begins with some dispute among individuals. Since we here deal with public law—with the relationships between the citizen and his government—most of the cases we discuss involve a dispute between a citizen and some institution of government. The case may begin, as most criminal cases do, with the government moving against a citizen, arresting and charging him with a crime. Or, as in the reapportionment cases, citizens may be dissatisfied with some policy being pursued by the government and decide to attempt to change these policies.[8] In any event, every case begins with some dispute or dissatisfaction. Quite early in the proceeding members of the legal profession are likely to become involved— private attorneys representing citizens, public attorneys representing the state. Thus, even before a case first goes to court, a substantial number of participants are likely to have become involved—police officers, members of legislative investigating committees, school-board officials, dissatisfied private citizens and their attorneys, and public attorneys representing the state. In addition, in many of the cases to be considered here, interest groups like the National Association for the Advancement of Colored People or the American Civil Liberties Union were important in putting citizen in contact with lawyer or in recruiting citizens to become parties to litigation.

A case then comes to court for the first time. A new group of participants becomes actively involved—the judge, his clerks, and the other personnel of the court system. A loser in the lower court may choose to leave the matter as it is, and the case will be over (which is the fate of the vast majority of all court cases). Or he may, should he choose, pursue the case higher up the

8. Though the categories become somewhat fuzzy at the margins, it may be useful to distinguish between "offensive" and "defensive" litigation. Offensive litigation begins at the behest of parties who wish to obtain a desired policy outcome through litigation: the policy or constitutional issues are apparent from the beginning. Defensive litigation begins at the behest of the government, as in the typical criminal prosecution. Broad issues emerge as the defendant attempts to use constitutional rights as a defense against the government's attempt to convict and punish him. Cases involving civil disobedience lie somewhere between these two categories, for the defendant may violate the law with the intention of testing its constitutionality, though the actual legal proceeding begins at the behest of the government.

appeals ladder. Again, since appeals require attorneys, time for preparation, and money for fees and preparation of briefs, interest groups may be crucial in the decision about whether to let a case die or to pursue it.

If a case is appealed, the personnel of the higher courts become involved. In the federal system the appeal from the lowest court (the district court) goes to the circuit court of appeals having jurisdiction over the district court. In most state systems appeals from trial courts go to the state supreme court.[9] The first appeal may involve changes in the attorneys for the state, for specialized agencies may represent the state in appeals courts, and the private citizen may also change attorneys.

The loser in the appeals court (whether circuit court of appeals or state supreme court) may then decide to appeal his case to the Supreme Court of the United States. Here, again, much winnowing occurs, for most cases are not appealed from the highest appeals court to the Supreme Court. If the loser chooses to appeal, he must prepare his request to the Supreme Court of the United States to hear his case. The Court has great discretion in deciding which cases to hear, and only 10–15 percent of these requests in any year will be granted.

Again, more participants become active. The justices of the Supreme Court and their clerks and administrative personnel must process the request for a hearing (most commonly a petition for *certiorari*) and decide whether they wish to grant it. And, again, the cast of lawyers may change. One private attorney may be replaced by another with more experience before the Supreme Court. Specialized appeals attorneys employed by the state, or the Solicitor General's Office in the federal system, may take over the case for the government.

If the request to be heard is granted, the case is then briefed and argued before the Supreme Court. Interest groups may attempt to enter the process formally, to file briefs *amicus curiae*, acting as "friend of the court" to urge one side or another. The justices of the Court will read the briefs, hear the oral arguments,

9. About a third of the states have intermediate courts of appeal between the trial court and the state supreme court.

and decide the case after conferring with one another and voting. They may issue an opinion or decide the case *per curiam,* simply ordering reversal or affirmance of the lower court decision without providing a detailed argument about their reasons for doing so. Justices disagreeing with the majority may issue dissenting opinions, and those agreeing with the result reached by the majority but for different reasons may issue concurring opinions.

Once the case is decided by the Court, it is sent back to the court from which it came. If the lower court has been affirmed, its decision stands. If its decision has been reversed in part or altogether, it is ordered to reconsider the case in light of the holding of the Supreme Court. The case then makes its way back down the same system it made its way up. Again, many individuals are involved, both lower court judges and the public officials (e.g., prison officials, police officers, members of a school board or legislature) whose conduct must change to conform to the Supreme Court ruling.

There is a common tendency to talk about the Supreme Court's doing this or that, but one must understand that both the opportunity for the Court to make a choice in the first place and the translation of its policy (or the failure of its policy to be carried out) are the products of a complex series of activities of a large number of participants in judicial policy-making.

Consider, for a moment, some of the most salient and important decisions of the Warren Court: *Brown v. Board of Education,*[10] which held that legal segregation of students in public schools was unconstitutional; *Miranda v. Arizona,*[11] which set forth rules governing custodial interrogation of suspects by police officers; *Reynolds v. Sims,*[12] which held that both houses of a state legislature must be apportioned on the basis of equal population districts; and *Abington Township v. Schempp,*[13] which held that the reading of the Bible in devotional services in public schools violated the provisions of the First Amendment. These

10. 347 U.S. 483 (1954).
11. 384 U.S. 436 (1966).
12. 377 U.S. 533 (1964).
13. 374 U.S. 203 (1963).

decisions have been the object of both criticism and applause. Much of the rhetoric and thinking has concentrated upon the Supreme Court: it went too far, it didn't go far enough, it interfered with the rightful activities of police officers, it violated the rights of states, it moved to protect the rights of oppressed minorities. But to focus exclusively upon the Court is to ignore the complexity of the process by which it attempts to fashion policy and to some extent imputes to it powers that it really doesn't possess.

The Court could never have made any of the policy suggested above unless a basic dispute existed in the first place and wound up in a lower court. The Court could not have decided these cases unless some individuals or groups in the society cared enough about the issue to pursue it up the appeals ladder, a process that often takes years and costs many thousands of dollars. Tens of thousands of cases die somewhere in the system for every one that eventually reaches the Court. Some die natural deaths when one party or the other chooses not to pursue the matter further. Many others die each year when the Court refuses to hear them.

The survivors—those that are decided by the Court—survive for reasons: because people care deeply about them and because members of the Court think they are important and wish to decide them. It must be kept in mind that these reasons do exist—the justices of the Court do not typically reach out and simply decide that they *want* to make policy about police practices or racial discrimination or reapportionment or Bible reading. They are *presented* with disputes from the broader society and asked to decide them. They can and do duck some issues by refusing to hear them, but when they do decide, they are not acting alone but are participants in a process in which many others have acted before them.

It is equally important to note that the decision of the Supreme Court is in many ways the beginning rather than the end of a case. Decisions of the Court are not self-executing. Just as the activities of many are the precursors of a decision of the

Court—of providing it an occasion to make policy—so the activities of others are required if the decision of the Court is to make a difference, is to change behavior in the society. Ten years after the *Brown* decision a relatively small percentage of black children in the South were attending schools with whites; after *Miranda* many police officers continued to interrogate suspects without providing the warnings the Court said they should; some states have still not completed the process of establishing equal population districts; and Bibles are still read in some schools in this country.

Thus a decision of the Court—a policy choice made by a majority of the justices—does not insure that behavior in the society will change. Noncompliance occurs all the time, for officials and individuals whose behavior must change if the Court's policy is to be carried out may resist. In addition, as we are seeing today, concern about policy made by the Court may be reflected in the appointment of new justices whose notions of policy are different, and past practice may be changed.[14]

It is because people care intensely about issues that they eventually arrive at the Supreme Court for decision. It is because they care intensely that the decisions of the Court do not by themselves resolve issues. Policy about race relations, about police practices, about reapportionment, about the relation between church and state—all are highly political issues; they affect who gets what in society and touch upon deeply felt values of broad segments of the population. And for this reason these issues are never finally "decided," by the Supreme Court or by any political institution. Because people care, because their preferences may undergo changes, such questions as these are continually undergoing scrutiny. Policies are promulgated and then reconsidered. Policy made by the Court becomes the subject for further debate and disagreement in just the same way that the activities of other governmental institutions were the subject for

14. For example, a recent decision of the Burger Court dealing with the introduction of statements obtained without adherence to the Miranda rules indicates a less restrictive attitude toward such admissions than had characterized the Warren Court. See Harris v. New York, 401 U.S. 222 (1971).

the debate and disagreement that led to the lawsuit in the first place. We never resolve issues of this character. Rather, our institutions of government—the Court, the legislature, the executive, the public at large—continually provide approximations of answers, tentative decisions about how to proceed that themselves become the focus for further debate and decisions.

Thus judicial policy-making is complex and involves many participants. Further, the decisions made by the Court stimulate further consideration by those affected by them and by other political institutions. We never finally "answer" questions of civil liberties and rights. We continually provide partial answers which themselves are reconsidered and modified.

As Jeremy Bentham noted, "The law is not made by judge alone, but by judge and company." And the law, especially in areas as far-reaching as civil liberties and civil rights, is never finally "made" but is always in a state of becoming. The important activities of the Warren Court represent one significant episode in this process, and we will here focus upon one group of the "company" who helped the judges make law. As this is written, there are indications that some of the law they made may be changing as new justices come to the Court. A look at the past will, it is hoped, help us better understand the present and the future.

A few words about the methodology of the study will serve as preface to a more detailed presentation of the data. The lawyers discussed here argued civil liberties and civil rights cases decided with opinion during the years 1957–66. The period was selected somewhat arbitrarily, but it did include many of the most important civil liberties decisions of the Warren Court. Civil liberties and civil rights cases are defined for purposes here as those in which claims were made before the Court under the Bill of Rights (particularly the First, Fourth, Fifth, Sixth, Eighth, and Ninth Amendments) and the Thirteenth, Fourteenth, and Fifteenth Amendments. All of these provisions of the Constitution deal with democratic rights, defining relationships between the citizen and his government and setting forth limits upon the activities of both. Though some of the disputes over these rights may have involved conflicts between private parties (e.g., racial discrimination by a private restaurateur), a governmental unit was almost always a party to the litigation.

Identification of the civil liberties and civil rights cases decided with opinion by the Supreme Court during the 1957–66 period (and thus of the lawyers who argued these cases) was made by examination of the Supreme Court reports. In case of doubt (i.e., where the opinion involved a highly technical issue and it was not clear that a civil liberties issue was involved), the briefs were consulted. During the period a total of 263 cases argued by 212 lawyers were decided by the Supreme Court. A large majority of these lawyers argued only one case during the period, though a few argued as many as eight.

In analyzing the cases and the lawyers, a somewhat different classification was used. Five categories of cases were developed: loyalty-security (60 cases), criminal justice (97), reapportionment (12), civil rights (43), other (51). The nature of the issues in each of the categories and the kinds of decisions that emerged from the litigation are discussed in detail in Chapter 2.

In grouping the lawyers, other categories could have been used, for example, their occupational position or type of practice. They are grouped by area of litigation because the focus here is upon their role in judicial policy-making, and the categories are designed to discriminate different areas of social and political policy. Two kinds of data were gathered. A mail questionnaire sent to the universe of 212 lawyers who argued civil liberties and civil rights cases gathered data on the socio-economic background characteristics of the respondent, his current position, organization memberships, and public policy preferences (a copy of the questionnaire is included in the Appendix).

The primary source of data utilized in the study was a series of interviews (conducted between February and October 1967) with a random sample of 82 of these lawyers. The interview (the schedule is presented in the Appendix) dealt with ways in which the lawyer became involved in the case he argued before the

Court, the goals and strategies he pursued, and his attitudes toward the law and the legal profession.

An obvious yet important caveat must be entered at this point. This study deals with only a small segment of the legal profession and of litigation. Even within the group of lawyers who were active in and had an impact upon civil liberties and civil rights litigation in the 1957–66 period, we deal with only a small segment, for a great deal of litigation does not reach the Supreme Court.

The justification for this restriction lies both in the need for parsimony—for confining research to manageable proportions —and in the judgment that the most important litigation reaches the Supreme Court. This point is arguable, but given the necessity of restricting the scope of litigation considered, concentrating upon cases that reach the Supreme Court seems at least one reasonable way to do so. The Court's rules for granting *certiorari* suggest that those cases that reach the Court's docket are likely to involve important policy issues. In addition, examination of the major changes in constitutional policy developed in recent years suggests that many of the important issues have, in fact, reached the Court.

Thus, though there is justification for restricting the study in this way, it must be stressed that the group here studied by no means exhausts the lawyers who were active and important in civil liberties and civil rights litigation during the 1957–66 period. The lawyers who argued before the Supreme Court were a highly select group. They were, to some extent, self-selected, for they chose to carry their cases to the Supreme Court; they were also selected by the Court itself, for their cases were chosen from among the many petitioning for a hearing. This caveat has implications not only for the relationship between the lawyers discussed and the bar generally but also for the respondents and their successors who will come before the Court. In the course of the study reference is made to trends that may be developing in the civil liberties and civil rights bar. The size and relative selectivity of the sample must be kept in mind in evaluating speculations about the future.

The bulk of the study is divided into two parts. Chapters 2 and 3 are preparatory, providing material that is a necessary prelude to the presentation of the data dealing with the lawyers. Chapter 2 presents an overview of the litigation argued during the 1957–66 period. Though it does not pretend to be a complete account, it is designed to suggest the trends in Court decisions and to point out their political and social significance. The outcomes in the litigation are important, for their comparison with the activities of the lawyers provides insight into the judicial policy-development process. Chapter 3 presents some of the basic concepts—clientele, legal ideology, etc.—used in analyzing the activities of the lawyers.

Chapters 4, 5, and 6 discuss the major clientele types: the Advocate, the Group Advocate, and the Civil Libertarian. The discussion of each focuses upon the nature of the clientele being served, how each is differentiated from the other types, the factors that produced the clientele type, and the kinds of litigation in which each was involved. The implications of each clientele type for judicial policy-making, for lawyer-client relationships, and for litigation as a political activity are also explored.

The concluding chapter draws together the data and analyses presented and returns to their implications for an understanding of the legal process.

2. The Litigation

This chapter provides an overview of the litigation argued by the lawyers discussed in this study. The focus of the chapter will be upon cases decided during the 1957–66 period, but we will also allude to decisions by the Warren Court that preceded and came after this decade. The 1957–66 period was chosen somewhat arbitrarily and does not demark any particular era in Supreme Court history. But it was at the heart of the Warren Court, and during this decade many of the decisions emerged that history will mark as the most significant of Warren's tenure. The brief description here does not purport to be a complete account of the decisions of the Warren Court; the activity of the Court was so great that such an undertaking would be a book in itself.[1] Rather, this chapter simply attempts to present an overview of the kinds of litigation decided by the Court, to describe some of the distinctive approaches to civil liberties and rights that characterized the Warren Court, and thus to provide a context for the discussion of the lawyers that follows.

Before turning to the litigation proper, something might be said about the general political climate in the country during this period. During this decade America was in a hiatus between

1. For a useful discussion of the work of the Warren Court in various areas of litigation, see Richard H. Sayler, Barry G. Boyer, and Robert E. Gooding, Jr., eds., *The Warren Court: A Critical Analysis* (New York: Chelsea House, 1969).

two periods of political and social polarization. As the decade began, in the late 1950s, the nation was emerging from the McCarthy period, from an era of extreme anticommunism and fear of internal subversion and external aggression.[2] The fear that gripped the country during the late 1940s and 1950s really needs little recounting here, for it is sufficiently close for most to recall vividly. As the decade we consider here came to a close, a new kind of polarization was beginning to be felt. Viet Nam had turned into a major conflict, and large segments of the population had begun to express their dissatisfaction with the war. The latest version of the generation gap was becoming a salient feature of American political and social life, with the emergence of the hippies as social style-setters and the rumblings of serious discontent on the nation's campuses. Finally, the civil rights movement—during the early 1960s a symbol of hope and fulfillment of the American Dream—had become disillusioned, with the riots in the North, the death or waning of influence of the established nonviolent leaders, and the rise of more militant black leadership.

For those who believe that there are patterns or cycles in the process by which political and civil rights develop, 1957–66 were years of activism and progress, a decade in which the major thrust of the society was toward extension of basic rights and liberties, not repression and attack. Though people may disagree about the role that the legal system plays in this process—whether it merely reflects developments in the broader political and social system or is an independent force—there seems to be no question that litigation and the opinions of the Supreme Court were an integral part of this flowering of civil liberties and rights.

Many minority groups were, during this decade, granted pro-

2. For a summary of data dealing with public attitudes in the mid-1950s toward Communists and other political nonconformists, see Samuel A. Stouffer, *Communism, Conformity and Civil Liberties* (New York: Doubleday, 1955). For contrasting views about Senator McCarthy's motivations, activities, and impact, see the following: Richard H. Rovere, *Senator Joseph McCarthy* (New York: Harcourt, Brace, 1959); William F. Buckley and L. Brent Bozell, *McCarthy and His Enemies* (New York: Henry Regnery, 1954); and Roy Cohn, *McCarthy: His Side of the Story* (New York: New American Library, 1968). Striking visual evocations of McCarthy can be found in two films by Emile De Antonio, *Point of Order* and *Charge and Countercharge*.

tections they had not before enjoyed. The blacks are, of course, the group that first comes to mind. Beginning with the *Brown* decision in 1954,[3] many of the forms of racial discrimination that permeated our society were attacked, if not eliminated. But this was not the only group whose rights were extended. Freedoms of political thought, belief, and association—especially for those of a radical persuasion—that had been under attack during the McCarthy period were to some extent expanded. The Court, in the past somewhat reluctant to interfere with the activities of the fearful majority, stepped in and began to put on the brakes. Another minority decidedly outside the mainstream of American social and political life—individuals accused of crime—was also the subject of important constitutional policy changes. Finally, the poor—what Michael Harrington has called the "other America"—were "discovered," and some first steps were taken toward ameliorating their condition and protecting their rights.[4]

Thus, if it is fair to characterize both a decade and a nation, the 1957–66 period was one in which the dominant trends in our society were toward equality and freedom. Litigation and the decisions of the Supreme Court of the United States were an integral part of this societal movement. What the future will bring is in doubt. Changes in the personnel of the Court and in administrations in Washington, the perhaps inevitable reaction of the majority that things have "gone too far," the changing character of the leadership of groups recently admitted to the political process, the movement from petitioning to demanding—all of these make the future hard to predict. But it does seem fair to say that the 1957–66 period was an important one in our legal and political history, that issues swept under the rug for too long—issues, as Chief Justice Warren has said, that were put off for future generations—were grappled with, though not resolved.

This study deals with four major areas of litigation: loyalty-security, criminal justice, reapportionment, and civil rights. In discussing each, the substantial changes in doctrine that emerged

3. Brown v. Board of Education, 347 U.S. 483 (1954).
4. Michael Harrington, *The Other America* (New York: Macmillan, 1963).

from the Warren Court are emphasized. In addition, some attention is paid to the particular political and social conditions that surrounded and provided a context for the litigation and the doctrinal change that emerged from it.

Litigation was an integral part of the political process during the period under consideration. The typical image of litigation as a conflict-resolving process, a mechanism for settling overt disputes between particular parties, may be by now simply a straw man. Civil liberties litigation before the Warren Court clearly did not perform only this limited and traditional function. It affected broad segments of the American polity, far beyond those involved as parties in particular disputes. The courts served as a forum in the broader political process in which groups denied access in other arenas got a hearing, and sometimes got their way.

That is, the litigation served not only to win cases but also to raise issues. In a sense it was as much a conflict-generating as a conflict-resolving process. This is not to say that the conflict that emerged after judicial decisions did not exist before. But the ability of issues to get a hearing in the judicial arena in a sense forced them into the open in other political arenas (and sometimes in the streets). Thus the importance of the litigation was not simply that, for example, segregation was declared unconstitutional, the accused were granted some rights, or legislative malapportionment was declared to violate the equal-protection clause of the Fourteenth Amendment. The Supreme Court can decide such matters in a doctrinal sense, but it cannot by itself resolve the basic clash of interests and groups that underlies such issues. What the Court can and did do was to insure that these basic political issues were placed upon the agendas of other political institutions.[5]

It is in this sense that the decisions were conflict-generating, were the catalyst by which a great deal of turmoil smoldering beneath the surface of the political system became the subject of open conflict. In this sense the Supreme Court during the 1957–

5. As reporter John MacKenzie suggests, "The Court's decisions are the start of an argument more often than they are the final, definitive word on a given subject." John P. MacKenzie, "The Warren Court and the Press," in Sayler, Boyer, and Gooding, eds., *The Warren Court*, p. 113.

66 period played a crucial role not only in beginning the process of extension of constitutional rights to minority groups but also as an institution important to the operation of the American political system.

LOYALTY-SECURITY LITIGATION

The loyalty-security litigation was very much the product of its time. Both the government programs that produced litigation and the climate that surrounded the cases themselves reflected the hostility and intolerance of a society filled with fear for the continued existence of its institutions. Though many questioned how much of the threat was real and how much was the product of entrepreneurial politicians who had found a readily marketable and exploitable issue, there can be no question that most Americans feared Communists.[6]

The wave of concern with subversive activities emerged in this country after World War II, when our erstwhile ally, Russia, suddenly became our enemy. Concern over internal subversion, exploited most notably by figures like Senator Joseph McCarthy of Wisconsin, reached its high point in the early 1950s.[7] This concern led to the institution of a number of governmental programs designed to protect against internal subversion. Such programs included federal antisubversive statutes (e.g., the Smith

6. See Stouffer, *Communism.* The following poll data indicate the degree of intolerance of Communists that developed in this country:

Should membership in the Communist party be forbidden by law?

Percentage of Respondents Saying "Yes"	Date of Survey	Survey
70.0	3/49	AIPO #438
78.4	12/50	AIPO #469
74.4	9/53	MINN #120

Should members of the Communist party be allowed to speak on the radio?

Percentage of Respondents Saying "No"	Date of Survey	Survey
43.7	3/46	NORC 49/141
57.3	4/48	NORC 75/157
73.2	1/54	NORC 136/351
75.5	1/56	NORC 150/382
75.1	4/57	NORC 156/404

7. When many of the important cases decided by the Supreme Court during the 1957–66 period were initiated.

and McCarran acts) and their analogues in the states, federal
and state employee screening programs and loyalty oaths, and
extensive investigative activities by federal and state legislative
committees.[8]

The potential constitutional infirmities of these loyalty-
security programs were manifest, and litigation was inevitable.
Many of the "subversive activities" that the government attempted to deal with involved speech, thought, and association.
Many of the legislative investigations appeared to be aimed at
exposure and punishment through publicity rather than at legislation. The employee screening programs lacked procedural
safeguards that many observers felt were essential in any matter
so serious as that of establishing the "loyalty" of an individual.
Thus the programs raised important First Amendment and due-
process issues. The Supreme Court agreed to hear and decide
many of the cases produced by the rash of litigation challenging
various aspects of the loyalty-security programs.[9]

Perspective suggests that the loyalty-security net caught many
different kinds of people, ranging from hard-core political radicals (and perhaps revolutionaries) to relatively nonideological
liberals. One phenomenon of particular importance here is the
role of the bar in the litigation that took place. Briefly, it may be
ventured that a large segment of the American bar was reluctant
to become involved in this type of litigation. There was a tendency for the lawyer to be tarred with the same brush as his client,[10]
and the reticence was perhaps understandable.[11] Defense of po-

8. For general background material on government loyalty-security programs,
see Bar Association of New York City, Special Committee on the Federal Loyalty-
Security Program, *Report* (New York: Dodd, Mead, 1956); Eleanor Bontecou,
The Federal Loyalty-Security Program (Ithaca, N.Y.: Cornell University Press,
1953); and Earl Latham, *The Communist Controversy in Washington* (Cambridge, Mass.: Harvard University Press, 1966). Walter Goodman, *The Committee* (New York: Farrar, Straus & Giroux, 1968), provides an entertaining
history of the House Un-American Activities Committee.

9. For a useful discussion of some of the issues raised by the loyalty-security
programs and an account of some of the litigation, see David Fellman, *The
Defendant's Rights* (New York: Rinehart, 1958), Ch. 12.

10. See, for example, U.S. Congress, House Un-American Activities Committee, *Communist Legal Subversion: The Role of the Communist Lawyer*, 86th
Cong., 1st sess., 1959, H. Rept. 41.

11. See Milnor Alexander, "The Right to Counsel for the Politically Un-

litical offenders thus devolved during the 1950s upon a small group of lawyers willing to become involved in this litigation and upon the few interest groups who supported them.[12] Chapter 5 discusses in detail the characteristics of this small group of lawyers—who are called here the Radical Bar—and some of the reasons why they were willing to participate when so many other attorneys were not.[13]

During the heyday of the loyalty-security effort the Supreme Court appeared to be reticent about intervening and tended to legitimate the various loyalty-security programs that came before it. After the more virulent strains of McCarthyism had begun to wane, the Supreme Court stepped in rather strongly to put the brakes upon what many felt to be the serious constitutional abuses of the loyalty-security programs.[14] In the 1956–57 terms, especially, the Supreme Court struck down or restricted a number of aspects of the loyalty-security effort, including state antisubversive activities statutes, legislative investigations, the use of faceless informers, and passport and travel restrictions. The Supreme Court may have misjudged the change in the political climate, though, for there followed a strong reaction in Congress and a number of efforts to pass legislation both reversing the particular decisions and restricting the Court's power generally. Though these proposals did not achieve the extensive goals of their proponents (most failed of passage), the Court did pull back in the 1959–61 period, upholding activities one might have expected them, on the basis of their recent decisions, to have overturned.[15] In the later part of the 1957–66 period the

popular," *Law in Transition Quarterly* 22 (1962): 19–45, and Jack H. Olender, "Let Us Admit Impediments," *University of Pittsburgh Law Review* 20 (1959): 749–53.

12. E.g., the National Lawyers' Guild, the Emergency Civil Liberties Committee (ECLC), the American Committee for the Foreign Born, and the Joint Anti-Fascist Refugee Committee.

13. See also Jonathan D. Casper, "Lawyers and Loyalty-Security Litigation," *Law and Society Review* 3 (1969): 575–96.

14. Compare Dennis v. United States, 341 U.S. 494 (1951), with Yates v. United States, 354 U.S. 298 (1957), and Garner v. Board of Public Works, 341 U.S. 716 (1951), with Slochower v. Board of Education, 350 U.S. 551 (1957).

15. See Walter Murphy, *Congress and the Court* (Chicago: University of Chicago Press, 1962), for an account of the Supreme Court decisions of the 1956–57 period, the congressional reaction, and the Supreme Court's retreat.

Court stepped in once again, striking down many of the remaining vestiges of the loyalty-security programs.

Thus the Supreme Court vacillated a good deal, with the political and social climate of the nation no doubt accounting in part for their varying approaches to the loyalty-security cases. By the end of the period, though, they were once more consistently upholding attacks upon the loyalty-security programs. This was partly a reflection of the change in the political and social climate in the society, in which fears of internal subversion and revolution had diminished greatly.[16] Concomitant with these changes in climate, different kinds of lawyers became active in the loyalty-security litigation toward the end of the period. What had once been the almost exclusive province of a small group of lawyers—the Radical Bar—became in the later period the province of many more lawyers from organizations like the ACLU. In a sense this litigation became more "respectable," the issues less directly tied with radical activity (e.g., Smith Act cases versus state loyalty-oath cases), and the possible professional and social sanctions applicable to lawyers involved became much less severe.

To provide a flavor of the litigation argued by lawyers during the 1957–66 period in the area of loyalty-security, we will now discuss some of the litigation and the Supreme Court opinions in more detail. First, we will examine legislative investigations, perhaps the most publicized form of ferreting out supposed subversives.

Legislative Investigations

The first major opinion during the 1957–66 period dealing with legislative investigations appeared to be a severe slap at the activities of legislative committees in attempting to expose internal subversion.[17] Watkins, a union organizer, freely testified before the House Un-American Activities Committee about his own

16. Though the response of the government to current antiwar protests, student radicals, and black militants seems disturbingly similar to much that took place during the height of the anti-Communist movement.
17. Watkins v. United States, 354 U.S. 178 (1957).

past political activities, denying previous testimony of others that he had been a member of the Communist party but admitting he had cooperated with the party on a number of occasions. He refused, however, to testify about acquaintances whom he knew to have been members of the party but who were no longer members. He based his refusal upon the First Amendment (specifically refusing to rely upon Fifth Amendment self-incrimination grounds), stating that he believed such questions to be beyond the proper scope of the committee's activities.[18]

With only Justice Clark dissenting, the Court overturned his subsequent conviction for contempt of Congress. The majority opinion, written by Chief Justice Warren, was, on the surface, a sweeping denunciation of many of the activities of legislative investigating committees. While admitting that the power of Congress to conduct investigations is "inherent in the legislative process" and that such power is "broad," the opinion stated, "But broad as is this power of inquiry, it is not unlimited. There is no general authority to expose the private affairs of individuals without justification in terms of the functions of the Congress."[19] It went on to say, "Investigations conducted solely for the personal aggrandizement of the investigators or to 'punish' those investigated are indefensible."[20]

Since many observers of the legislative hearings into loyalty-security affairs were inclined to believe that punishment was in fact a major purpose of most investigations, and that personal aggrandizement was an integral part as well, the opinion appeared to go right to the heart of the legislative investigating process. Warren went on to note that the provisions of the Bill of Rights, including the First Amendment, were applicable to such investigations: "The First Amendment may be invoked against infringement of the protected freedoms by law or by law-

18. He told the committee, "I do not believe that such questions are relevant to the work of this committee nor do I believe that this committee has the right to undertake the public exposure of persons because of their past activities. I may be wrong, and the committee may have this power, but until and unless a court of law so holds and directs me to answer, I most firmly refuse to discuss the political activities of my past associates" 354 U.S. 185.
19. 354 U.S. 187.
20. Ibid.

making."[21] Further, "We have no doubt that there is no congressional power to expose for the sake of exposure."[22]

But when it came to actually deciding the case, Warren chose rather more limited grounds. Since the contempt statute required that a conviction be based upon refusal to answer a question "pertinent to the question under inquiry,"[23] the majority opinion reasoned that a question's pertinence must be made clear to the witness so that he could know whether he was in violation of the law or not. Citing the vagueness of the resolution authorizing the activities of HUAC[24] and the lack of explicit statements of relevance and pertinence by the chairman and committee members, the majority opinion held that the pertinence of the questions had not been made clear to the witness and therefore that his contempt conviction could not stand: "Unless the subject matter has been made to appear with undisputable clarity, it is the duty of the investigative body, upon objection of the witness on the grounds of pertinency, to state for the record the subject under inquiry at that time and the manner in which the propounded questions are pertinent thereto."[25] Thus, though the rhetoric of the opinion was sweeping, the actual holding was much less broad. The next major HUAC case decided—*Barenblatt v. U.S.*[26]—made clear how narrow the holding might be.

Barenblatt, an instructor at Vassar, was asked by the committee about his alleged Communist activities while a graduate student at the University of Michigan. He refused to answer, among others, questions about his own memberships, claiming that the

21. 354 U.S. 197.
22. 354 U.S. 200.
23. 2 United States Code, Section 192.
24. The House resolution (passed in 1938) authorizing the establishment of HUAC, Rule XI, defined the committee's authority as follows: "The Committee on Un-American Activities, as a whole or by sub-committee, is authorized to make from time to time investigations of (i) the extent, character, and objects of un-American propaganda activities in the United States, (ii) the diffusion within the United States of subversive and anti-American propaganda that is instigated from foreign countries or of a domestic origin and attacks the principle of the form of government as guaranteed by our Constitution, and (iii) all other questions in relation thereto that would aid Congress in any necessary remedial legislation."
25. 354 U.S. 214–15.
26. 360 U.S. 109 (1959).

committee did not have the power to inquire into such subjects, and he expressly disclaimed any reliance on the Fifth Amendment. In his appeal to the Supreme Court he argued that *Watkins* had in effect stripped HUAC of its power to compel this type of testimony because of the vagueness of Rule XI. The majority of the Court in *Barenblatt* (in an opinion by Justice Harlan) held that *Watkins* had been decided solely on the issue of whether the witness had been apprised adequately of the relevance of the questions asked him to the specific investigation being carried on. The Court in *Watkins*, Harlan argued, was dealing with Rule XI not in general but only in the context of that particular hearing.

The majority opinion went on to hold that there was nothing in legislative history indicating that the House did not approve of the committee's investigation of subversion in educational institutions and that, in general, Rule XI could not "be said to be constitutionally infirm on the score of vagueness."[27] The opinion noted that Barenblatt had made no objection at the hearing on the ground of pertinency to the questions asked of him, and that in fact the members of the committee had made the relevance of the questions to the subject under investigation quite clear.

In dealing with the constitutional dimension of the First Amendment claim, the Court adopted the approach of balancing the interest of Congress in gathering the information requested from the witness against the interest of the witness in remaining silent. Given what the Court asserted to be the nature of the Communist menace, the balance was struck in favor of the government, and the conviction was upheld.

Four justices (Warren, Black, Douglas, and Brennan) dissented from the *Barenblatt* decision. The major dissenting opinion (by Black) argued that Rule XI was so broad and vague as to void any contempt conviction. He went on to attack the balancing approach to the First Amendment, arguing his "absolutist" position that when the First Amendment says "no law," it means simply that. But even under the balancing test, he argued, the case had been wrongly decided, since the test should balance

27. 360 U.S. 122–23.

not just the individual witness's interest but also the interest of "the people as a whole in being able to join organizations, advocate causes and make political 'mistakes' without later being subject to governmental penalties for having dared to think for themselves."[28] Finally, he argued that the basic purpose of such hearings was to punish by "humiliation and public shame": "Thus if communism is to be made a crime and communists are to be subjected to 'pains and penalties,' I would still hold this conviction bad, for the crime of communism, like all others, can be punished only by court and jury after trial and with all judicial safeguards."[29] Thus the *Barenblatt* case suggests the widespread division on the Court in dealing with legislative investigations, with a sizable minority in favor of substantial restrictions upon the power of Congress to engage in such investigations.

The *Barenblatt* case was followed by a number of Court decisions dealing with legislative investigations. In most of them[30] the Court overturned the convictions of witnesses convicted of contempt, but never did a majority accept Black's position. The convictions were overturned on the basis of a number of technical issues, including defects in indictments,[31] failure to act upon a request for an executive session,[32] and failure to delegate power clearly to a subcommittee.[33] Generally, in the area of federal legislative investigations, the Court moved gingerly, overturning many of the convictions that came before it but never rendering majority opinions that went to the heart of the power of such committees to compel testimony.[34]

28. 360 U.S. 144.
29. 360 U.S. 160.
30. With the major exceptions being two 1961 cases, Wilkinson v. United States, 365 U.S. 399, and Braden v. United States, 365 U.S. 399.
31. Russell v. United States, 369 U.S. 749 (1962).
32. Yellin v. United States, 374 U.S. 109 (1963).
33. Gojack v. United States, 384 U.S. 702 (1966).
34. A pattern quite similar to that in the Watkins and Barenblatt cases emerged in state legislative investigation cases. In 1957, Sweezy v. New Hampshire, 354 U.S. 234, the Court overturned a contempt conviction for refusing to answer questions before the attorney general of New Hampshire, acting as a one-man investigating committee. The Court held that the authorizing resolution of the state legislature had not authorized the questions put to Sweezy, which dealt with some lectures he had delivered at the state university and with his general political activities. In 1959 in Uphaus v. Wyman, 360 U.S. 72, the defendant had been convicted for contempt after refusing to produce the guest list

Federal Antisubversive Activities Statutes

During the 1957–66 period the Court also dealt with two of the pillars of the federal government's loyalty-security program, the Smith and McCarran acts. In the *Dennis* case in 1951[35] the Court had upheld the conviction under the Smith Act of eleven prominent members of the American Communist party for allegedly conspiring to advocate the violent overthrow of the government of the United States. In rather broad language the majority opinion held that the government had the right to protect itself against such activities, even though they involved speech rather than actual attempts at overthrow. Distinguishing between "mere discussion" and "advocacy," the majority opinion stated, "Obviously the words [of the First Amendment] cannot mean that before the Government may act, it must wait until the *putsch* is about to be executed, the plans have been laid and the signal is awaited. If Government is aware that a group aiming at its overthrow is attempting to indoctrinate its members and commit them to a course whereby they will strike when the leaders feel the circumstances permit, action by the Government is required."[36] As the date of the opinion suggests, it was tendered during the height of the scare over internal subversion that gripped this country during the late 1940s and early 1950s. The Court returned to the Smith Act in 1957,[37] and, as in the legislative investigation cases of that year, attempted to pull in the reins a bit.

The *Yates* opinions are extremely complex and will only be briefly summarized here. Fourteen members of the Communist party had been convicted under the Smith Act just as eleven had been convicted in *Dennis*. In the *Yates* opinion, however, the Court overturned the convictions of five and ordered acquittal;

---

of a summer camp he ran that was suspected of being a "Communist front." The conviction was upheld by the Supreme Court in a five–four decision. The majority used the balancing technique and held that the state's interest in delving into subversive activities outweighed the probable invasion of freedom of association involved in production of the lists.

35. 341 U.S. 494.
36. 341 U.S. 509.
37. Yates v. United States, 354 U.S. 298.

for the other nine, the convictions were overturned and new trials were ordered. The conditions for conviction set forth in the Supreme Court opinion led the government to drop the charges against all of the defendants.

The majority opinion in *Yates*, written by Justice Harlan, tightened up the requirements for what constituted "advocacy" of overthrow. The Court held that mere abstract doctrine of overthrow was not sufficient, that there must be advocacy of action to that end. In addition, the majority held that the term "organize" in the Smith Act applied only to the creation of new organizations. Since the American Communist party was "organized" in 1945 and the indictment against these defendants was not returned until 1951, the statute of limitations had tolled and they could not be indicted. These holdings were sufficient to require reversal of the convictions of all fourteen, but the Court went further and examined the evidence against the defendants. In finding that most of the evidence produced (which generally went to the character of the party, not to individual acts) dealt with no more than abstract advocacy and teaching of forcible overthrow, the Court not only ordered acquittal of five of the defendants but made it quite difficult to prove violation of the statute for the others.

Thus *Yates*, like *Watkins* in the same year, restricted the power to abridge speech and association in the name of national security. But, as with the legislative investigation cases, the Court later reversed itself to some extent. In 1961 in *Scales v. U.S.*[38] the defendant was convicted not under the conspiracy provisions of the Smith Act, as in *Dennis* and *Yates*, but under the provisions making *membership* in "any organization which advocates the overthrow of the Government of the United States by force and violence" a crime.[39] Scales had been convicted by a jury charged that conviction required "active" membership in an organization (the Communist party) that advocated overthrow, in the sense of "advocacy of action" to accomplish the end as soon as possible, and that he must have been aware of this illegal advocacy and

38. 367 U.S. 203.
39. 18 United States Code, Section 2385.

have intended to bring about the overthrow as "speedily as circumstances would permit."

The Court upheld the conviction, construing the statute to require such active and knowledgeable membership. The majority opinion also held that such restrictions upon association and speech that might be the result of the application of the law were permissible under the First Amendment. In addition, the Court appeared to reinterpret the *Yates* evidentiary requirements, making them somewhat less rigorous. Thus the eventual demise of the Smith Act was not directly related to the rulings of the Court, for it has never been declared unconstitutional, and its major provisions are still operative. Rather, its disuse was at the behest of a government that apparently felt that it was no longer necessary to invoke it.[40]

The other major pillar of the federal government's loyalty-security program was the McCarran Act (the Subversive Activities Control Act) of 1950. Briefly, the act created the Subversive Activities Control Board and empowered it to hold hearings to determine whether various organizations were either Communist-action or Communist-front organizations. Upon such a finding, an organization was required by the act to register, providing information about its officers, moneys received and spent, names and addresses of members, a list of all printing devices in the possession of the organization, etc. Once an organization had registered, or a final order from SACB to do so had been filed, the organization and its members had to fulfill certain other requirements as well. For example, any publication of the organization sent through the mails had to be in an envelope indicating that it was being sent by a "Communist organization." It was likewise not entitled to a tax exemption under the Internal Revenue Code, nor were contributions to it tax-deductible. In addition to many restrictions upon employment of members of such organizations, members could not apply for passports or use ones they already had.

40. Though, as noted before, some of the indictments for recent antiwar activity (e.g., Spock and Coffin, the Chicago Eight) suggest crimes similar to those involved in the Smith Act cases.

In 1961 the Supreme Court upheld the constitutionality of the act against a First Amendment attack in a five–four decision.[41] But gradually thereafter, the major provisions of the act were declared unconstitutional. In 1964 in *Aptheker v. Rusk*[42] the passport provisions of the act were declared unconstitutional for being too broad. In banning passports to all members, the Court held that the act failed to take into account whether the individual knew and subscribed to the purposes of the party, whether he participated in its activities, whether the proposed trip was innocent, and whether he wished to travel to a security-sensitive area. In *Albertson v. SACB*[43] the Court overturned the registration provisions of the act. Dealing with an issue that it had refused to decide in the 1961 opinion, the Court held that the provisions of the act requiring individual members to register in the event the officers refused to do so violated the privilege against self-incrimination protected by the Fifth Amendment.[44]

Thus the two major pieces of federal legislation dealing with alleged internal subversion—the Smith and McCarran acts—were dealt with extensively by the Court during this period. The Smith Act cases, though skipping around a bit, resulted in the upholding of the basic statute, but it has atrophied through disuse. The other program—the registration scheme of the McCarran Act—was substantially emasculated by the Court.

Government Employee Screening Programs

Federal, state, and municipal units of government established programs for screening employees aimed at keeping disloyal individuals off the public payrolls and out of sensitive positions.

A number of cases grew out of municipal programs for dealing

41. Communist Party v. Subversive Activities Control Board, 367 U.S. 1. Recall that this was the same term in which the HUAC contempt convictions of Wilkinson and Braden and the Smith Act membership conviction of Scales were upheld.

42. 378 U.S. 500.

43. 382 U.S. 70 (1965).

44. In 1967, United States v. Robel, 389 U.S. 258, the Court struck down the provision of the McCarran Act that made it criminal for any member of an organization ordered to register as a Communist-action organization by the SACB to engage in employment in any defense facility.

with employees. In 1951 the Supreme Court upheld a loyalty oath administered to municipal employees in Los Angeles.[45] The oath required employees to swear that they did not and had not for five years previously "advised, advocated or taught, the overthrow by force, violence or other unlawful means, of the Government of the United States or of the State of California" and had not been members of organizations which did so. The program also required execution of an affidavit stating whether the employee had ever been a member of the Communist party of the United States and, if so, when. Holding that the affidavit was relevant to competency for employment, and reading in a requirement *scienter* (knowledge and intent) to the oath about memberships, the program was upheld.

In a 1957 case, *Slochower v. Board of Education*,[46] the Court overturned the New York City Charter provision that required automatic discharge of any public employee who invoked the Fifth Amendment privilege against self-incrimination to avoid answering questions relating to his official conduct. Slochower had refused to answer questions about his membership in the Communist party in 1940–41. The Court held that the application of the law to him was unconstitutional, since it was not clear that the questions he was asked were relevant to his competency to hold his position as professor at Brooklyn College. Differentiating the case from *Garner*, the majority opinion held that there must be a showing that the information sought was in fact relevant to the competency of the individual to hold his position, if the requirements of due process were to be met.

In three cases that followed, however, the Court came out on the other side. In the 1958 cases of *Lerner v. Casey*[47] and *Beilan v. Board of Public Instruction*,[48] municipal employee firings were upheld. In *Lerner* a subway conductor in New York City had been fired for refusing (on Fifth Amendment grounds) to answer a superior's question about whether he was a member of the Communist party. In *Beilan* a teacher in Pennsylvania had been

45. Garner v. Board of Public Works, 341 U.S. 716.
46. 350 U.S. 551.
47. 357 U.S. 468.
48. 357 U.S. 299.

fired for statutory "incompetency" because of failure to answer
a superintendent's questions about past Communist party activity and similar questions asked by a congressional committee.
In both cases the Supreme Court held that the construction by
state courts of terms like "competency" was not so unreasonable
as to be unconstitutional. By implication, then, the Court agreed
that such questions were relevant to the employee's fitness for
state employment.

In the third case, *Nelson v. Los Angeles*,[49] a social worker had
been discharged for "insubordination" for failure to obey a superior's instruction to answer questions before HUAC. The
employee's dismissal was upheld on the ground that he was
discharged for insubordination, not for the Fifth Amendment
claim, and that such discharge did not have a built-in inference
of guilt resulting from assertion of the privilege. The key to the
difference in the Court's treatment of the various cases appears
to lie in whether or not the state could demonstrate some interest
in gaining the information and in the relevance of it to state
employment. Lumping subway conductors, social workers, and
teachers together, the Court granted the states a good deal of
latitude in determining what was relevant and what was not.

Beginning in 1961, the Court moved against a variety of
loyalty oaths that were a condition for state employment in many
jurisdictions. The major grounds used by the Court in these cases
stressed the ambiguities and vagueness of the oaths and hence
their potential infringement upon protected activity. In *Cramp
v. Board of Public Instruction*[50] the Court overturned a Florida
oath that required teachers to swear that they had never aided,
supported, or abetted the Communist party. The Court held that
the oath was unconstitutionally vague, since terms like "aided"
or "supported" could involve such innocent acts as endorsing
candidates for office or writing in support of the rights of
Communists. A similar problem of potential overbreadth of
the statute was held in 1964 to render a Washington oath
unconstitutional.[51]

49. 362 U.S. 1 (1960).
50. 368 U.S. 278 (1961).
51. Baggett v. Bullitt, 377 U.S. 360 (1964).

In *Elfbrandt v. Russell*[52] the Court went even further, over-turning an Arizona oath that proscribed knowing membership in subversive organizations. The interpretation of the oath offered by Arizona courts made it clear that it was not intended to reach the protected activities alluded to in *Cramp*. The Court found the oath unconstitutional on the ground that its application could involve the firing of state teachers even if they did not subscribe to the unlawful ends of the organization (a reflection of the *Yates* doctrine). In 1967 the Court also overturned a New York law which made Communist party membership, as such, grounds for firing of teachers. Citing *Elfbrandt*, the Court held that the statute, because it did not permit rebuttal of the disqualification for employment on grounds of either lack of knowledge of the organization's intent or nonactive membership, was unconstitutional.[53]

A long line of cases emerged from the federal loyalty-security programs as well. Most of these cases did not reach the implicit constitutional issues, but were decided upon somewhat technical issues (e.g., whether or not an official was empowered to dismiss an employee rather than the broader issue of whether, assuming that he had been empowered to do so, he could constitutionally do it).

Perhaps the major decision dealing with constitutional issues came out of the Circuit Court for the District of Columbia, not the Supreme Court of the United States.[54] Miss Bailey, an employee of the U.S. Employment Service, was served with a series of questions dealing with her past membership in the Communist party and other organizations. She replied and denied the allegations of Communist party membership. She requested and was granted an administrative hearing in which she denied the charges and professed her loyalty. She also presented a variety of character witnesses. No adverse witnesses appeared. The Regional Board of the Civil Service Commission then found that

52. 384 U.S. 11 (1966).

53. Keyishian v. Board of Regents, 385 U.S. 589 (1967). A similar decision the same year overturned a Maryland loyalty oath: Whitehill v. Elkins, 389 U.S. 54 (1967).

54. Bailey v. Richardson, 182 F. 2d (D.C. Cir.) 46 (1950). Affirmed by an equally divided Supreme Court in Bailey v. Richardson, 341 U.S. 918 (1951).

"reasonable grounds exist for belief that [she] is disloyal to the Government of the U.S." This finding was upheld by the Loyalty Review Board, and she was dismissed. Clearly she was found disloyal on the basis of testimony by informers whom she had no opportunity to confront. The circuit court opinion, upholding her dismissal, argued that government employment is neither property nor contract nor liberty. Therefore, it concluded that "the due process clause [of the Fifth Amendment] does not apply to the holding of a Government office."[55] The opinion went on to reject her claim that the dismissal violated her First Amendment rights: "But the plain hard fact is that so far as the Constitution is concerned there is no prohibition against the dismissal of Government employees because of their political beliefs, activities, or affiliations."[56] The Supreme Court affirmed this case by an equally divided vote.

The Court dealt with a number of similar cases during the 1957–66 period.[57] In *Service v. Dulles*[58] the discharge of a State Department employee was overturned on the grounds that the Secretary of State, in ordering the dismissal, had not followed the procedures set forth in the department's own regulations.

In *Greene v. McElroy*[59] a revocation of a security clearance was reversed. The Supreme Court ruled that neither the president nor the Congress had given the Department of Defense authority to establish a program by which people could lose their jobs in proceedings in which they were not permitted confrontation and cross-examination of adverse witnesses. Warren, writing for the majority, suggested that when programs and proceedings *might* involve infringements of constitutional rights, explicit congressional or presidential authorization was necessary. The Supreme Court in a sense really ducked the constitutional issue, since the apparent authorization of such programs

55. 182 F. 2d 57.
56. 182 F. 2d 59.
57. Two federal employee screening cases occurring between Bailey and those discussed here include Peters v. Hobby, 349 U.S. 331 (1955), and Cole v. Young, 351 U.S. 536 (1956).
58. 354 U.S. 363 (1957).
59. 360 U.S. 474 (1959).

was as clear as it was in many areas in which Congress delegated authority to executive agencies.

In 1961 the Court again dealt with the loyalty-security programs in *Cafeteria Workers v. McElroy*.[60] Here a cook in a cafeteria had been summarily fired from her position at the Naval Gun Factory in Washington, D.C. The Supreme Court upheld this exclusion, arguing that naval regulations and history supported the right of a commander to summarily exclude civilians from his base. Thus, the Court held, there was no constitutional requirement for a hearing and a specification of grounds for discharge.

The Supreme Court treated employee screening programs somewhat gingerly, not reflecting the pronounced "activist" desire to intervene that is often said to have characterized the Warren Court. The cases were generally decided on nonconstitutional grounds, and the broad language of the circuit court in *Bailey* was never explicitly overruled.

In general, then, the Court followed a checkered path in the area of loyalty-security cases, intervening in 1956–57, stepping back in 1959–61, and then later reasserting itself. A shift in the kinds of lawyers who argued these cases and the clienteles they were serving is discussed in detail in Chapters 5 and 6.

CRIMINAL JUSTICE

The decisions of the Warren Court dealing with the administration of the system of criminal justice were among its most controversial. The decisions touched almost every aspect of the criminal justice system, from a suspect's first encounter with the police to his appeals to higher courts.[61] The major thrust of the decisions was an attempt to make the actual administration of justice in this country more closely approximate the ideals and values embodied in the Bill of Rights. There is an obvi-

60. 367 U.S. 886.
61. For a useful summary and evaluation of some of the major cases, see A. Kenneth Pye, "The Warren Court and Criminal Procedure," in Sayler, Boyer, and Gooding, eds., *The Warren Court*, pp. 58–77.

ous and perhaps inevitable tension between the need to appre-
hend and punish social offenders and the procedural values
embodied in the Constitution and in the conscience of a civilized
people.[62] The American system has in practice long appeared to
emphasize crime control over due process. The Warren Court
began the attempt to redress the balance, to reduce discrimination between rich and poor and black and white in the administration of criminal justice, to provide some practical import to
those protections and procedural safeguards putatively available
to defendants. Decisions of the Court are by no means self-
executing, and the reality of criminal justice today does not
meet the ideals expressed in the Constitution. Given the tension
between the values of crime control and due process, though,
the Warren Court did succeed in making significant strides toward more adequate protection of the rights of persons accused
of crime.

In addition to their direct effects upon the administration of
criminal justice, the decisions themselves became matters of
hot political dispute. They were held up as models of the kinds
of excesses in which some said the Warren Court engaged, of
the coddling of criminals, of the sacrifice of the rights of society
to those of the individual. The decisions, combined with a social
and political climate in which the rights of criminals were fertile
ground for political dispute, produced a "new" political issue—
commonly referred to as "crime in the streets" or "law and order."

In a sense, then, the criminal justice cases were a paradigm of
the conflict-generating phenomenon that characterized much
of the civil liberties and civil rights litigation that came before
the Warren Court. Court decisions did not simply resolve disputes between John Smith (accused) and the state, nor did they
only produce some new rules governing the conduct of law enforcement in America. In a sense they brought to the surface a
latent political issue—the rights of a group of citizens far out-

62. For important discussions of this point, see Thurman Arnold, *The Symbols
of Government* (New Haven, Conn.: Yale University Press, 1935), Chs. 6–7, and
Herbert Packer, *The Limits of the Criminal Sanction* (Stanford, Calif.: Stanford
University Press, 1968), Chs. 8–12.

side the mainstream of American social and political life. The decisions did not resolve the conflict between law and order and individual rights, nor did they make America live up to its ideals. But they did force other governmental institutions and perhaps a broad segment of the population at large to face up to an important "political" issue that before was very much beneath the surface of our lives. What the resolution will be—for the offender, for society, and for the Court itself—is still a matter of doubt. But there can be no doubt that the decisions have been vitally important and controversial.

The following sections treat briefly the decisions in a few selected areas of criminal justice: the right to counsel, arrest and interrogation, and search and seizure. The accounts give the outlines of the law before the 1957–66 period and describe the important steps taken by the Court during this decade.

The 1957–66 decade was characterized by two major departures in the Court's approach to issues of criminal justice. The first was a rapid increase in the pace of the process by which provisions of the Bill of Rights were made applicable to state proceedings. The second was an increased willingness by the Court to abandon a previously dominant *ad hoc*, case-by-case approach to issues of criminal justice, and to replace it with the use of individual cases as vehicles for the enunciation of broad guidelines for law enforcement officials.

Early in the nineteenth century the Court had held that the provisions of the Bill of Rights were applicable only to federal government activities, not to those of the states.[63] The passage after the Civil War of the Fourteenth Amendment, with its restrictions upon state action that violated "due process," opened an avenue for the application of the provisions of the Bill of Rights to state proceedings. Not until the twentieth century, though, did the Supreme Court begin this process of "incorporation"—including within the meaning of "due process" the rights specified in the Bill of Rights.[64] During this century the

63. See Barron v. Baltimore, 7 Peters 243 (1833).
64. The first case, incorporating the provisions of the First Amendment dealing with freedom of speech, came in 1925: Gitlow v. New York, 268 U.S. 652.

Court has gradually incorporated nearly all of these provisions.[65]

A major dispute has raged on the Court over the process of incorporation. One group, led by Justice Black, has argued that the due-process clause incorporates directly *all* of the provisions of the Bill of Rights. This view has never gained the adherence of a majority, and the Court has pursued a course of "selective incorporation," making the provisions applicable one at a time.[66] As noted above, the two positions have today arrived at essentially the same result, for the Court has by now "selectively" incorporated almost all provisions of the Bill of Rights. In any event, the 1957–66 period saw a very rapid incorporation of procedural safeguards that had not before been applicable to state criminal proceedings.

The second departure was the increased willingness to use individual cases as vehicles for broad policy-making. This change is described in detail below in the areas of right to counsel and interrogation. This change in approach is of particular interest for the discussion in Chapter 4 of the lawyers who argued criminal justice cases.

Thus the Warren Court not only made substantively important decisions in the area of criminal justice but also began to treat individual cases differently.[67] Now we may turn to a discussion of some of the litigation.

The Right to Counsel

The Sixth Amendment provides that "in all criminal prosecutions, the accused shall enjoy the right . . . to have the assistance

65. As of this writing, the only provision relating to criminal procedure not incorporated is the right to indictment by grand jury.

66. See, for example, the opinions by the majority and dissenters in Adamson v. California, 332 U.S. 46 (1947). See also Henry Friendly, "The Bill of Rights as a Code of Criminal Procedure," *California Law Review* 53 (1965): 929–58; William Crosskey, "Charles Fairman, 'Legislative History' and the Constitutional Limitations on State Authority," *Chicago Law Review* 22 (1954): 1–143; and Charles Fairman, "A Reply to Professor Crosskey," ibid., pp. 144–56.

67. As this is written, there are indications that the Burger Court is beginning to take a somewhat different approach to issues of criminal justice. For example, the recent decision in Harris v. New York, 401 U.S. 222 (1971), appears to undercut the celebrated Miranda decision discussed below.

of counsel for his defense."[68] The major legal issue in this century dealing with the right to counsel involved the provision of counsel to indigent defendants. Such a right has long prevailed in federal courts,[69] and the controversy centered around the obligation of states to provide counsel to indigents in their proceedings.

In the Scottsboro case[70] the Supreme Court first held that the due-process clause of the Fourteenth Amendment did include the right to counsel in state criminal proceedings. But the decision was limited to capital cases and stressed particular characteristics of the defendants and the offense: young, illiterate blacks accused of the rape of white girls in a hostile southern community. Though limited, the *Powell* case was an important milestone in the gradual process by which the provisions of the Bill of Rights were incorporated into the Fourteenth Amendment and made applicable in state proceedings.

The limited nature of the obligation of states to provide counsel in criminal cases was made clear in *Betts v. Brady* in 1942.[71] A majority of six justices[72] held that due process was not always denied when a state court refused to appoint counsel for an indigent defendant. Stressing that the requirements of the due-process clause were more flexible than those of the Sixth Amendment, the majority held that the question of whether denial of counsel amounted to denial of due process depended upon "an appraisal of the totality of facts in a given case"[73] (the test became known as the "special circumstances" rule). Characteristics of the case and the defendant were to determine whether the

68. For general treatments of the right to counsel, see Fellman, *The Defendant's Rights*, Ch. 7; William M. Beaney, *The Right to Counsel in American Courts* (Ann Arbor: University of Michigan Press, 1955); and Lee Silverstein, *Defense of the Poor in Criminal Cases in American State Courts* (Chicago: American Bar Foundation, 1965).

69. See Rule 44 of the Rules of Criminal Procedure for U.S. district courts.

70. Powell v. Alabama, 287 U.S. 45 (1932). For a detailed and fascinating account of this celebrated incident, see Dan T. Carter, *Scottsboro* (Baton Rouge: Louisiana State University Press, 1969).

71. 316 U.S. 455.

72. Over a dissent by Justice Black, who was 20 years later to write the opinion reversing Betts.

73. 316 U.S. 462.

state was constitutionally obligated to provide him a lawyer: his age, intelligence, experience, familiarity with courtroom procedure, the complexity of the case against him, the nature of the charge. Only in capital cases did the state have an absolute obligation to provide the indigent defendant with a lawyer.

A number of cases were subsequently decided under the special-circumstances test, each one turning not upon a general principle but upon the particular facts of the case. In 1958 one careful scholar of this area of the law characterized the current status of constitutional policy as follows:

The federal rule [regarding requirements for provision of counsel to indigent defendants in state criminal proceedings] comes to this: so far as the cases involving capital offense are concerned, the Fourteenth Amendment requires of state courts that they observe the strict rule prevailing in federal courts[74] by virtue of the explicit command of the Sixth Amendment. But in noncapital cases the absence of counsel vitiates the proceedings only if there were special circumstances present which resulted in injustice. The approach is a case-to-case method in which an attempt is made [by the Supreme Court] to weigh degrees of prejudicial error.[75]

But there were distinct straws in the wind pointing toward a more strict rule for the states. First, in 1956 the Supreme Court ruled it a violation of due process and equal protection for a state requiring a stenographic proceeding of the trial to be part of the appeal record to refuse to provide such a record free to those who could not afford to have one printed.[76] The Court asserted in *Griffin*, "In criminal trials, a state can no more discriminate on account of poverty than on account of religion, race, or color. Plainly the ability to pay costs in advance bears no rational relationship to a defendant's guilt or innocence and could not be used as an excuse to deprive him of a fair trial."[77] The potential relevance of this approach to the issue of providing counsel to indigent defendants was obvious.

74. The court must advise the defendant of his right to counsel and must assign him counsel unless he elects to proceed without counsel or is in a position to obtain counsel on his own.
75. Fellman, *The Defendant's Rights*, p. 117.
76. Griffin v. Illinois, 351 U.S. 12.
77. 351 U.S. 17–18.

In addition, the Court was using the special-circumstances test consistently in favor of defendants. Between 1950 and the *Gideon* case decision in 1963, not a single case came before the Supreme Court in which circumstances were found to justify a denial of counsel. Relatedly, though still deciding cases in terms of prejudicial errors that occurred, the Court appeared to be paying less and less attention to weighing the importance of the error in the determination of whether due process had been denied. The direction of the right-to-counsel cases and of other related cases was apparently pointed toward the view that the failure to provide counsel to an indigent defendant was itself a denial of fundamental fairness, and hence grounds for a new trial, and away from the *ad hoc* special-circumstances test.[78]

Finally, in 1963 the Court abandoned the *ad hoc* special-circumstances approach and adopted a broad rule requiring the provision of counsel to all indigent defendants in state felony proceedings. In writing the *Gideon* opinion,[79] Justice Black vindicated his dissent in the *Betts* case 20 years earlier. Concluding that the provision of counsel to indigent defendants in state proceedings violated the value of fundamental fairness embodied in the due-process clause of the Fourteenth Amendment, *Betts* was overruled. The Court also moved to grant the right to counsel to

78. Cases illustrating this movement away from close scrutiny of the degree of prejudicial error involved in a particular denial of counsel include Cash v. Culver, 350 U.S. 633 (1959), and Hudson v. North Carolina, 363 U.S. 697 (1960).

Hudson is a particularly interesting case. It was argued before the Court, as some others before it had also been, both on special-circumstances grounds and as a generalized attack upon the Betts rule. As one of the lawyers in Hudson indicated, "Well, I argued the thing on a pretty broad basis. I argued it on the basis of overruling Betts and Brady. I argued the same thing they decided finally in the Gideon case. But they weren't quite ready to go that far then, so they decided it on a narrow ground. It was almost identical with Gideon, about as close as you'd ever get one" [10]. After he left the Court, Chief Justice Warren suggested that though the Supreme Court does make important policy choices, it does not do so consciously: "It doesn't make [law] consciously, it doesn't do it by intending to usurp the role of Congress, but because of the very nature of the job." *New York Times*, 27 June 1969. The fact that the Court, after several opportunities, finally resolved the right-to-counsel issue, suggests that the Court's control over its docket and opinion provides it with a good deal more flexibility than Warren's remarks might imply.

79. Gideon v. Wainwright, 372 U.S. 335 (1963). For a fascinating account of this case, see Anthony Lewis, *Gideon's Trumpet* (New York: Random House, 1964).

defendants at other stages of the proceeding, both before and after trial. The Court ruled that under certain circumstances counsel must be provided at arraignment,[80] at the preliminary hearing,[81] at the first appeal of a criminal conviction,[82] and at a lineup.[83]

Thus the right-to-counsel cases proceeded from an *ad hoc* approach turning upon the circumstances of the particular case to the fashioning of a broad rule applying prospectively to all prosecutions. This movement is particularly important because of the way in which the Court shortly began to intertwine the right to counsel with the voluntariness of confessions, the next area of litigation to be discussed. Before moving on, though, it is worth noting that the right-to-counsel cases illustrate the movement toward a stress upon the value of equality—of removing discrimination based upon economic status—that was characteristic of the Warren Court generally.

Interrogations and Confessions

The decisions dealing with the protection of the rights of the accused against police attempts to obtain confessions were perhaps the most controversial of the Warren Court's work in the area of criminal administration.[84] As David Fellman points out, the Court had used essentially two justifications for banning coerced confessions: "On the one hand, a confession is bad if it is untrustworthy in the light of the confessor's power to resist the methods used to induce him to confess. On the other hand, a confession may be regarded as inadmissible if it was obtained by methods offensive to due process, without regard to the question

80. Hamilton v. Alabama, 368 U.S. 52 (1961).
81. White v. Maryland, 373 U.S. 59 (1963).
82. Douglas v. California, 372 U.S. 535 (1963).
83. U.S. v. Wade, 388 U.S. 218 (1967).
84. For discussions of police interrogation techniques and the notion of "voluntary" confessions, see the following: Fred E. Inbau and John E. Reid, *Criminal Interrogation and Confessions* (Baltimore: Williams and Wilkins Co., 1962); Yale Kamisar, "What Is an 'Involuntary' Confession? Some Comments on Inbau and Reid's *Criminal Interrogation and Confessions*," *Rutgers Law Review* 18 (1963): 728–59; and Yale Kamisar, "A Dissent from the Miranda Dissents: Some Comments on the 'New' Fifth Amendment and the Old 'Voluntariness' Test," *Michigan Law Review* 65 (1966): 59–104.

of the probable falsity of the confession. The first test is concerned with the danger of erroneous convictions, the second with the danger of tolerating uncivilized police methods."[85]

The line of cases dealing with station-house interrogation of defendants by state officers that culminated in the controversial *Miranda* decision began with more objectionable police practices, including use of various forms of torture and the third degree.[86] The state interrogation cases were not decided upon the application of the privilege against self-incrimination to state proceedings[87] but, rather, upon notions of "fundamental fairness" that the Court imputed to the meaning of due process.

The first important confession case was *Brown v. Mississippi*.[88] Mississippi police had used third-degree methods to extort a confession. The Supreme Court overturned the conviction, making it clear that the use of such a confession in a state proceeding violated the due-process clause of the Fourteenth Amendment. The Court clearly eschewed reliance upon the self-incrimination clause of the Fifth Amendment. In 1940 the Court again threw out a state conviction, this time in a case involving somewhat less obvious methods of coercion but including arrest on suspicion without a warrant, denial of contact with friends or attorneys, and long periods of questioning by different squads of police officers.[89]

A long line of cases followed, proceeding well into the 1957–66 period. As in the right-to-counsel cases, the Court had adopted an *ad hoc* rule for evaluating the admissibility of confessions in state proceedings. Commonly called the "totality of circumstances" rule, it involved an evaluation by the Court (or, at the

85. Fellman, *The Defendant's Rights*, p. 181.

86. There was also a similar line of federal cases based upon the Court's power to supervise federal law enforcement and interpret the federal Rules of Criminal Procedure. See, for example, McNabb v. United States, 318 U.S. 332 (1943), and Mallory v. United States, 354 U.S. 449 (1957). See also James E. Hogan and Joseph M. Snee, "The McNabb-Mallory Rule: Its Rise, Rationale and Rescue," *Georgetown Law Journal* 47 (1958): 1–46.

87. Indeed, the privilege was not incorporated against the states until 1964: Malloy v. Hogan, 378 U.S. 1. In two earlier cases, Twining v. New Jersey, 211 U.S. 78 (1908), and Adamson v. California, 332 U.S. 46 (1947), the Court had refused to incorporate the privilege against self-incrimination.

88. 297 U.S. 278 (1936).

89. Chambers v. Florida, 309 U.S. 227.

trial level, by the judge or jury) in each case of the circumstances surrounding the obtaining of a particular confession—the age and maturity of the defendant, the nature of the charge, the kinds of subtle or not so subtle pressures put upon the defendant, the length of interrogation—and an evaluation of whether its admission violated due process. Again, as in the right-to-counsel cases, when the 1957–66 period began, the Court was increasingly tending to reverse convictions using this test, though they had not ceased applying it. The Court ruled inadmissible confessions involving relatively sophisticated and "subtle" forms of coercion, such as long questioning and attempts at gaining the sympathy of a defendant via an old friend on the police force,[90] threats to bring in a defendant's wife for questioning,[91] threats to take away a defendant's young children,[92] use of a so-called "truth serum" upon a wounded suspect,[93] and refusal to permit a defendant to call his wife or lawyer during an extensive period of interrogation.[94]

Thus in 1964 three different doctrinal developments converged in the development of the rights of defendants during interrogation. First, as noted above, the Court had been sharpening its totality-of-circumstances test, using it to throw out increasingly subtle techniques for inducing defendants to confess. Second, the right-to-counsel cases, culminating in the *Gideon* decision of the year before, pointed to a possible combining of the right to counsel with the protection of the defendant in interrogation. Finally, the Fifth Amendment privilege against self-incrimination had finally been made applicable to state proceedings.

In the *Escobedo* case[95] the Court faced again the problem of an individual who made damaging admissions under interrogation, in this case after he had asked for and been refused time to

90. Spano v. New York, 360 U.S. 315 (1959).
91. Rogers v. Richmond, 365 U.S. 534 (1961).
92. Lynumn v. Illinois, 372 U.S. 528 (1963).
93. Townsend v. Sain, 372 U.S. 293 (1963).
94. Haynes v. Washington, 373 U.S. 503 (1963).
95. 378 U.S. 478 (1964). For a related development in federal law dealing with the relationship of the right to counsel and self-incriminatory statements, see Massiah v. United States, 377 U.S. 201 (1964).

consult with an attorney.[96] The Court overturned the conviction, saying,

> We hold, therefore, that where, as here, the investigation is no longer a general inquiry into an unsolved crime but has begun to focus on a particular suspect, the suspect has been taken into police custody, the police carry out a process of interrogations that lends itself to eliciting incriminating statements, the suspect has requested and been denied an opportunity to consult his lawyer, and the police have not effectively warned him of his absolute constitutional right to remain silent, the accused has been denied the "assistance of Counsel" in violation of the Sixth Amendment to the Constitution as made obligatory upon the states by the Fourteenth Amendment, *Gideon v. Wainwright*, and that no statement elicited by the police during the interrogation may be used against him at a criminal trial. . . .[97]

Though a big step, the *Escobedo* ruling, as indicated in Justice Goldberg's remarks above, was still couched in the particularized language of the totality-of-circumstances rule. Two years later the Court drew the lines of development alluded to here to their logical conclusion in the highly controversial *Miranda* decision.[98]

Miranda was actually four cases decided together, from New York, Arizona, California, and a federal case out of the Ninth Circuit Court of Appeals. In the *Miranda* opinion the Court attempted to answer some of the questions *Escobedo* had raised but not resolved. Exactly what rights did the defendant have? Was it a constitutional requirement that he be informed of them? Was the state obligated to provide an attorney if an indigent defendant undergoing interrogation desired but could not afford one?

The *Miranda* rules, based upon the Fifth Amendment privilege against self-incrimination (*Escobedo* had been based upon

96. An earlier case, decided the other way, had presented somewhat similar circumstances: Crooker v. California, 357 U.S. 433 (1958). Unlike Escobedo, though, Crooker was a more highly educated defendant and indeed had some law school training. For a detailed account of the Crooker case, see Barrett Prettyman, Jr., *Death and the Supreme Court* (New York: Harcourt, Brace & World, 1961), Ch. 5.
97. 378 U.S. 490–91.
98. Miranda v. Arizona, 384 U.S. 436 (1966).

the Sixth Amendment right to counsel), were a distinct break from past cases, for the Court dropped the *ad hoc* totality-of-circumstances rule. In place of this approach, the Court spelled out some behavioral guidelines for law enforcement officials and held that if these procedures were not followed, any statement elicited would be inadmissible. The *Miranda* rules were as follows:

To summarize, we hold that when an individual is taken into custody or otherwise deprived of his freedom by the authorities in any significant way and is subjected to questioning, the privilege against self-incrimination is jeopardized. Procedural safeguards must be employed to protect the privilege, and unless other fully effective means are adopted to notify the person of his right of silence and to assure that the exercise of the right will be scrupulously honored, the following measures are required. He must be warned prior to any questioning that he has the right to remain silent, that anything he says can be used against him in a court of law, that he has the right to the presence of an attorney, and that if he cannot afford an attorney one will be appointed for him prior to any questioning if he so desires. Opportunity to exercise the rights must be afforded to him throughout the interrogation. After such warnings have been given, and such opportunity afforded him, the individual may knowingly and intelligently waive these rights and agree to answer questions or make a statement. But unless and until such warnings and waiver are demonstrated by the prosecution at trial, no evidence obtained as a result of interrogation can be used against him.[99]

Miranda raised a storm of controversy, for many law enforcement officers claimed that confessions were essential to the solution of the majority of crimes and that interrogation was essential to obtaining such confessions. *Miranda*, it was argued, would hamstring the police and make solution of crimes much more difficult.[100]

99. 384 U.S. 478–79.
100. Several empirical investigations dealing with the importance of confessions to law enforcement and the effects of the Miranda rules suggest that the decision may not in fact hinder law enforcement as much as many critics have proposed. A combination of failure to give the warnings, failure of defendants to understand or take advantage of their rights to silence and the presence of an attorney, willingness of defendants to waive their rights and confess even after

Search and Seizure

A third area in which the Supreme Court took important steps in the administration of criminal justice involved searches and seizures by law enforcement officers. The Fourth Amendment to the Constitution provides that "the right of the people to be secure in their persons, houses, papers, and effects, against unreasonable searches and seizures, shall not be violated. . . ." As with the other provisions of the Bill of Rights, the protection against unreasonable searches and seizures was applicable only to actions of the federal government until it was explicitly incorporated into the due-process clause of the Fourteenth Amendment.[101]

Among the obvious questions raised by the Fourth Amendment were, what was an "unreasonable" search and, relatedly, when was a warrant required before a search could be made (and when could searches proceed without warrants)? Finally, what were the penalties to be assessed if the police did engage in an unreasonable search? The latter question had been answered, as far as federal officers were concerned, in the 1914 case of *Weeks v. U.S.*[102] The Court enunciated what came to be known as the exclusionary rule, holding that evidence secured illegally must be suppressed at trial (i.e., could not be admitted against the defendant). The justification for the rule was essentially pragmatic, based upon the notion that without such a rule the protection against unreasonable searches and seizures would have no meaning.

The other thorny issues surrounding the Fourth Amendment have been harder to resolve, even for the federal system. In a

---

the warnings, and the ability of police to solve crimes without confessions suggests that the critics of Miranda may have overstated their case. See the following studies: "Interrogations in New Haven," *Yale Law Journal* 76 (1967): 1521–1648; Albert Reiss and Donald Black, "Interrogation and the Criminal Process," *Annals of the American Academy of Political and Social Science* 374 (1967): 47–57; and Richard J. Medalie, Leonard Zeitz, and Paul Alexander, "Custodial Police Interrogation in Our Nation's Capital: The Attempt to Implement Miranda," *Michigan Law Review* 66 (1968): 1347–1422.

101. See the discussion below of Wolf v. Colorado, 338 U.S. 25 (1949), and Mapp v. Ohio, 367 U.S. 643 (1961).

102. 232 U.S. 383.

long line of cases the Court wrestled with the problem of when a warrant was or was not required.[103] The Court skipped around a good deal in the federal search and seizure cases, enunciating the rule that a warrant had to be obtained if there was time available (*Trupiano*), rejecting the rule a couple of years later (*Rabinowitz*), and then gradually appearing to return to it. The Court has also long grappled, again somewhat confusingly, with the related issue of what constituted a lawful search incident to arrest.[104]

The Court also had to grapple with the problem we have discussed in the areas of right to counsel and interrogation: what were the rights of defendants in state proceedings under the due-process clause of the Fourteenth Amendment? The Court first faced the issue squarely in 1949 in *Wolf v. Colorado*.[105] In *Wolf* a six-member majority held that the Fourteenth Amendment did protect the privacy of individuals from arbitrary intrusions by state law enforcement officers. At the same time, though, the majority refused to declare that the federal remedy—exclusion of illegally obtained evidence—was also applicable to state proceedings. The majority argued that the due-process clause guaranteed basic rights essential to a free society but that exclusion of evidence was not necessarily one of these. The opinion stressed the flexibility in experimenting with various remedies (e.g., civil actions against offending officers) that federalism required. The dissenting justices pointed out that the other remedies had generally proved ineffective, and that in the absence of the exclusionary rule the incorporation of the protection of the Fourth Amendment against state officers was close to meaningless.

The Warren Court had occasion to reconsider the *Wolf* ruling a few years later and upheld it.[106] Though the actions of the police in this case (forced entry and installation of a listening device) were obviously lawless, the five-man majority stood

103. See, for example, Harris v. United States, 331 U.S. 145 (1947); Trupiano v. United States, 334 U.S. 699 (1948); United States v. Rabinowitz, 339 U.S. 56 (1950); and Chapman v. United States, 365 U.S. 610 (1961).
104. See, for example, Agnello v. United States, 269 U.S. 20 (1925), and Go-Bart v. United States, 282 U.S. 344 (1931).
105. 338 U.S. 25.
106. Irvine v. California, 347 U.S. 128 (1954).

by the *Wolf* holding that illegal activity was not itself sufficient to require exclusion. But during the next few years the Court did move against collaboration by state and federal officers and eliminated the so-called "silver platter" doctrine, a practice in which state officers would engage in illegal searches and turn the evidence over to federal authorities for use in federal prosecutions.[107]

In 1961 the Court finally decided to apply the exclusionary rule to state proceedings. Citing the movement in many states toward the exclusionary rule, and the lack of other effective remedies, the Court concluded that the Fourth Amendment protection made applicable to states in the *Wolf* case now required the federal remedy as well.[108] Later decisions restricted state practices in arresting without warrants[109] and applied to state proceedings the federal rules about probable cause for issuance of a search warrant.[110] In a 1963 case the Court appeared to apply a standard somewhat less rigorous than that prevailing in federal cases to searches by state police officers.[111] Then in the final days of Chief Justice Warren's term the Court appeared to tighten the standards to be applied to state searches and seizures.[112]

Thus, in dealing with searches and seizures, as in other areas, the Court moved toward protection of the rights of defendants in criminal proceedings. The invocation of the exclusionary rule evinces its tendency to substitute broad rules for a previously *ad hoc* approach.

107. See, for example, Rea v. United States, 350 U.S. 214 (1956); Benanti v. United States, 355 U.S. 96 (1957); and Elkins v. United States, 364 U.S. 206 (1960).

108. Mapp v. Ohio, 367 U.S. 383 (1961). See also Peter H. Wolf, "A Survey of the Expanded Exclusionary Rule," *George Washington Law Review* 32 (1963): 193–242, for a discussion of the development of rules dealing with search and seizure, with special emphasis upon the relationship of the Mapp and Wolf decisions.

109. E.g., Beck v. Ohio, 379 U.S. 89 (1964).

110. Aguilar v. Texas, 378 U.S. 108 (1964).

111. Ker v. California, 374 U.S. 23.

112. See, for example, Chimel v. California, 395 U.S. 752 (1969). Though tightening controls over searches of premises, the Court loosened restrictions upon warrantless searches of the person designed to detect weapons—the so-called "stop and frisk" practice. See Terry v. Ohio, 392 U.S. 1 (1968).

Other Criminal Justice Litigation

The Court also dealt with a number of other rights of persons accused of crime. Though there is not space here to discuss them in detail, brief mention of some of them indicate the breadth of the Warren Court's attempt to reform the area of criminal justice. The Court incorporated the Sixth Amendment right of confrontation of witnesses in state proceedings.[113] It moved to protect the rights of juvenile offenders[114] and to outlaw the practice by which prosecutors commented adversely upon the choice of a defendant not to take the stand in his own defense.[115]

The Court wrestled with the thorny issue of publicity and a fair trial, a clash between the provisions of the First and Sixth Amendments.[116] It also dealt with the protection of the Fifth Amendment against double jeopardy, finally applying this protection to state defendants in 1969.[117] The Eighth Amendment protection against cruel and unusual punishments was held to be incorporated into the due-process clause.[118] The Court grappled with the constitutional issues raised by police use of informers and of wiretapping and other forms of eavesdropping, arduously attempting to begin the fashioning of some rules.[119] Finally, the Court dealt with the issue of the retroactivity of its decisions, holding that most would apply only prospectively.[120]

This brief laundry list of Court decisions is obviously not complete, nor does it convey adequately the scope of the Court's

113. Pointer v. Texas, 380 U.S. 400 (1965), and Douglas v. Alabama, 380 U.S. 415 (1965).

114. In re Gault, 387 U.S. 1 (1967).

115. Griffin v. California, 381 U.S. 957 (1965).

116. E.g., Irvin v. Dowd, 366 U.S. 717 (1961); Estes v. Texas, 381 U.S. 532 (1965); and Sheppard v. Ohio, 384 U.S. 333 (1966).

117. See Benton v. Maryland, 395 U.S. 784 (1969), and North Carolina v. Pearce, 395 U.S. 711 (1969).

118. Robinson v. California, 370 U.S. 660 (1962).

119. See, for example, Lopez v. United States, 373 U.S. 427 (1963); Hoffa v. United States, 385 U.S. 293 (1966); Osborn v. United States, 385 U.S. 323 (1966); Berger v. New York, 388 U.S. 41 (1967); and Katz v. United States, 389 U.S. 347 (1967).

120. See, for example, Linkletter v. Walker, 381 U.S. 618 (1965), dealing with the Mapp decision; Tehan v. Shott, 382 U.S. 406 (1966), dealing with Griffin v. California; and Johnson v. New Jersey, 384 U.S. 719 (1966), dealing with Miranda.

dealings with criminal justice in the 1957–66 period. But it does at least suggest that the Court in criminal justice cases did move quickly and widely in extending the protections of the Bill of Rights to defendants in both state and federal proceedings. As suggested at the outset, this movement was characterized by rapid incorporation of new provisions of the Bill of Rights against state proceedings and by a switch in approach, from an essentially *ad hoc*, case-by-case approach to the fashioning of broad behavioral guides affecting the whole criminal justice system.

REAPPORTIONMENT

Chief Justice Warren stated on several occasions that he considered the Supreme Court decisions dealing with reapportionment to have been the most significant of his tenure. The cases and their most publicized expression—"one man–one vote"— have a fulfilling democratic ring to them, exemplars of the invocation of judicial review to protect the democratic process itself.

As in other areas of civil liberties and civil rights litigation discussed here, the reapportionment decisions of the 1957–66 period marked a break with past practice and a movement toward the development of new doctrine with profound legal, political, and social significance. The Court stepped into the "political thicket" that it had in the past avoided, delving into an issue that directly touched the fortunes of state and national parties in electoral politics. The litigation, again a characteristic of much in which the Warren Court became involved, was highly acrimonious, and the decisions led both to generalized attacks upon the Court and to attempts to reverse its decisions by constitutional amendment.[121]

Ironically, though, some of the research that followed the movement toward reapportionment in this country raises ques-

121. For a discussion of the reapportionment litigation and response to the Supreme Court's decisions, see Robert Dixon, *Democratic Representation* (New York: Oxford University Press, 1969), especially Chs. 15–21; Arthur E. Bonfield, "The Dirksen Amendment and the Article V Convention Process," *Michigan Law Review* 66 (1968): 949–1000; and Robert McKay, "Court, Congress and Reapportionment," ibid. 63 (1964): 255–78.

tions about whether the shifts in districting mandated by the Court had any important impact either upon party balances in state legislatures or upon the kinds of public policies that emerged from those legislatures.[122] Still, the cases were hard fought, raised a great deal of controversy, and became one of the most publicized symbols of the Warren Court, for both its supporters (who hailed the decisions as protection of our democratic system) and its opponents (who attacked the decisions as but one more example of judicial usurpation and interference in the affairs of other institutions of government).

Malapportionment—inequality in representation in legislative districts—is itself enshrined in the Constitution of the United States, for the Senate is a legislative body designed to produce such inequalities. But in the House of Representatives and in many state legislatures malapportionment became widespread not by constitutional design but by history and demographics. In legislatures whose district apportionments were putatively based upon equality of population, a combination of retention of old apportionment schemes and massive shifts in population (from farm to city and city to suburb) produced great inequalities, with rural areas typically being highly overrepresented. Malapportionment, once it developed because of population shifts, tended to maintain itself because the power to reapportion (either by statute or by amendment of the state constitutions) lay in the hands of the guilty parties themselves—the state legislatures. Controlling majorities in the legislature

122. The following books are examples of work by proponents of reapportionment, who urge that it would affect party balances and legislative policy: William C. Havard and Loren P. Beth, *The Politics of Mis-Representation* (Baton Rouge: Louisiana State University Press, 1962), and Malcolm Jewell, *State Legislatures: Politics and Practice* (New York: Random House, 1962).

The following work by political scientists attempting to assess the impact of reapportionment suggests that its effects are not particularly great, either on party competition or on public policy: Thomas R. Dye, "Malapportionment and Public Policy in the States," *Journal of Politics* 27 (1965): 586–601, and Richard Hofferbert, "The Relation between Public Policy and Some Structural and Environmental Variables in the American States," *American Political Science Review* 60 (1966): 73–82. For a somewhat contrasting view, using similar research techniques, see Allan G. Pulsipher and James L. Weatherby, Jr., "Malapportionment, Party Competition, and the Functional Distribution of Governmental Expenditures," ibid. 62 (1968): 1207–19.

had much to lose and little to gain by reapportioning themselves. Thus a kind of stalemate existed, and one might have expected the legal system to step in and vindicate the rights of equality that were being denied. The Court did so in the 1957–66 period, but it was a break with past practice, and a brief discussion of previous litigation in this area will provide a backdrop for the decisions of the Warren Court.

In 1946 the Court had been asked to enjoin election for members of Congress from Illinois on the grounds that the congressional districts were malapportioned (the state was still operating upon an apportionment passed in 1901, though great shifts in population from rural areas to cities and suburbs had taken place). The Supreme Court upheld the lower court's refusal to issue the injunction.[123] The seven justices who participated in the decision were divided into three blocs, with a four-to-three majority against intervention. Two justices concurred with an opinion by Justice Frankfurter holding that the issue was not "justiciable," was not an issue which courts ought to attempt to resolve. Relying on the doctrine of political questions—the notion that there are certain kinds of disputes in which courts should not become involved—the Frankfurter opinion asserted, "Nothing is clearer than that this controversy concerns matters that bring courts into immediate and active relations with party contests. From the determination of such issues this Court has traditionally held aloof. It is hostile to a democratic system to involve the judiciary in the politics of the people."[124]

The Frankfurter opinion also stressed the constitutional provisions that authorized Congress to determine whether its members had been elected properly and were fairly representative: "To sustain this action would cut very deep into the very being of Congress. Courts ought not to enter this political thicket. The remedy for unfairness in districting is to secure State legislatures that will apportion properly, or to invoke the ample powers of Congress. The Constitution has many commands that are not enforceable by courts because they clearly fall outside the

123. Colegrove v. Green, 328 U.S. 549 (1946).
124. 328 U.S. 553–54.

conditions and purposes that circumscribe judicial action."[125]

The proposition that appeared to dominate the Frankfurter opinion was that the matter of legislative apportionment was simply one in which courts would not intervene. But the holding of the case was muddied somewhat by the fact that Justice Rutledge—who cast the crucial vote—concurred in the outcome on somewhat different grounds. Concluding that the issue was in fact justiciable, Rutledge reasoned that the shortness of time before the election and the possibility of an at-large election after a declaration of unconstitutionality of the current scheme made it doubtful that any equitable relief could be obtained in court, and therefore the Court should decline to rule.

In any event, *Colegrove* was followed by several cases in which the Court refused to interfere with elections and legislative apportionment schemes.[126] One of the first intimations of a shift in approach came in 1960 in an attack upon a gerrymandering of Tuskegee, Alabama.[127] Though the decision did not rely upon the equal-protection clause of the Fourteenth Amendment but, rather, upon the right-to-vote guarantees of the Fifteenth Amendment, in overturning the gerrymandering scheme the Court did appear to weaken its blanket prohibition against dealing with issues of legislative apportionment and voting. The case was different from the malapportionment cases, for it involved not the usual unequal weighting of votes but an attempt to prevent blacks from voting in a municipal election. Thus it mixed together the issues of gerrymandering and racial discrimination. But it was a straw in the wind and augured changes soon to come.

The landmark opinion in *Baker v. Carr*[128] established the proposition that legislative malapportionment was an issue with which the federal courts could and would deal. Holding that the issue was not one that fell under the rubric of "political questions," and hence nonjusticiable, the Court ruled that an

125. 328 U.S. 556.
126. E.g., McDougall v. Green, 335 U.S. 281 (1948), and South v. Peters, 339 U.S. 276 (1950).
127. Gomillion v. Lightfoot, 364 U.S. 339.
128. 369 U.S. 186 (1962).

attack upon legislative malapportionment (in this case upon the apportionment of the Tennessee legislature), as a violation of the equal-protection clause, was properly a matter for the federal courts. The major question that *Baker* left open was, what standards for apportionment did the Fourteenth Amendment impose upon states? In the next year the Court made its first statements about what was required.

In *Gray v. Sanders*,[129] an attack upon the Georgia county unit system, the Court said the following: "Once the geographical unit for which a representative is to be chosen is designated, all who participate in the election are to have an equal vote—whatever their race, whatever their sex, whatever their occupation, whatever their income, wherever their home may be in that geographical unit. This is required by the Equal protection Clause of the Fourteenth Amendment."[130]

In 1964 the Court further clarified the standards imposed by the equal-protection clause. First, in a case dealing with the apportionment of congressional districts,[131] the Court held that Article I, Section 2, of the Constitution, requiring that representatives be chosen "by the People of the Several States," meant that as nearly as possible one man's vote in a congressional election counted for the same as another's. Black's opinion argued that it would "defeat the principle solemnly embodied in the Great Compromise—equal representation in the House for equal number of people—for us to hold that, within the States, legislatures may draw the lines of congressional districts in such a way as to give some voters a greater voice in choosing a Congressman than others."[132]

On the same day the Court decided six cases dealing with malapportionment in state legislatures.[133] In the words of the

---

129. 372 U.S. 368 (1963).
130. 372 U.S. 379.
131. Wesberry v. Sanders, 376 U.S. 1 (1964).
132. 376 U.S. 14.
133. Alabama: Reynolds v. Sims, 377 U.S. 533 (1964); New York: WMCA v. Lomenzo, 377 U.S. 633 (1964); Colorado: Lucas v. Colorado General Assembly, 377 U.S. 713 (1964); Maryland: Maryland Committee for Fair Representation v. Tawes, 377 U.S. 656 (1964); Virginia: Davis v. Mann, 377 U.S. 678 (1964); Delaware: Roman v. Sincock, 377 U.S. 695 (1964).

now famous "one man–one vote" opinion by Chief Justice Warren: "We hold that, as a basic constitutional standard, the Equal Protection Clause requires that the seats in both houses of a bicameral state legislature must be apportioned on a population basis. Simply stated, an individual's right to vote for state legislators is unconstitutionally impaired when its weight is in a substantial fashion diluted when compared with the votes of citizens living in other parts of the State."[134] Rejecting the so-called federal analogy, which suggested that if the Constitution permitted—in fact required—apportionment of one house of the federal legislature on a basis other than population, then it was anomalous to hold that it did not permit similar schemes in state legislatures, the Court held that both houses of state legislatures must be apportioned on the basis of equal population districts. One week later, on 22 June 1964, the Court declared unconstitutional (either directly or by affirming lower court judgments) the legislative apportionments of nine other states. In a week, then, the Court had overturned apportionments of legislatures in nearly a third of the states. By 1968 congressional redistricting had taken place in 37 of the 50 states, and every state had taken at least some steps toward equalizing population in its legislative districts.[135] In a later decision, *Avery v. Midland County*,[136] the Court held that the one man–one vote principle applied to the drawing of districts for some municipal governmental units as well.

The major question left open by the decisions was that of precisely how much deviation from exact numerical equality was to be tolerated. The Court opinions eschewed mathematical exactness and implied that some deviations were constitutionally tolerable. The issue is still not resolved. A recent case dealing with congressional apportionment indicated that a deviation of only 6 percent from equality is not permissible.[137] The Court has gradually narrowed the limits of deviation but has never actually

134. 377 U.S. 568.
135. Robert McKay, "Reapportionment: Success Story of the Warren Court," in Sayler, Boyer, and Gooding, eds., *The Warren Court*, p. 38.
136. 390 U.S. 474 (1968).
137. Kirkpatrick v. Preisler, 394 U.S. 526 (1969).

agreed upon a mathematical standard (i.e., stated that any deviation greater than x percent is constitutionally impermissible).

Because it will be of interest when we discuss the lawyers who argued the reapportionment cases, it is worth noting here the positions taken by the different justices in dealing with the question of malapportionment. With the exception of Justice Harlan (who, following the Frankfurter approach, argued that the Court simply had no business taking up reapportionment cases at all), all members of the Court agreed that some degree of malapportionment was constitutionally impermissible. But various justices differed on the question of exactly how the constitutional judgment should be reached.

One group, led by Chief Justice Warren (exemplified in his majority opinion in *Reynolds*), attempted to apply a general principle, the one man–one vote formula. Population was taken as the standard, and apportionments were to be judged on the basis of their deviation from equal population in all districts. Though, as noted above, it is still unclear how much deviation from equality this position finds constitutionally acceptable, the approach had at least the semblance of a neutral and principled criterion.

Justices Stewart and Clark, on the other hand, tended to reject what they considered an overly mechanical approach and adopted their own approach. One is tempted to characterize their approach (like Stewart's text for hard-core pornography)[138] as essentially "I can't say exactly what it is, but I know it when I see it." Using phrases like "crazy quilt," "invidious discrimination," and "lack of rational basis," their test viewed each state's apportionment individually and attempted to evaluate it in terms of whether or not it possessed some kind of rationality, whether some reasonable justification for the scheme could be discovered. Refusing to apply mechanical (and perhaps more clear and general) formulae, the Clark-Stewart approach asserted that the states must be granted some latitude. In the six *Reynolds* cases, for example, Clark and Stewart concurred in holding the Alabama, Delaware, and Virginia apportionments

138. See Jacobellis v. Ohio, 378 U.S. 194 (1964).

unconstitutional, dissented in the holding of the Colorado and New York schemes invalid, and split on the Maryland plan.

The two types of tests not only applied different criteria (and were based upon differing notions about what the constitutional justification for reapportionment was), but they came out differently as well. In general, the Warren position more consistently decided in favor of reapportionment. The views of the lawyers who argued the reapportionment cases toward the two positions are discussed in detail in Chapter 5.

Thus the reapportionment suits did represent a distinct break with past practice. Though to many they appeared simply inevitable—given the lack of other remedies to deal with malapportionment—they were hotly contested in the courts and in the broader political context. In a sense, though, the decisions differed from others involving civil liberties and civil rights. Many of the other areas of litigation dealt with the protection of rights of minorities; the reapportionment cases dealt to some extent with the rights of a majority. Perhaps for this reason, though the decisions were attacked by many politicians, the decisions did not make as much of an impact upon public opinion as did some of the other Warren Court decisions.[139]

As suggested before, the impact of reapportionment upon the policy outputs of American legislative institutions is still in doubt. But there can be no doubt that the reapportionment cases did represent one of the more significant doctrinal departures of the Warren Court and were an important component of the

139. Survey research dealing with public perceptions and evaluations of Supreme Court decisions suggests that the reapportionment decisions—as compared, for example, with those dealing with segregation, school prayer, and the rights of persons accused of crime—did not make a particularly great impression upon the public at large. See, for example, Walter F. Murphy and Joseph Tanenhaus, "Public Opinion and the United States Supreme Court," *Law and Society Review* 2 (1968): 357–84, and Kenneth M. Dolbeare, "The Public Views the Supreme Court," in Herbert Jacob, ed., *Law, Politics, and the Federal Courts* (Boston: Little, Brown, 1967), pp. 194–212.

The relative lack of public interest in the reapportionment cases contrasts sharply with Chief Justice Warren's view that they were the most important decisions of his tenure: "I think the reapportionment, not only of state legislatures but of representative government in this country, is perhaps the most important issue we have had before the Supreme Court." *New York Times,* 27 June 1969. "I think Baker v. Carr was the most important case that we decided in my time." *New York Times Magazine,* 19 October 1969, p. 130.

image of the "activist court" that has come to be identified with Warren's tenure.

CIVIL RIGHTS

The struggle against racial discrimination in America has been dotted with important litigation: the *Dred Scott* case,[140] the *Civil Rights Cases,*[141] *Plessy v. Ferguson,*[142] the Scottsboro case,[143] *Shelley v. Kraemer,*[144] *Brown v. Board of Education.*[145] The black man, excluded from the normal channels of the political process, has frequently turned to the legal system to vindicate his rights. During the past 40 years civil rights litigation has achieved considerable success. The *Brown* case was probably seminal in the development of the activist civil rights movement, with its freedom rides, marches, sit-ins, and eventual success in the legislative arena.

During the 1957–66 period the Supreme Court struck down racial discrimination in a variety of contexts. This litigation was probably the most controversial of all that came before the Court, and in the long run it will likely prove to be the most politically and socially significant action of the Warren era. The great variety of litigation makes our description here necessarily rather cursory, but it will provide at least the flavor of the scope of litigation and decision in this vital area of social and constitutional policy.

Since the school cases, culminating in *Brown*, were the breakthrough in civil rights litigation, they will be treated first. The doctrine of "separate but equal" long dominated constitutional policy dealing with race relations. First clearly enunciated in the 1896 *Plessy v. Ferguson* decision, the policy amounted to an endorsement of racial discrimination. School segregation was explicitly condoned in 1908.[146] So long as facilities were equal (and this requirement was, for a long period, never really closely ex-

---

140. Dred Scott v. Sanford, 19 How. 393 (1857).
141. 109 U.S. 3 (1883).
142. 163 U.S. 537 (1896).
143. Powell v. Alabama, 287 U.S. 45 (1932).
144. 334 U.S. 1 (1948).
145. 347 U.S. 483 (1954).
146. Berea College v. Kentucky, 221 U.S. 45.

amined), the equal-protection clause was not violated by racial discrimination enforced by state action. Beginning in 1938, though, the Supreme Court began to cast a more critical eye at segregation in state-supported schools. Though the separate-but-equal doctrine was not abandoned, the Court began to look more closely at facilities which blacks were forced to attend, to make the doctrine more than a mere shibboleth. In a series of cases dealing with graduate and professional education the Court struck down systems of segregation in public educational facilities.[147]

The more careful scrutiny of segregation in public education, combined with a number of decisions dealing with other forms of racial discrimination,[148] suggested that constitutional tolerance of racial discrimination was being re-evaluated. The major break, now familiar, came in the 1954 decision, *Brown v. Board of Education.* In the *Brown* decision, and an accompanying case dealing with segregation in the District of Columbia,[149] the Court declared that segregation by race in the public schools was in violation of the equal-protection clause of the Fourteenth Amendment. Thus the whole fabric of life of a substantial section of the country was called into question. But the Court somewhat blunted the impact of the decisions dealing with schools in its implementation decision the following year.[150] Rather than following standard practice, under which a violation of a constitutional right was subject to immediate relief, the Court, with its famous "all deliberate speed" phrase, in effect turned control over the pace of school desegregation to the lower federal court judges.

Given the intense political contention over the decision and over the general issue of racial discrimination, and given the broad scope of life affected by the decision, the Court's course of

147. For example, Missouri ex rel. Gaines v. Canada, 305 U.S. 337 (1938); McLaurin v. Oklahoma, 339 U.S. 637 (1950); and Sweatt v. Painter, 339 U.S. 629 (1950).

148. For example, in the area of housing the Court struck down enforcement of restrictive covenants in Shelley v. Kraemer; in the area of voting rights the Court upheld attacks upon the white primary in Smith v. Allwright, 321 U.S. 649 (1944).

149. Bolling v. Sharpe, 347 U.S. 497 (1954).

150. Brown v. Board of Education, 349 U.S. 294 (1955).

action is perhaps understandable, though debatable. In any event, in the years that followed the *Brown* implementation decision the Supreme Court ducked many of the cases that arose in the lower federal courts, leaving district and circuit court judges to exercise their own prejudices or to be subjected to the often intense pressures of their local communities.[151] Various kinds of evasive schemes—pupil placement laws, transfer plans, grade-a-year plans, school closings, and private school systems—were condoned by lower courts and not challenged by the Supreme Court. The Court did speak out in 1958, condemning the obviously evasive scheme concocted in Little Rock[152] and forcing a somewhat recalcitrant President Eisenhower to utilize the power of the federal executive in favor of what was now constitutional policy.

In 1963 the Court finally began to deal directly with the evasive schemes that had to a large extent nullified its holding in *Brown*. In a series of cases the Court began to express its dissatisfaction with the pace of desegregation and with the countenancing of evasive schemes by lower courts.[153]

Though the Court did not press the pace of integration in the public schools, it did move with a good deal more swiftness in striking down racial discrimination in other contexts. A simple laundry list of some of the major cases demonstrates the breadth of areas of social and political life affected by Court decisions. The Court struck down racial discrimination in public parks,[154] interstate buses,[155] public golf courses,[156] airports,[157] libraries,[158]

151. For a fascinating account of the role played by lower federal court judges in the implementation of the Brown decision—and its evasion—see Jack Peltason, *Fifty-eight Lonely Men* (New York: Harcourt, Brace & World, 1961).

152. Cooper v. Aaron, 358 U.S. 1 (1958).

153. For example, Goss v. Board of Education, 373 U.S. 683 (1963); Griffin v. School Board of Prince Edward County, 377 U.S. 218 (1964); Bradley v. Richmond, 382 U.S. 103 (1965); and Green v. School Board of New Kent County, 391 U.S. 430 (1968). In 1969 the Court finally declared that the standard of "all deliberate speed" was no longer applicable: Alexander v. Holmes County Board of Education, 396 U.S. 19.

154. E.g., Watson v. Memphis, 373 U.S. 526 (1963).

155. Boynton v. Virginia, 364 U.S. 454 (1960).

156. Holmes v. Atlanta, 350 U.S. 879 (1955).

157. Turner v. Memphis, 369 U.S. 762 (1962).

158. E.g., Brown v. Louisiana, 383 U.S. 131 (1966).

courtrooms,[159] marriage and sexual relations,[160] and voting.[161] In a series of cases the Court dealt with attempts by governmental institutions to disrupt the activities of the interest groups— particularly the NAACP—which were promoting much of the litigation alluded to above. The Court consistently vindicated the activities of civil rights organizations in the face of these attacks.[162] The Court also moved quickly to validate the public accommodations section (Title II) of the Civil Rights Act of 1964[163] and the Voting Rights Act of 1965.[164]

During the period under consideration here the Court concentrated its civil rights decisions upon problems arising out of discrimination in the South. It refused to grant hearings in cases arising out of lower courts in the North dealing with the issue of *de facto* segregation and what responsibility, if any, there was to alleviate it.[165]

Finally, in a line of cases that will be of particular interest when we discuss the lawyers who argued civil rights cases, the Court dealt extensively with the public demonstration and sit-in aspects of the civil rights movement in the South.[166] In the public demonstration cases the Court generally sidestepped the First Amendment issues and used more technical grounds (e.g., lack of evidence that an offense like breach of the peace had occurred) to decide the cases. During the early part of the period

159. Johnson v. Virginia, 373 U.S. 61 (1963).

160. McLaughlin v. Florida, 379 U.S. 184 (1964), and Loving v. Virginia, 388 U.S. 1 (1967).

161. E.g., Harper v. Virginia, 383 U.S. 663 (1966).

162. E.g., NAACP v. Alabama, 357 U.S. 449 (1958); Bates v. Little Rock, 361 U.S. 516 (1960); Shelton v. Tucker, 364 U.S. 479 (1960); NAACP v. Button, 371 U.S. 415 (1963); and Gibson v. Florida Investigation Committee, 372 U.S. 539 (1964).

163. Heart of Atlanta Motel v. U.S., 379 U.S. 241 (1964), and Katzenbach v. McClung, 379 U.S. 294 (1964).

164. South Carolina v. Katzenbach, 383 U.S. 301 (1966).

165. See, for example, Bell v. Gary, 324 F. 2d 209 (7th Cir., 1963), *cert.* denied, 377 U.S. 294 (1964); and Balaban v. Rubin, 14 N.Y. 2d 193 (1964), *cert.* denied, 379 U.S. 881 (1964).

166. For a very imaginative treatment of the Court's decisions dealing with civil rights demonstrators, see Joel B. Grossman, "A Model for Judicial Policy Analysis: The Supreme Court and the Sit-In Cases," in Joel B. Grossman and Joseph Tanenhaus, eds., *Frontiers of Judicial Research* (New York: John Wiley and Sons, 1969), pp. 405–60.

the Court found consistently in favor of the demonstrators, though upon relatively narrow grounds.[167] Toward the end of the 1957–66 period, though, the Court did uphold some convictions growing out of the public demonstration aspects of the civil rights movement.[168]

In the sit-in cases, mainly involving racial discrimination in public accommodations like lunch counters and restaurants, the Court also found consistently in favor of the demonstrators, but often on fairly narrow grounds. Briefly, there were typically three possible grounds upon which a sit-in case might be won. First, using settled principles of constitutional law, overt state action (e.g., enforcement of a statute requiring segregation) in favor of discrimination in public accommodations could be overturned under the equal-protection clause of the Fourteenth Amendment. Two other approaches were pressed upon the Court which would have somewhat expanded the law. Second, the doctrine of *Shelley v. Kraemer* was urged upon the Court as a means for throwing out sit-in convictions. Under the *Shelley* approach, state action in enforcing generally recognized and constitutional laws (e.g., trespass or breach-of-peace statutes) for the purpose of preventing racial integration would be declared unconstitutional. This was obviously one step beyond holding that state action in enforcing laws directly related to racial discrimination was unconstitutional. The third, and most far-reaching, approach urged upon the Court suggested that racial discrimination in a public accommodation—in the absence of any overt state action and simply by virtue of the fact that an establishment held itself out as a public accommodation—did itself violate the equal-protection clause. This, in effect, would have made a matter of constitutional right the policy that emerged in the public accommodations section of the 1964 Civil Rights Act.

A majority of the Court was never willing to decide the constitutional issues implicit in the second and third approaches.

167. E.g., Garner v. Louisiana, 368 U.S. 157 (1961); Edwards v. South Carolina, 372 U.S. 229 (1963); and Brown v. Louisiana, 383 U.S. 131 (1966). On the demonstration cases generally, see Harry Kalven, Jr., *The Negro and the First Amendment* (Columbus: Ohio State University Press, 1965).

168. E.g., Adderley v. Florida, 385 U.S. 39 (1966).

Thus the sit-in cases were typically decided in favor of the demonstrators, but upon relatively technical grounds. In some of the cases the existence of an ordinance requiring discrimination made the Court's decision fairly easy.[169] In some cases, though, the Court had to reach rather far to find the requisite state action: statements by local officials apparently urging discrimination,[170] some obscure toilet regulations requiring separate washrooms for white and black employees,[171] or the fact that a special policeman making an arrest in an amusement park was also a deputy sheriff.[172] In *Bell v. Maryland*[173] the Court remanded a sit-in conviction for reconsideration in light of the passage of a state public accommodation law subsequent to the arrest. Finally, the Court effectively ended the public accommodations litigation by holding that all such prosecutions not completed and appealed were abated by the passage of the public accommodations section of the 1964 Civil Rights Act.[174]

A majority of the Court was typically willing to find in favor of the demonstrators but was not willing to take the rather broad constitutional steps urged upon the Court by some lawyers. The tactics of the lawyers and their expectations and goals in the sit-in cases are discussed in Chapter 5.

Thus, in the area of civil rights, the Court moved to strike down many important aspects of racial discrimination. The Court moved more cautiously in some areas than others (e.g., schools versus public accommodations) and sometimes did not go so far as some of the advocates of desegregation might have wished. An important aspect of this litigation, and one that is discussed in subsequent chapters, was the role of litigating interest groups—like the Legal Defense Fund of the NAACP—in initiating, promoting, and supporting the litigation that eventually came before the Supreme Court. In some areas of civil

169. See for example, Peterson v. Greenvile, 373 U.S. 244 (1963).
170. E.g., Lombard v. Louisiana, 373 U.S. 267 (1963).
171. E.g., Robinson v. Florida, 378 U.S. 153 (1964).
172. E.g., Griffin v. Maryland, 378 U.S. 130 (1964).
173. 378 U.S. 226 (1964).
174. Hamm v. Rock Hill, 379 U.S. 306 (1964). For a critical treatment of the Court's handling of the sit-in cases, see Monrad G. Paulson, "The Sit-In Cases of 1964: 'But Answer There Came None,'" *Supreme Court Review* 1964: 137–70.

rights litigation (school segregation is the best example) the suits were planned, initiated, and coordinated by such litigating interest groups. In other areas, especially the public demonstration cases, the lawyers entered the litigation at a later stage, and legal strategy had to be improvised along the way. But in nearly all of the civil rights litigation the process by which a lawyer was recruited and a suit pursued up the appeals ladder depended upon the activities of interest groups. Their success in litigation and in using the doors opened by litigation to mobilize a movement active in other institutional arenas and in the streets is in large part the story of the genesis and success of the civil rights movement in this country.[175]

OTHER LITIGATION

The four areas of litigation discussed thus far encompass the most legally, socially, and politically significant decisions of the Warren Court during the 1957–66 period. Yet the Court was also active in other litigation dealing with important civil liberties and rights, and in terms of public reaction, its decisions in areas like obscenity and freedom of religion were among the most salient.[176]

The Court dealt extensively with the free-exercise and establishment provisions of the First Amendment: "Congress shall make no law respecting an establishment of religion or prohibiting the free exercise thereof. . . ." In interpreting the free-exercise clause, the Court voided a test oath for notaries public in Maryland,[177] dealt somewhat ambiguously with the indirect effects of state laws upon the practice of religion,[178] and expanded the

175. For a sharply contrasting view of the role of the Supreme Court vis-à-vis racial discrimination, see Lewis M. Steel, "Nine Men in Black Who Think White," *New York Times Magazine*, 13 October 1968, p. 56.

176. See Murphy and Tanenhaus, "Public Opinion," and Dolbeare, "The Public Views the Court."

177. Torcaso v. Watkins, 367 U.S. 488 (1961).

178. Contrast Braunfeld v. Brown, 366 U.S. 599 (1961)—upholding a Sunday closing law in the face of a challenge by Orthodox Jews who closed their businesses on Saturdays—with Sherbert v. Verner, 374 U.S. 398 (1963)—overturning the denial of workman's compensation benefits to a Seventh-Day Adventist who refused to accept employment on Saturdays.

availability of conscientious objector provisions under the Selective Service Act.[179]

In two of the most controversial cases decided by the Warren
Court, dealing with the establishment clause, the Court held
unconstitutional the reading of the Regent's Prayer in New York
schools[180] and the reading of the Bible in devotional exercises
in public schools.[181] Though the religion decisions probably will
not have the lasting social and political significance of those
dealing with racial discrimination, reapportionment, or criminal
justice, they were among the most salient and widely unpopular
of those rendered by the Warren Court. In 1968, in two cases
dealing with aid to parochial schools, the Court did deal with
the religion issue in a context with important political ramifications. They upheld a New York program providing for the loan of
textbooks to parochial school students[182] and opened the way for
taxpayers' suits against federal aid to parochial schools.[183]

The Court also dealt with the freedom of speech and press
provisions of the First Amendment in the context of control of
allegedly obscene materials. As with the religion cases, although
the political significance of the litigation was probably slight
compared with other areas of litigation, the cases were themselves the subject of a tremendous amount of public concern
and condemnation. After declaring that obscene material did not
enjoy the protection of the First Amendment in 1957,[184] the
Court then faced the thorny problem of providing a legal definition of what in fact constituted material that was obscene and
hence did not enjoy the protection of the First Amendment. In
a series of decisions a highly divided Court wrestled somewhat
unsatisfactorily with this perhaps intractable problem.[185] The

179. E.g., United States v. Seeger, 380 U.S. 163 (1965), and Welsh v. United
States, 398 U.S. 333 (1969). The Court later denied the validity of the so-
called "selective conscientious objector" position; see Gillette v. United States,
401 U.S. 437 (1971).
180. Engel v. Vitale, 370 U.S. 421 (1962).
181. Abington Township v. Schempp and Murray v. Curtlett, 374 U.S. 203
(1963).
182. Board of Education v. Allen, 392 U.S. 236 (1968).
183. Flast v. Cohen, 392 U.S. 83 (1968).
184. Roth v. United States and Alberts v. California, 354 U.S. 476 (1957).
185. See, for example, Kingsley Pictures v. New York, 360 U.S. 684 (1959);

net result of the decisions was to greatly expand the area of protected material, though the Court never reached a very clear standard defining what was or was not within the bounds of First Amendment protection. The Court also dealt with various forms of direct and indirect censorship of books and movies.[186] Again, the net result of the decisions was to put significant procedural and substantive restraints upon formal and informal schemes for prior restraint of obscene material.

The Court also began exploring the dimensions of the right to privacy—the right to be left alone in a highly complex technological society. They dealt with invasions of privacy under the guise of law enforcement,[187] the clash between publicity and the individual's reputation and right to be left alone,[188] and interference with marital relations.[189]

SUMMARY

This concludes our brief review of the civil liberties and civil rights litigation before the Warren Court during the 1957–66 period. What the review has done is to provide an introduction to the kinds of issues before the Court during the period, and to suggest their breadth and importance not only as legal and constitutional issues but also as political and social issues affecting the lives of most Americans. However one evaluates the Warren Court, there can be no doubt that it did decide cases of tremendous significance for political and social life in this country.

The discussion suggests that the "activist" image of the Warren Court does have strong bases in the doctrine that was devel-

---

Manual Enterprises v. Day, 370 U.S. 478 (1962); Jacobellis v. Ohio, 378 U.S. 194 (1964); Ginzburg v. U.S., 383 U.S. 463 (1966); Memoirs v. Massachusetts, 383 U.S. 413 (1966); and Mishkin v. New York, 383 U.S. 502 (1966).

186. See, for example, Butler v. Michigan, 352 U.S. 380 (1957); Smith v. California, 361 U.S. 147 (1959); Times Film v. Chicago, 365 U.S. 43 (1961); and Freedman v. Maryland, 380 U.S. 51 (1965).

187. Berger v. New York and Katz v. United States for wiretapping and Schmerber v. California, 384 U.S. 757 (1966), for mandatory blood tests for those suspected of driving under the influence of alcohol.

188. E.g., New York Times v. Sullivan, 376 U.S. 254 (1964), and Time v. Hill, 385 U.S. 374 (1967).

189. Griswold v. Connecticut, 381 U.S. 479 (1965).

oped. The Court did move to expand and protect the rights of minorities and, in doing so, did intervene in the affairs of other branches of the federal and state governments. The discussion also suggests that the Court is not immune to the pressures of the political context in which it operates. For example, the checkered path followed in the loyalty-security litigation and the failure to require vigorous compliance with its desegregation decisions indicate that the Court is influenced by and must take account of the preferences of the polity and the support or opposition of other governmental institutions. By the same token, recent changes in Court personnel, in part a result of the 1968 election, have ended the Warren Court and replaced it with one that may be moving toward a different view of the protection of civil liberties and rights. Finally, it is clear that the decisions of the Court are not self-executing, i.e., do not meet with the compliance that would be required were the Court in a position to authoritatively and finally "decide" the questions implicit in the cases that come before it.

Thus, both in obtaining occasions for policy-making and in having its decisions complied with (or modified or ignored), the Warren Court—like all others—interacted with other individuals and political institutions. The rest of this book is devoted to the activities of one group of individuals, the lawyers who argued many of these cases before the Court.

3. Concepts

This chapter discusses some of the concepts utilized in the analysis of the activities of the lawyers who argued civil liberties and civil rights cases before the Supreme Court. In the course of explaining these concepts, an overview of some of the interview data is presented.

CLIENTELE

There is a variety of ways of conceptualizing what a lawyer is trying to achieve in his litigation. We might talk about *goals*, referring to what particular outcome the lawyer was trying to achieve (to win? to win on a particular point of law? to secure some social or political policy?). The notion of *role* might be useful, for self-expectations and those of others may be very important in shaping the lawyer's perception of his case and his notions of how he ought to approach it. Another useful concept might be *reference groups or individuals*, for there may be particular individuals or groups whose expectations and preferences are particularly important to the lawyer. Finally, we could use the concept of *clientele*, which deals with the set of persons (ranging from an individual to all of society) that the lawyer perceives as having a stake in the case and as being likely to be affected importantly by its outcome.

Most of the concepts suggested above are theoretically distinct and separable, but all are related to some extent. One of these concepts, clientele, is the focus of this study. The discussion in this chapter of theoretical material is not the product of the particular complexity of the concepts. Rather, the discussion is necessary because the concepts draw rather fine distinctions, ones that are perhaps more apparent in the abstract than when applied, and it is, therefore, important to indicate what is intended when they are used. In addition, since the "made up" concept used here—"clientele"—is in fact close to concepts about which there is an extensive literature, it is important both to justify the use of something new and to distinguish it from those that are more familiar.

The term "clientele" is not used here in the restricted sense usually applied to the principal for whom the lawyer acts as agent. The clientele of a lawyer (as distinguished from his client) is not simply the person, group, or organization that formally retains and pays him. Rather, clientele is defined by the lawyer's perceptions of what group or interest he is serving. Obviously, a lawyer's clientele in a particular case may be his client, but the two need not be the same. In fact, a lawyer's clientele could range along a continuum from one person (usually his client) to all of society. In analyzing the responses to questions designed to tap the respondent's clientele, lawyers with three different classes of clienteles were distinguished: the *Advocate*, the *Group Advocate*, and the *Civil Libertarian*.[1]

The Advocate is close to the paradigm often associated with the legal profession. He uses his training and skills in litigation on behalf of his client. He is concerned simply with winning the case for his client, and he will use any legal and ethical means, raise any issue, seek any satisfactory result (e.g., agree to a plea bargain before trial,[2] be satisfied with winning an appeal on a

1. The questions in the interview schedule dealing most directly with clientele were as follows: (1) *Did you consider the case primarily important for your client or for broader social considerations?* (2) *Were you interested in winning the case on any possible ground or in establishing a particular point of law?* (3) *Were you satisfied with the results of this litigation?*

2. Though the literature dealing with plea bargaining suggests that the lawyer may be pursuing goals of his own (financial, interpersonal, etc.) that may not always coincide with those of his client. See, especially, Abraham Blumberg,

technicality or with a remand to a lower court for further proceedings). The Advocate is essentially indifferent about whom he represents; the characteristics of his client are of little interest to him. The Advocate views his own policy preferences as irrelevant to his activity as an attorney, and the ramifications of his case for others in society are also of little concern, unless they affect directly his chances for winning. The Advocate's clientele is his client.

The Group Advocate sees himself as a representative of some particular group and uses his skills in the case he argues to further the aims of that group. This is not to imply that the Group Advocate is simply an Advocate with a group as his client. Rather, the Group Advocate perceives himself as having long-term commitments to the group involved, and, more important, the group may not even be a formal party to the litigation. In a sense, then, the Group Advocate is serving *his* group in litigation (though he may not formally be a member of the group—e.g., the white civil rights lawyer representing black clients).[3] Thus the Group Advocate's clientele is somewhat wider than that of the Advocate, but it still numbers less than all of society. The Group Advocate perceives himself as a member of a specific group and his activity in litigation as representative of the group interest.

The Civil Libertarian[4] views his clientele as all of society and

Criminal Justice (Chicago: Quadrangle Books, 1967), and "The Practice of Law as a Confidence Game," *Law and Society Review* 1 (1967): 15–39.

3. Though, if David Truman's definition of group membership—shared attitudes and interaction—is adopted, the white civil rights lawyer and his black clientele are members of the same group. See Truman, *The Governmental Process* (New York: Alfred A. Knopf, 1951), Ch. 2.

4. Some recent discussions of changing patterns in legal practice have used the term "public interest lawyer." Discussions of this type of attorney and practice suggest that lawyers in this category might be acting—in specific cases—as Civil Libertarians (for example, in some consumer protection suits) or as Group Advocates (for example, in some conservation suits designed to protect localities from specific environmental threats). Thus the term "public interest lawyer," though focusing upon some of the same traits as the clientele types discussed here, is somewhat less specific in its referent. For useful discussions of these developments in legal practice, see Edgar S. and Jean Camper Cahn, "Power to the People or the Profession: The Public Interest in Public Law," *Yale Law Journal* 79 (1970): 1005–48, and "The New Public Interest Lawyers," ibid., pp. 1069–1152.

his case as a vehicle by which democratic principles important to all of society may be vindicated. The principles are general: "freedom of religion" or "freedom of speech." The lawyer is something of a gadfly, using his expertise to promote democratic principles. The ACLU is an organization—staffed largely by lawyers—dedicated to using litigation to promote such principles. The Civil Libertarian, like other lawyers, is involved in litigation that affects specific individuals, but he is primarily concerned with the results of the litigation upon society generally—not "free speech for John Doe" or "free speech for those with whom I am associated" but "free speech for all."

The distinction between the Advocate and the Group Advocate and Civil Libertarian is sharper than that between the Group Advocate and the Civil Libertarian. This is especially true because some of the cases in which Group Advocates have become involved—those dealing with racial discrimination, speech and association rights of political radicals, and reapportionment—do appear to involve principles obviously important to the whole society. But the key to the distinction between the Group Advocate and the Civil Libertarian is not the *issue* that appears to be involved in the case but the lawyer's perception of the group interest at stake. As is pointed out in some detail in the discussions of Group Advocates and Civil Libertarians, this is not meant to imply that Group Advocates are indifferent to the effects of their cases upon society generally, but simply that their primary concern deals with the effects upon a particular group rather than upon society at large.

The distinction between the Group Advocate and the Civil Libertarian may be further illuminated by contrasting two litigating interest groups, the NAACP Legal Defense Fund (LDF) and the ACLU. Lawyers of both organizations become involved in litigation dealing with similar issues. For the LDF the operative factor in its involvement has typically been the presence of an issue involving black people (i.e., an issue affecting this *particular* group of people); for the ACLU the operative factor has been the presence of some democratic principle. The services of the LDF have, in a sense, not been available to all, for the organization was set up and has functioned primarily as an advocate for a particular minority.[5] The ACLU, on the other hand, has professed to be indifferent to the characteristics of its clients —ACLU lawyers have represented fascists and Communists, blacks and white racists.[6] For the one organization, a particular group of people has brought it into action, for the other, a type of principle.[7] The differences between the activities of the two organizations correspond rather closely to the distinction between the Group Advocate and the Civil Libertarian.

Clienteles and Goals

Though empirically there is a relationship between the clienteles of lawyers and the goals they profess, the two concepts are theoretically distinct. Thus, for example, lawyers might report the following goals, if asked what they were trying to accomplish: (1) win my case, regardless of the ground upon which decision is based; (2) win my case and thereby establish a particular point of law; (3) get John Smith out of jail; (4) integrate the public schools; (5) reform the politics of South Dakota; (6) protect freedom of religion.

Theoretically, at least, any of the three types of clientele could be associated with any of the above goals. To take a couple of examples, a lawyer could be working toward a fairly limited goal (e.g., win regardless of grounds; get Smith out of jail) and still perceive his clientele as all of society (if, for example, he felt that Smith was an important national political figure whose freedom and activities were important to the country). Or a

5. Though this has been changing in the past few years. The LDF has moved into issue areas—criminal justice, welfare, hunger, attachment and garnishment proceedings—that affect classes of citizens much broader than blacks alone.

6. A recent discussion of the controversy within the ACLU over the provision of counsel to Dr. Spock and his co-defendants charged that its policy may be changing. See Joseph W. Bishop, Jr., "The Reverend Mr. Coffin, Dr. Spock, and the ACLU," *Harper's* (May 1968), pp. 57–68. Others active in the ACLU dispute Bishop's contention.

7. Of course, LDF cases have typically involved a principle—racial equality. But the thrust of the organization has been toward dealing with discrimination against a *particular* group, blacks, not against other minority groups like Indians, etc. As suggested in note 5, though, this emphasis upon one group has been changing in recent years.

lawyer could be seeking to force reapportionment in a state legislature, with his clientele being a particular political figure, perhaps because the lawyer felt strong personal or ideological attachments to that individual. Thus, although lawyers with very limited goals are typically Advocates and those with rather sweeping social or political goals are Group Advocates or Civil Libertarians, the concepts are theoretically distinct. When the factors that appear to determine a lawyer's clientele in particular cases are discussed, some reasons for the empirical relationship between goals and clienteles will emerge more clearly. But, on the conceptual level, the concepts are distinguishable and distinct. It may be useful to conceive of clientele as the *social domain of a goal*, indicating that different combinations of the concepts are theoretically possible.

One of the reasons for focusing upon clientele rather than goals is the fact that it is easier to operationalize the concept of clientele. The primary advantage of the notion of clientele is that it has an intuitively plausible dimension to it involving the number of individuals that constitute the clientele. The concept of goal also has a kind of "breadth" dimension to it, but it seems easier to tap clientele and to distinguish between differing clienteles than among a variety of goals. In asking a lawyer what he was trying to accomplish, and then attempting to characterize and compare goals, confusions are likely to arise. For example, consider two lawyers involved in loyalty-security cases, one dealing with the House Un-American Activities Committee and the other with a state loyalty oath. When asked why they felt the cases were important or what they were trying to accomplish, both might well respond that they were dealing with the protection of the right of speech or association. But the cases may have very different meanings to the lawyers. One may perceive his case as essentially a holding action for political radicals (with whom the lawyer is, to some extent, in agreement) against unwarranted governmental harassment. The other may be concerned not with particular applications of the principle of free speech to a particular group but with the effects of the application of such oaths on society at large. This kind of difference can be better understood with the concept of clientele, while it might well be obscured if we concentrated upon reported goals.

Clientele also lends itself to integration with the so-called "group theory" of the legal process.[8] Although clientele deals with the perception of the lawyer, not the overt activity of interest groups, it does to some extent illuminate the degree to which the representation of a "group interest" (and the nature of the group involved) was a factor in the lawyer's reasons for pursuing his case up the appeals ladder. Thus clientele will be useful in further assessing the relevance of the group theory of the legal process and of some of its recent critics.[9]

To recapitulate, clienteles and goals are theoretically distinct but do have an empirical relationship (discussed in detail later). Because of a greater amenability to operationalization and because of the relationship of clientele to the group theory of the legal process, clientele rather than goals is the organizing concept used here.

Clienteles and Roles

Role is another concept, fashionable in current social science research, that might have been an organizing concept for the study of the behavior and goals of the lawyers under consideration here.[10] Roles are defined by expectations about the behavior of actors in a social system. The expectations that define a role may be the self-expectations of the actor or the expectations of other members of the social system of which he is a member.

There is, without question, a role attached to the activities of

8. See, for example, Jack Peltason, *Federal Courts in the Political Process* (New York: Random House, 1955), and Clement E. Vose, "Litigation as a Form of Pressure Group Activity," *Annals of the American Academy of Political and Social Science* 319 (1958): 20–31.

9. See, for example, Nathan Hakman, "The Supreme Court's Political Environment: The Processing of Noncommercial Litigation," in Joel B. Grossman and Joseph Tanenhaus, eds., *Frontiers of Judicial Research* (New York: John Wiley and Sons, 1969), pp. 199–253.

10. A useful general introduction to role theory is found in Neal Gross, Ward Mason, and Alexander McEachern, *Explorations in Role Analysis* (New York: John Wiley and Sons, 1958), Ch. 4. Role theory has been extensively used in the analysis of the behavior of congressmen. See, for example, Richard Fenno, Jr., *The Power of the Purse* (Boston: Little, Brown, 1966).

an attorney in litigation. The expectations (of the bar in general, court personnel, or the public) are, in fact, codified in the Canons of Legal Ethics. The responsibilities of the lawyer in litigation and the restrictions upon what behavior is permissible are defined in some detail. Although actual behavior may be at variance with that defined by the role,[11] a role does exist, defined in terms of both self-expectations and expectations of others. However, for purposes of this study, the concept does not seem of great utility. The role of the lawyer is to a large extent undifferentiated; as a general rule, the lawyer is expected to behave in a certain fashion regardless of the type of litigation in which he is involved.[12] Since this study seeks to analyze differences in the activities and expectations of lawyers and to relate their activities to the kinds of litigation in which they are involved, an organizing concept that differentiates relevantly among the lawyers is required.

Clienteles and Reference Groups

Clientele is very closely related to the concepts of reference groups and reference individuals.[13] Reference groups and individuals provide people with standards of comparison for self-appraisal (comparative reference groups) and serve as a source of an individual's norms, attitudes, and values (normative reference groups). The concepts of reference groups and individuals have been used extensively in the analysis of various kinds of political behavior.

A lawyer's clientele is, in fact, one of his reference individuals

11. The contrast between the norms of the Canons of Ethics and the behavior of many lawyers is discussed in Jerome Carlin, *Lawyers' Ethics* (New York: Russell Sage Foundation, 1966) and *Lawyers on Their Own* (New Brunswick, N.J.: Rutgers University Press, 1962).

12. Though some recent court decisions dealing with the activities of litigating interest groups and the development of group practice of law suggest that the norms dealing with ethical behavior are very much in a state of flux. See, especially, NAACP v. Button, 371 U.S. 415 (1963), and Brotherhood of R. Trainmen v. Virginia, 377 U.S. 1 (1964).

13. For an introduction to reference-group theory, see Herbert Hyman, "Reference Groups," *International Encyclopedia of the Social Sciences* (New York: Macmillan and the Free Press, 1968), 13: 353–61, and Robert Merton, *Social Theory and Social Structure* (Glencoe, Ill.: Free Press, 1957), Ch. 8.

or groups. In any particular case a lawyer's reference groups and individuals probably include his formal client, other members of the bar, and the judges before whom he argues. His *clientele* in a case *may* be one of these reference groups or individuals common to all lawyers (e.g., the Advocate whose clientele is his client), but it may not. For example, in a civil rights case a lawyer may take cues about his behavior from his formal client, from the bar and judges, but, most important, from his perceptions of the needs of blacks generally. Clientele, then, attempts to focus upon the reference group or individual that is most salient to the lawyer in a particular case.

Reference-group theory recognizes that an individual with multiple reference groups and individuals may experience conflict. This phenomenon, discussed in terms of clientele, is relevant to the lawyers discussed here. For example, a Civil Libertarian, viewing his case as essentially vindicating principles important for society at large, would obviously be under some cross-pressuring if he were representing on appeal an individual convicted of a capital crime.

Thus the basic organizing concept used in this study to differentiate the lawyers' approaches to their litigation, their goals, their expectations, their perceptions of why their cases are important, is clientele. It is related to other concepts that might have been used, but clientele appears to have certain advantages that recommend it rather than the others.

Lawyers with the three types of clienteles were not randomly distributed among the various areas of litigation. Table 1 presents the distribution of clienteles by area of litigation. The pat-

TABLE 1. CLIENTELES BY TYPE OF CASE ARGUED.

	Advocate	Group Advocate	Civil Libertarian	Total
Criminal justice	20	1	7	28
Reapportionment	0	8	0	8
Loyalty-security	2	12	7	21
Civil rights	1	12	1	14
Other	2	1	8	11
Total	25	34	23	82

$x^2 = 62.1$ (significant at .001 level)

terns of distribution—the overrepresentation of Advocates in criminal justice cases, the predominance of Group Advocates in reapportionment and civil rights cases, etc.—are the subject of detailed analysis in the chapters dealing with the three clientele types.

The classification of a lawyer's clientele is based upon a series of questions dealing with his perceptions of the case that he argued before the Supreme Court. Thus, when we speak of a lawyer's being an Advocate, Group Advocate, or Civil Libertarian, we are referring to his perception of the particular case that he argued. In the discussion of the connection between a lawyer's clientele and his attitudes toward the role of the law and the legal profession, it is suggested that a lawyer's clientele is not typically the product simply of factors idiosyncratic to the case he argued but is, in part, the product of enduring attitudes about what it is to be a lawyer. But this is not to say that a lawyer approaches *all* his cases with the clientele that he serves in the litigation discussed in the interview. Other factors may be at work —the context in which a case comes to an attorney, his experience with the type of litigation, cues provided by the Court itself —that also affect a lawyer's clientele. Thus the data here can only support the proposition that varying patterns of clienteles occurred in different areas of litigation, not that a lawyer who is called an Advocate, Group Advocate, or Civil Libertarian *always* approaches his cases with this clientele. Since we are interested in exploring the relationship between the recruitment and the goals of lawyers as actors in the judicial policy-making process —and hence interested in contrasting clienteles with outcomes of cases in various areas of litigation—this limitation upon the ability to more broadly characterize a lawyer's approach to *all* his litigation is less severe than it might be if we were interested in offering generalizations about the character of the bar.

LEGAL IDEOLOGY

Clientele deals with the lawyer's approach to his litigation, with his perceptions of whom he is representing. In addition to discussing the behavior of lawyers having different clienteles and the types of litigation in which they were involved, we will explore some of the factors that appear to affect a lawyer's clientele. The most important factor is the lawyer's attitudes toward the role of law and the legal profession in society, referred to here as his *legal ideology*. The implicit hypothesis is that a lawyer's clientele is not simply a discrete phenomenon, particular to a given case, but is in some measure the product of an enduring attitude structure that informs his approach to his professional activities.

Two variables designed to tap legal ideology were developed, and questions pertaining to them were included in the interview schedule. The first deals with a lawyer's perception of the role of law in our society, the second with the role of the legal profession. Combination of these variables produced a typology of lawyers.

The Role of Law

The question dealing most directly with the role of law in society was as follows:

What do you think should be the primary role of the law and the judicial process in American society today?

The question is extremely open-ended and amenable to a variety of answers. Some of the respondents had obviously given the issue a good deal of thought over the years; others had seemingly never thought about it at all. Though an almost infinite variety of replies is conceivable, certain patterns of response emerged quite clearly. The most common types of response were (1) social control/prevent anarchy; (2) do justice and reach the truth in specific disputes; (3) protect the rights of the individual from infringement by government; (4) provide the basic mechanisms for the maintenance of a democratic society and political system; (5) provide a mechanism for social change and reform of society.

The basic dimension of these responses seems to involve a dichotomy between views of the law as a mechanism for conflict resolution and control (categories 1 and 2) and as a mechanism for maintaining a democratic political system and for promoting social change (categories 3, 4, and 5). A few of the responses may illustrate the two views:

Well, I think it should be the referee by which society plays the game . . . that has been laid out in our fundamental laws. In other words, beginning with your local statutes, your constitutions and statutes, I think the role of the courts is, and should be, to see that these laws are applied as they have been intended to, to keep a well-ordered society. [20]

. . . I think that the purpose of the law should be to promote justice. And that the function of a court and of a jury is the application and declaration of the truth. And as long as we have the truth come out in each case—and every man who's guilty is found guilty, and every man who's innocent is acquitted, then the law is doing a 100% perfect job, and no one can camplain. [2]

. . . the purpose of law in our society is not to protect the state's society, but enable the society in which we live to live up to its best potential. In other words, I think the law can be protective and that, in a democratic society, the law ought to be for people, disadvantaged people, and people should be and are entitled to equal opportunities, and the law ought to be the vehicle by which they can secure it. The judicial process should make that easy. Unfortunately, as in most societies, the law is geared to maintain the status quo. And I think that through constitutional education, in our society, that it is not as broad as it should be and I suppose that is why we are here. [35]

I feel that the law should be moulded always to do the greatest justice and progress for those who have the least, and that the law should favor those with the least and work against those with the most. [58]

I feel quite strongly that the courts have a very affirmative role to play, that it is their function to develop principles, to apply those principles forcefully, to positively operate to maintain those ground rules that protect the individual and which underlie a democratic process. [30]

Thus the lawyers were classified into two categories in terms of their attitudes toward the role of law—those who stressed law as a mechanism for social control and conflict resolution versus those who viewed law as a mechanism for democracy and promoting social change. It is clear that, if pressed, those who responded in terms of one of these categories would acknowledge that the law also serves the function stressed by those in the other category. This is a phenomenon often encountered with such open-ended questions. But the ability of this dichotomy to differentiate lawyers who also are differentiable on another dimension—clientele—suggests that the concept of legal ideology does have some theoretical utility.

The Legal Profession

Data were also gathered dealing with the attitudes of the respondents toward the role of the lawyer and the legal profession in society. The dimension examined was a preference for an active versus a passive legal profession. Perceptions of the respondents of the role the bar should play in shaping society *through litigation* (not the respondents' views about the role of lawyers, as citizens, in the development of public policy) were explored.

The legal profession has developed a series of norms which severely restricts the activities of attorneys in initiating and intervening in litigation. The Canons of Legal Ethics forbid such practices as soliciting clients (either directly or through lay intermediaries), stirring up litigation, and advertising. The philosophy embodied in the canons is that of a passive bar, a group of professionals willing to exercise their expertise in behalf of those who seek them out but unwilling to exercise initiative in seeking out clients or raising legal issues.

Though the norm of passivity is adhered to in varying degrees by different economic and status strata of the bar, the norm does seem fairly pervasive. Recent legal developments in noncommercial areas of the law have to some degree legitimated more active conduct by lawyers. In the *Button* case, for example, the Supreme Court sanctioned initiatives by the NAACP which would violate the canons if practiced in the area of personal injury litigation. The development of legal services offices under the auspices of the Poverty Program that view themselves as legal lobbyists for the underprivileged may further expand the initiatives which will be considered proper.

A series of questions was directed at the respondents to elicit their attitudes toward the posture of the legal profession general-ly and toward certain specified initiatives by attorneys in hypo-thetical situations. In all questions it was implied that the attorney would have no financial interest in the outcome of the litigation and that it would involve some broad social issue. Re-spondents were divided into those who preferred an active and those who preferred a passive legal profession.[14]

Legal Types

The dichotomous variables produce four legal types. As the presentation of Table 2 suggests, though four types are theoreti-

TABLE 2. FOUR LEGAL TYPES.

Law as:	The Bar as:		
	Passive	Active	
Conflict resolution/social control	Traditionalist 24	10	34
Democracy/change	6	Reformer 42	48
	30	52	82

$x^2 = 28.9$ (significant at .001 level)

cally possible, only two of them (containing about 81 percent of the respondents) are used here. These two, called the *Tradi-*

14. See Appendix for the interview schedule. Questions 10 and 12–16 dealt with attitudes toward the role of the legal profession. Because of time limitations in interviews, not all respondents were asked all six questions. The four questions (10, 13, 14, 16) with the highest response rate (the average nonresponse was 7 percent) were analyzed. Responses were dichotomized (initiative proper or im-proper), and a satisfactory Guttman Scale was constructed (CR = .92; CS = .72). Though none of the items produced a majority of negative responses, some respondents did reply negatively to all questions. The respondents were placed into two groups on the basis of their response to the fourth item (to which 37 percent responded negatively).

tionalist and the *Reformer,* combine attitudes toward the law and the legal profession in a fashion that is intuitively plausible. The other two "types" possess what may be called "equivocal" legal ideologies, combining the two dimensions in ways that do not have as obvious interpretations. Because they did not occur frequently, they will not be the subject of close scrutiny here.[15]

The Traditionalist, as the name implies, adheres to rather traditional views about both the law and his profession. He sees the law as primarily a mechanism for resolving disputes in society, and he feels that the lawyer should remain passive in his relations with potential clients, waiting for a client with a complaint to come to him rather than going out looking for cases. The Reformer, his opposite on both dimensions, views the law as a

15. Though the small numbers of respondents in each category make even speculation risky, some observations about the two types with "equivocal" legal ideologies may be made. The group falling in the lower left cell (passive bar and law as democracy/change) might be called Theoreticians, for they aspire to law promoting social change but do not condone initiatives by attorneys. Five of the six Theoreticians encountered had argued criminal justice cases. None of them practiced criminal law (or civil liberties law generally) regularly; they were in commercial and corporate practice and became involved by means of appointment or retainer clients. Thus their involvement was to some extent "accidental." It is possible that this type might be quite prevalent among young members of large firms. Though they do not practice much civil liberties law themselves, they are members of a generation of lawyers likely to accept the function of law as a vehicle for social change, perhaps because many spent their formative years in a period that saw law used for such purposes. The characteristics of their regular law practice—their noninvolvement in civil liberties litigation—and the importance of the Canons of Ethics in areas of commercial and corporate practice may be related to their perhaps anomalous views about the propriety of initiatives by attorneys.

The other group of ten lawyers (combining a preference for an active bar with a view of law as a mechanism for social control and conflict resolution) might be called Activists. A number of these attorneys were in solo practice or with small firms and did primarily personal injury and divorce work. Though many were financially successful, their practices were highly competitive, and the struggle for clients was an integral part of their legal experience. Significantly, many interpreted the questions dealing with initiatives by attorneys—all of which explicitly or tacitly dealt with litigation involving social or political issues —as involving legal initiatives generally. Some spoke of their preference for competitive advertising by lawyers, for example. These lawyers, then, may represent another stratum of the bar that does not typically become involved in civil liberties litigation (only two of the ten reported any regular involvement in that area). This type may be found frequently among lawyers with practices in which competition for cases is strong.

The determinants of clienteles for both these types with "equivocal" legal ideologies are discussed in detail in subsequent chapters.

mechanism for promoting social change and protecting democracy and tends to reject traditional norms of complete passivity.

It is of some interest to note that in an entirely different context Zechariah Chaffee concluded that lawyers fall into groups
quite like those presented here:

> Thoughtful lawyers in their attitudes toward social and economic
> problems fall roughly into three groups. The first is composed of men
> who are satisfied with the existing situation and anxious to keep
> things as they are. . . . At the opposite extreme are lawyers who are
> very much dissatisfied with existing conditions and anxious to change
> them. . . . In between these two extremes falls an intermediate group
> of lawyers who, though reasonably comfortable themselves, are
> nevertheless troubled by inequalities in power and fortune and are
> skeptical as to the eternal merits of the present rules of the game.[16]
> Perhaps they would not do much themselves to change the existing
> situation, for example, if they were legislators. Yet they are reluctant
> to stop other men from trying to make things better. They are not
> sure enough of their own ideas to be certain that the reformers are
> wrong.[17]

Clientele and Legal Ideology

The combination of the two groups of lawyers with differing
legal ideologies—the Traditionalists and the Reformers—and
their clienteles in the cases they argued before the Supreme
Court, suggests that these two variables are not independent of
one another. As is obvious from simple inspection of Table 3

TABLE 3. CLIENTELE AND LEGAL IDEOLOGY.

	Traditionalist	Reformer	Total
Advocate	13	4	17
Group Advocate	7	25	32
Civil Libertarian	4	13	17
Total	24	42	66

$$x^2 = 14.8 \text{ (significant at .001 level)}$$

16. This "intermediate group" corresponds closely to the Theoreticians discussed above.

17. Zechariah Chaffee, Jr., *Free Speech in the United States* (Cambridge,
Mass.: Harvard University Press, 1941), p. 360.

(and is reflected in the x^2), the Traditionalists are more likely to be Advocates and the Reformers to be Group Advocates or Civil Libertarians.[18]

In the succeeding chapters, as the three clientele groups are discussed in detail, the meaning of these relationships will be explored more fully. At this point the gross statistical relationship suggests that the two concepts discussed here—clientele and legal ideology—are not independent. Later it is argued that legal ideology is, in fact, the basic variable determining a lawyer's clientele, to some extent shaping his practice generally. Other factors—including the nature of the particular case, circumstances surrounding the lawyer's involvement, and cues provided by the Supreme Court—also affect the lawyer's clientele, but they operate at the margins. In addition, these other factors are crucial to the difference between the Group Advocate and the Civil Libertarian, since both these groups are characterized by similar legal ideologies.

INVOLVEMENT IN LITIGATION

Another aspect of the lawyers' participation in their cases deals with their involvement in the litigation that they eventually argued before the Supreme Court. Two aspects of recruitment are of particular interest: the *stage* at which a lawyer becomes initially involved in the case and the *means* by which he becomes involved.

There are essentially three stages at which a lawyer can become involved in a case that eventually reaches the Supreme Court: (1) before or at the time of the initial trial; (2) during the period between the initial trial and the first appeal (either

18. Since the distinction between the Advocates and the Group Advocates and Civil Libertarians is conceptually somewhat greater than the difference between the Group Advocate and the Civil Libertarian, it may be useful to present a similar contingency table, combining Group Advocates and Civil Libertarians:

	Traditionalist	*Reformer*	*Total*
Advocate	13	4	17
Group Advocate or Civil Libertarian	11	38	49
Total	24	42	66

$$x^2 = 15.8 \text{ (significant at .001 level)}$$

to a state supreme court or to a federal circuit court of appeals);[19] (3) during the period between the first appeal and the appeal to the Supreme Court of the United States.

The data pertaining to the stage at which the lawyers interviewed became involved are presented in Table 4. A substantial

TABLE 4. LAWYERS' STAGE OF INVOLVEMENT.

Type of Case	Initial Trial	First Appeal	Supreme Court	
Criminal justice	42.8%	35.7%	21.5%	(n=28)
Reapportionment	87.5	12.5	———	(n=8)
Loyalty-security	85.7	9.5	4.8	(n=21)
Civil rights	64.3	———	35.7	(n=14)
Other	72.7	———	27.3	(n=11)
Total	65.8	15.8	18.3	
	(54)	(13)	(15)	(n=82)

proportion of the lawyers handled these cases from their inception. With the possible exception of civil rights litigation, these cases were not argued before the Supreme Court by a specialized appeal bar.

The second kind of data pertaining to involvement concerns the manner in which an attorney becomes involved in a case. Analysis of responses to questions about involvement reveals five patterns: (1) appointment by a court (referred to hereafter as "appointment"); (2) referral of the client by another attorney ("referral"); (3) representation of a client whom the lawyer had previously represented ("previous client");[20] (4) referral to a lawyer by a group in which he was active, e.g., the ACLU, the NAACP Legal Defense and Educational Fund, Inc. ("group"); (5) a request to the lawyer to represent an individual with whom he has had social contact or friendship ties ("friendship").[21] The

19. In about a third of the states there is an intermediate appeals court between the trial court and the state supreme court. But all of the respondents interviewed became involved at one of the three stages indicated here.

20. This category includes representation of retainer clients, as, for example, representation of an official of a union that retains the lawyer for all its legal work.

21. There were occasional overlaps between involvement through "friendship" and through "previous client." The classification in each case was made upon the

distribution of means of involvement is shown in Table 5. Certain patterns are striking. Appointment, as would be expected,

TABLE 5. LAWYERS' MEANS OF INVOLVEMENT.

Type of Case	How Involved					
	Appointment	Referral	Previous Client	Group	Friendship	
Criminal justice	42.8%	28.6%	3.6%	10.7%[a]	14.3%	(n=28)
Reapportionment	———	———	12.5	37.5[b]	50.0	(n=8)
Loyalty-security	———	4.8	14.3[c]	33.4[d]	47.6	(n=21)
Civil rights	———	14.3	7.1	78.6[e]	———	(n=14)
Other	———	18.2	18.2	36.4[f]	27.3	(n=11)
Total	14.6	15.8	9.8	34.1	25.6	(n=82)

[a] One through ACLU, one through New York Legal Aid Society, one through local committee to abolish capital punishment.
[b] Three through various local political clubs.
[c] All three were officials of unions which were retainer clients.
[d] Six through ACLU, one through local bar association.
[e] Eight through NAACP, two through ACLU, one through CORE.
[f] Three through ACLU, one through Planned Parenthood group.

was important in the criminal justice litigation, and friendship ties seem to have been crucial in the loyalty-security and reapportionment litigation. The significance of these patterns is treated in detail in the chapters dealing with the three clientele types.

These, then, are some of the major concepts that will be used in analyzing the data gathered about the lawyers. Now we shall turn to a detailed discussion of the three clientele types.

---

basis of the factor the lawyer stressed most in reporting the circumstances of his involvement.

4. The Advocate

Judicial power is frequently invoked by parties for reasons that have nothing to do with the promotion of large values. For example, a man on trial for murder may raise the claim that he was denied his constitutional right to assistance of counsel and in so doing represent an interest of a much wider scope than he himself is aware. His own reasons for his activity may be unrelated to, and certainly not designed to promote, any wider interest.[1]

The Advocate is closest to the traditional image of the lawyer, the attorney acting simply as agent for his client. Since most of the Advocates were active in one area of litigation—criminal justice—this chapter is also in large part about the criminal justice cases argued before the Warren Court.

The first part of the chapter describes in detail exactly what is meant by the term "Advocate" and describes how the Advocate (as opposed to lawyers with other clientele types) approaches his litigation. The discussion then turns to some suggestions of *why* lawyers become Advocates. Several factors are discussed, including the lawyer's perceptions of the role of law and the legal profession (his legal ideology); the degree of experience he has had with the field of litigation in which he becomes involved; the stakes of his client (i.e., the lawyer's perception of

1. Jack Peltason, *Federal Courts in the Political Process* (New York: Random House, 1955), p. 44.

how much his client stands to lose by defeat in court); and cues provided by the Supreme Court suggesting to the lawyer how he ought to treat his case. The major factor producing an Advocate is a particular legal ideology (the Traditionalist) that tends to focus his perspective on his case. The other factors operate at the margin, making the relationship between legal ideology and clientele far from perfect. Some lawyers with the legal ideology associated with being an Advocate do not behave like Advocates; some lawyers with legal ideologies associated with other clientele types behave like Advocates. Thus both the connection between legal ideology and clientele and other intervening factors are discussed.

After consideration of the reasons why some lawyers tend to be Advocates, the discussion moves to the question of why Advocates become involved predominantly in one area of litigation, criminal justice. The same factors that tend to produce Advocates (i.e., Traditionalists, or lawyers with equivocal legal ideologies who become involved on a temporary basis in cases in which the stakes of their clients appear high) have been associated with the recruitment of many lawyers into criminal justice litigation argued before the Supreme Court.

The argument then moves to another, yet related, question. How does the activity of this group of lawyers in this area of litigation illuminate a view of the judicial system as a policy-developing process? In the area of criminal justice the legal reforms that occurred during the 1957–66 period (and they were of no little consequence) were largely unintended by-products of the activities of attorneys neither very much aware of nor concerned with policy development. This discontinuity between the goals of lawyers and the policy that emerged differentiates criminal justice from the other areas of litigation discussed here.

One major consequence of the important decisions that came out of the Court in the area of criminal justice goes beyond the protection of the rights of defendants. These decisions have directly affected the recruitment and goals of lawyers who will be involved in criminal justice litigation in the future. To use the terms developed here, in the future fewer Advocates and more

Group Advocates and Civil Libertarians may, largely as a consequence of the decisions of the Court (especially those dealing with provision of counsel to indigent defendants), become involved in this litigation. To put it more generally, although in the past a large proportion of criminal justice cases were argued by "casuals" serving by court appointment, in the future more and more may be argued by specialists, operating out of institutions designed to act as legal lobbyists for the rights of criminal defendants. Litigation in criminal justice, then, may become more like that in other areas of civil liberties, with individual cases being vehicles for the vindication of broad policy goals. The lawyers may become more like the image usually associated with "civil liberties" lawyers—they will be interested in policy as well as in their clients.

Finally, this chapter makes a first exploration of some of the consequences of such a development, for the lawyer-client relationship, for the role of litigation as a political phenomenon, for the protection of civil liberties and civil rights. Different evaluations might be made depending upon the perspective one adopts. Somewhat perversely (though quite plausibly), one might conclude that one kind of lawyer is "desirable" if one is the defendant, another "desirable" from the perspective of society as a whole.

THE ADVOCATE

What is an Advocate? Or, more precisely, what is it about this group of lawyers that makes them different from the other lawyers with whom we deal? The Advocate perceives his function in litigation as protecting and promoting the interests of but one individual, his client. He is not necessarily particularly fond of his client, nor does he admire his activities; many Advocates interviewed spoke of their clients with distaste if not antipathy. Moreover, an Advocate is not necessarily unaware that his case may involve extremely important social and political issues. But he will consciously deny that this fact is important to his function in litigation. Rather, he perceives his function as simply that of serving the interest of his client, as he and his client see it. If this interest is served by a guilty plea rather than a trial, this is what the Advocate thinks he ought to advise. If the case goes to trial and then appeal, any issue, however technical or sweeping, should be stressed, and victory on any ground is to a large extent sweet. What the Advocate wants is to *win*. What counts for him is his *client*. Though his is to some extent an ideal type (as are the others), this perspective does differentiate one group of lawyers from the others, and it is this difference that defines the Advocate.

The following quotations give the flavor of the Advocate's approach to his litigation:

Well, I think [the case] had questions of law and some issues in it that were of real consequence, but as far as the facts of this case, we were just representing a client. . . . I was interested in winning the case, and that's all. Any reversal would have suited me fine. [12]

Well, I think any lawyer who's appointed to defend a client in a case is primarily interested in his client. . . . It may be very interesting to vindicate principles of the law, and if you can, one frequently tries to—but it's the interest of the client that has to be paramount. If his interest doesn't happen to coincide with vindicating some great principle, the attorney has no business trying to vindicate the principle at the expense of his client. The client must come first. [73]

No, I am a professional. . . . I have represented guys who I would have locked up and put in the death house myself, if it were left to me. . . . It is my job to win when I represent a guy. This is the difference between, let's say, an ACLU lawyer and myself. My commitment to civil liberties is the commitment to represent the guy and what represents his cause is of no importance to me, and following that route, I am trying to win. . . . That is my job, and if I have to convince the Court to overrule the First Amendment, that's what I'll try to do. And if I convince the Court to overrule the First Amendment, then I have won the case. [32]

The points suggested above emerge more clearly when the lawyers themselves are allowed to speak. The Advocate wants to win; he is largely indifferent to the broader ramifications the case may possess. In his role as attorney, he neither condones nor condemns the activities of his client, for such considerations are perceived to be irrelevant to his performance. This last point is especially important, for the absence of any commitment (personal or ideological) by the lawyer to his client differentiates many Advocates from Group Advocates.

As respondent 32 indicates starkly, the ground for decision in his case is of little interest to the Advocate—what counts is the outcome. If a favorable decision requires that he convince the Court to take a broad step—to overrule an important precedent —then he will try to induce it to do so. If, on the other hand, alternative grounds are available, he perceives it to be his responsibility to raise all of them. In fact, if there is a choice between stressing a broad ground or a narrow one, the Advocate is likely to be attracted to the narrow alternative.[2] He is so attracted because of some kind of law of parsimony. He is interested in the result and feels intuitively that he is more likely to win if he asks the Court to take only a small step rather than to reconsider precedent or enunciate a broad new rule. This view, emerging from his professional socialization, is probably related to the rules for decision adopted by the Court, which in general require the Court to decide cases as narrowly as possible.[3]

2. This statement would admittedly be difficult to prove. Such proof would require content analysis of briefs and oral arguments. The analysis of briefs is not particularly revealing, because often the attorney will attempt to cover all possible arguments. The oral arguments would appear to be a better source of data on this point—one could attempt to see what issues, among those available, the lawyer stressed. But such analysis is difficult. Transcripts of oral arguments are not always available. In addition, in many oral arguments the lawyer does not have the opportunity to make a coherent presentation. The justices are likely to take control of the argument and require the attorney to discuss those points which they think are important (and to use "questions" as means to argue among themselves). Thus this statement is only suggestive. It is based upon discussions with lawyers, examination of briefs and some oral argument transcripts, and personal observations of oral argument before the Court.

3. The Court has developed norms for decision that are putatively designed to avoid deciding broad issues unless they must be confronted. Thus the norms suggest that if a narrow and a broad ground are both available to decide a case, the Court ought to choose the former. Moreover, the norm of self-restraint may be invoked to avoid deciding an issue if it is not "ripe," that is, if the case does not frame the issues in such a way that it is presented clearly and there are compelling reasons to confront it. For statements of these principles, see United Public Workers v. Mitchell, 330 U.S. 79 (1941); Justice Brandeis's concurring opinion in Ashwander v. T.V.A., 297 U.S. 288 (1936); and Poe v. Ullman, 367 U.S. 487 (1961). The discussion in this chapter of criminal justice cases in

On some occasions an Advocate may not even be aware that his litigation could potentially become the vehicle by which a broad principle will be enunciated. One example will serve to point up this phenomenon. (Unfortunately, in order to preserve the anonymity of the lawyer involved, the account must be severely cut and robbed of some of its impact.) The lawyer was representing a defendant in a criminal case on appeal to his state supreme court. During the appeal he raised a fundamental issue of procedure and argued that the rights of his client had been violated. He based his claim on the provisions of the state constitution. After losing in the highest state court, the lawyer resolved to petition for *certiorari* to the Supreme Court of the United States. His major reason for doing so was a sense of indignation at the curt treatment his argument had been accorded in the state supreme court. In his words:

[My appeal to the state supreme court] was thrown out, rejected out of hand. And it made me mad, so I decided to appeal it. On petition for *certiorari*, instead of going on the broad grounds used in the state court appeal—which I should have been astute enough to know . . . I rationalized that if I was going to get a hearing at all, it would have to be real close. I went on [another case, dealing with right to counsel]. Anyway, I felt that if I was going to get a hearing, it would probably be a little *per curiam* deal, and I would use [the right to counsel case]. That's the way I was pitching it, hoping to get a little *per curiam* opinion out of it. And pitching it to the conservatives. Rather than take it that way, well, they decided to make an issue of it. And Mr. Justice "Smith" wrote a beautiful brief for me on [the major issue upon which the Supreme Court decided the case].

Thus the attorney petitioned for *certiorari* and wrote his brief stressing a narrow and fairly well-established technical point, never alluding to the very broad issue upon which the Court eventually ruled:

When did it become apparent to you—if at all before the opinion— that the Supreme Court was going to use the [broad issue]? Was it raised in oral argument?

---

which the Court quite clearly reached out to decide issues that they might have avoided indicates that these principles of self-restraint are by no means completely unambiguous or invariably obeyed.

No, they didn't. I received a rumor. Where it came from, I'm not sure. Probably the [state] Attorney General's office. The case filed in March, I believe. In October they granted *cert.*, and the Attorney General's office or somebody—I guess that's where it was—said the Supreme Court was in a hurry to decide it. They wanted to get it up there. And I thought that was a little strange. I couldn't read between the lines, though, that there was anything more to it than that. I'm sorry that I can't take credit for this thing and say I was brilliant, you know. I just can't do it. I was a little brilliant in another case, but not this case.

No, they very coyly hid it all from me. They didn't treat me like they did Abe Fortas, and say, "Here's the question we want you to present." Now, that would have been nice if they'd done that. I thought they wouldn't. . . . I would have probably botched it if they had. . . .

They knew what they wanted and they knew how they were going to get it. . . . I think they had the opinion written before I talked to them. [8]

This account points up the fact that Advocates are typically not concerned with (and may not even be aware of) the broader implications of the litigation in which they become involved. Incidents as clear as the one recounted are probably rare,[4] but they do serve to emphasize the distinctive quality of the Advocate.

As noted before, Advocates were not distributed randomly across the various categories of litigation under study here. Rather, they appeared primarily in one kind of case—criminal justice. Table 6 contrasts the incidence of the three clientele

TABLE 6. CLIENTELES: CRIMINAL JUSTICE VERSUS ALL OTHER LITIGATION.

	Advocate	Group Advocate	Civil Libertarian	Total
Criminal justice	20	1	7	28
All other cases	5	33	16	54
Total	25	34	23	82

$$x^2 = 38.4 \text{ (significant at .001 level)}$$

4. Though in another important incorporation case involving criminal justice the major issue was not raised at all in the petitioner's brief but, rather, in an *amicus* brief filed by the ACLU.

types in criminal justice cases with the other types of litigation (combining reapportionment, loyalty-security, civil rights, and other).

In the area of criminal justice, as in other areas of civil liberties and civil rights during the 1957–66 period, a great deal of important litigation took place. The litigation was important because much of it dealt not just with the particular cases but with the development of sweeping new policy in the administration of criminal justice. Using individual cases as vehicles for the enunciation of important constitutional policy, the Court fashioned broad behavioral rules governing the administration of justice from a defendant's initial encounter with law enforcement officials to his rights in appellate hearings. In such areas as arrest, interrogation, search and seizure, right to counsel, and confrontation of witnesses, important changes in the system of criminal justice emerged from Supreme Court decisions. Perhaps as a result of the extent of the reform inherent in the Supreme Court's decisions, they were among the most controversial of the period, producing both violent opposition and impassioned defense. The issue of "law and order," which became a potent campaign slogan in electoral politics from the national to the local levels, was linked to the constitutional policy that emerged from these decisions.

Two questions immediately occur. First, why was this particular type of lawyer—the Advocate—so prominent in this particular area of litigation? Second, given the fact that Advocates—with their limited goals and expectations—were so prominent, what does this suggest about the nature of the process by which these important reforms took place in the area of criminal justice? Before getting to them, and by way of a preface, we shall treat another question: why is a lawyer an Advocate? More precisely, having defined this particular approach to litigation, this particular clientele, what factors appear to make a lawyer assume it?

In seeking to understand why some lawyers assume the clientele of the Advocate, that is, view their cases in terms of the interests of the particular client rather than broader social or political considerations, several factors appear important. First, and probably most important, is the legal ideology of the lawyer. Legal ideology refers to a lawyer's attitudes toward the role of the law and the legal system. The legal ideology of lawyers who are Advocates provides for them an enduring frame of reference that focuses their views on the individual cases in which they become involved.

Several other factors also appear to be of some consequence, making the relationship between legal ideology and clientele by no means perfect. One of the factors involves the characteristics of the client in a particular case: how much he stands to lose by defeat in court (e.g., the seriousness of the penalty), whether the client himself is interested simply in winning or in broader issues involved in the case, the presence or absence of personal or ideological ties between lawyer and client. Another factor apparently quite important in the way a lawyer perceives his litigation is the amount of experience he has had with similar litigation and the expectation (or lack of it) that he will continue to be involved in such litigation. If a lawyer is highly experienced with a particular type of case (whether criminal, loyalty-security, or civil rights), and if he expects that in the future he will continue to be involved, he is more likely both to perceive and to be concerned with the broader legal, social, or political issues that the case represents. He is therefore more likely to view his case not as a discrete matter to be resolved but as a vehicle by which broader issues may be confronted.[5] A final factor that may affect a lawyer's clientele involves cues provided by the Supreme Court itself. By a variety of techniques the Court may indicate to an attorney that the litigation in which he is in-

5. It might be hypothesized that the relationship between experience and clientele would go the other way: that to the experienced (and perhaps jaded) practitioner, each case would be a run-of-the-mill matter of routine, and for the inexperienced (and perhaps more curious) "casual," the case would be of more interest and concern. The findings here suggest that the relationship between clientele and experience runs the other way. These data deal with lawyers in cases on appeal—when issues are naturally broadened—and might not be as applicable to experienced criminal lawyers at the pretrial and trial stages. For the inexperienced lawyer, it is, in fact, the very novelty of the litigation that contributes to his concern for winning and relative lack of concern for broader issues that may be implicit in his case.

volved should be viewed not as simply another case but as a vehicle by which the Court can confront some broad policy question.

LEGAL IDEOLOGY: TRADITIONALISTS AND ADVOCATES

The legal ideology associated with the Advocate is that of the Traditionalist. The Traditionalist views the law in a fairly conventional way, stressing its function as the mediator of disputes and as a means for social control. He also adheres to rather traditional views about the role of the bar in society, preferring lawyers to remain passive, waiting for potential litigants to seek them out rather than taking initiatives to promote litigation dealing with social issues. There were 25 Advocates among the 82 lawyers interviewed. Thirteen of these Advocates had the Traditionalist legal ideology. Of the remaining 12, 4 were Reformers and 8 had equivocal legal ideologies. In the group of lawyers who had unequivocal legal ideologies (either Traditionalists or Reformers)—the major subject of inquiry here—we find that 13 of the 17 Advocates were Traditionalists. Thus there appears to be a connection between being an Advocate and having the legal ideology of the Traditionalist.

When a lawyer with the Traditionalist ideology becomes involved in a particular case, he is predisposed to view the case in the context of his more general attitudes toward what he is about as a lawyer; he will view his function in the litigation as that of representative of, and partisan in, the cause of his particular client. This, then, is one of the major explanations of the relationship between the particular legal ideology and the particular clientele, between the Traditionalist and the Advocate. The lawyer's clientele, as might be expected, is not simply the product of idiosyncratic characteristics of particular cases in which he becomes involved, but is in part the product of enduring notions of what it is to be a lawyer. Clearly, though, the relationship between clientele and legal ideology is complex, for legal ideology is by no means an unambiguous predictor of clientele. Here, then, we must introduce other factors to explain why a lawyer becomes an Advocate. In this chapter we will be particularly concerned with those cases that appear to be exceptions to the general relationship between legal ideology and clientele.

Advocates Who Are Not Traditionalists: The Client's Stake

This group includes lawyers who are Advocates—who perceive their cases as important simply for their clients—but whose legal ideology is not that typically associated with this view of litigation. Included are four lawyers whose legal ideology is that of the Reformer—a view of the law as an instrument for social and political change and a preference for an active legal profession —and eight lawyers with equivocal legal ideologies.[6] For all of these lawyers we have either a "contradiction" between legal ideology and clientele or an equivocal legal ideology that does not help much in explaining why the lawyer assumed his clientele.

One factor that appears to be quite important in producing Advocates—and in explaining their high incidence in criminal cases—is the stake of the client in the case. Defendants in criminal cases have a great deal to lose, often their freedom for long periods of time and sometimes even their lives. Though defendants in other kinds of civil liberties and civil rights cases sometimes have much to lose, by comparison their material losses are less substantial. In the loyalty-security cases, though sometimes jail terms were meted out, they were typically not of long duration. Perhaps more important, the real losses to defendants in this kind of litigation were the product of the mere institution of the proceeding against the individual—the taint of allegations of disloyalty, the obloquy and scorn that one branded unpatriotic (or worse) had to suffer. To a large extent these penalties—and none can deny that they were indeed harsh—did not depend upon the outcome of the cases, were not washed away by a Supreme Court reversal in the same way that a ten-year term in jail can be. The same was true to some extent for the defendants in civil rights cases, for, again, the penalties themselves were

6. See note 15, Chapter 3.

typically not harsh (at least in terms of jail sentences, though no doubt many would conclude that they were terribly excessive in light of the "crimes" for which they were meted out).

In the cases that did not involve criminal proceedings but, rather, civil suits to force or enjoin some activity (reapportionment, school prayer, some of the later loyalty-oath cases), though the litigant stood to lose much in terms of his policy preferences, an adverse decision did not involve incarceration. Relatedly, in many of the types of cases discussed above— loyalty-security, reapportionment, civil rights, religion—the litigants themselves were not so much interested simply in winning as they were in establishing a particular social or political policy. In the criminal cases, though, these factors were not so prevalent. The sentences themselves were harsh; the litigants were men primarily interested (and not unreasonably so) in avoiding jail. Though some criminal defendants are interested in legal principles, most probably could care less what legal or constitutional grounds get them out of jail, so long as they are in fact released.

Thus the stake of the client is an important factor in causing a lawyer in a criminal case to treat his litigation as an Advocate, to try to get his client off whatever the grounds. This is particularly true for lawyers who have had little experience in criminal litigation. To the lawyer who regularly practices criminal law, a sentence of ten years may appear routine (and perhaps even light, given similar cases in which he has been involved). Knowing the typical sentence handed down for the type of crime and the circumstances surrounding it, being familiar with the parole system and knowledgeable about time to be served as distinct from time sentenced, the regular criminal practitioner may regard ten years as yet another sentence, not especially noteworthy. To the inexperienced practitioner in criminal law, though, it may seem an awfully harsh sentence, for ten years seems like a long time. Whether a lawyer is inexperienced in criminal law because he is just beginning his practice or because he regularly practices in another field of law and happens to become involved in a criminal case, this lack of experience may lead him to become very concerned with the stake of his client. This is not to suggest that regular criminal lawyers are hardened men who don't care about the fates of their clients; rather, the severity of the sentence is likely to be much more salient to the inexperienced lawyer than it is to the criminal lawyer.

A mechanism peculiar to criminal cases—court appointment —has tended to bring a fairly large number of lawyers inexperienced in the field into these kinds of cases. Thus we have discovered that a number of lawyers who do not have the Traditionalist legal ideology do in fact act as Advocates. For the bulk of these lawyers, inexperience in the type of litigation, combined with the fact that they become involved in criminal cases in which the penalties are, to their eyes at least, shockingly severe, suggests why they approach their litigants as Advocates. The penalties focus the lawyer's attention upon the potential risks of defeat, upon obligation to secure victory whatever the grounds: in short, he becomes an Advocate.

Traditionalists Who Are Not Advocates: Experience, Cues, and Context

Continuing our discussion of the relationship between legal ideology and clientele, and of the Advocate clientele in particular, we now turn to the other "exceptions"—lawyers whose legal ideology might be expected to make them Advocates but who assumed another clientele. The Group Advocate and the Civil Libertarian are the subjects of the next two chapters, but since our focus is upon the Traditionalist/Advocate relationship, it seems reasonable to discuss this important group of exceptions here.

Again, the bulk of this group of lawyers is drawn from those who argued criminal justice cases. Just as it was argued above that lack of experience tends to focus a lawyer's perspective upon the stakes for his client (particularly in a criminal case where the stakes are often so high), extensive experience tends to focus his attention upon the broader issues involved. Not only is the sentence itself likely to be less salient to the experienced lawyer, but he has become steeped in the issues that a particular case is likely to involve. Further, he anticipates that his practice will likely in the future continue to involve these issues. As a consequence, though his legal ideology may predispose him to view his practice and his cases narrowly, his career experience may lead him to view them as involving not his clients so much as principles and issues with which he will continue to be confronted. Thus one criminal lawyer, who was clearly a Traditionalist, still acted as a Civil Libertarian in his criminal case, and commented as follows:

> I was interested in the appeal in establishing this broad point of law as a principle, as well as for the defendant. In the appeal, I definitely wanted this rule. . . .
>
> So yes, these principles are important to us in the trial of cases. And the good cops aren't hurt by these decisions. Because you see it today—in 90% of the cases where there's a confession, the guy has been advised of his rights, but he's busting to tell his story. He's got his conscience, and it's a catharsis for him. . . . So this is the kind of principle that we're fighting for in these cases, and 90% of the time, the individual that's in the case, whether he be Cahan or he be Dorado, or Escobedo—they're pretty scurvy little creatures, and what *they* are doesn't matter a whole hell of a lot. It's the principle that we're going to be able to use these people for that's important. [2]

Another factor that may cause a Traditionalist to be a Group Advocate or a Civil Libertarian is cues provided by the Supreme Court. The Court provides two types of cues. First, it may specify in granting a petition for *certiorari* that it wants the lawyers to concentrate upon a particular issue. In this way it informs the lawyer, for example, that the case is to be decided upon broad policy grounds (or at least that the Supreme Court may be interested in this), and hence what to stress in his brief. The second cueing technique is somewhat more subtle. At times the Court will group together for argument and decision a number of similar cases from different localities. When the Court does this, it suggests to the various lawyers that it is interested in deciding the issue common to all the cases. Thus, though there may be a variety of technical issues idiosyncratic to each case, the grouping technique indicates that it is the common issue that is likely to be crucial in the Court's decision.

Examples of both these techniques are discussed in Chapter 6. At this point, note that by cues the Supreme Court may induce a kind of shift in the clientele of the lawyer, from focus simply on result to focus on some broader issue. In this fashion some Traditionalists act as Civil Libertarians or Group Advocates.

The final factor, also discussed in more detail in later chapters, is simply the context surrounding the lawyer's involvement in a particular case. If a lawyer (in this connection, especially if he is a Traditionalist) receives a case in the context of his connection with a particular group[7] and, especially, if the case comes to him as one involving the fortunes of *his* group, then he is likely not to treat it in the way his legal ideology predisposes him to treat most of his litigation.

The argument thus far, then, is relatively simple. We have sketched out a particular style of lawyering, of approaching one's litigation, and called the lawyer with this style an Advocate. We have addressed the question of *why* a lawyer is likely to take this approach to his litigation. The basic influence is his legal ideology, his views about what it is to be a lawyer. One particular set of these views—the set called Traditionalist—appears to characterize lawyers who are Advocates. The relationship is by no means perfect, and we have suggested some other factors— including the stake of the client, degree of experience with the type of litigation, cues provided by the Court, and the context of involvement—to help explain why lawyers become (or fail to become) Advocates.

Now we may move on to a question raised earlier: why do so

7. This is particularly important for some of the southern black attorneys. They were among the most conservative of those interviewed in terms of legal ideology, but they acted as Group Advocates in their litigation. It is also relevant for some of the reapportionment lawyers, who were also Traditionalists but acted as Group Advocates for political factions to which they perceived themselves as tied. Both of these groups are treated in Chapter 6.

many Advocates become involved in one particular type of litigation, criminal justice?

ADVOCATES AND CRIMINAL JUSTICE LITIGATION

The means by which the 28 lawyers interviewed who argued criminal justice cases initially became involved in their litigation are distributed as follows: twelve were appointed to represent indigent defendants, eight received their cases by referral from another attorney, one was representing a previous client, three received cases as a result of their affiliation with institutions or groups, and four had social or friendship ties with their clients. What these data suggest is that there were in fact two major groups of lawyers who argued criminal justice cases, with a third very small (yet potentially significant) one tacked on. The groups are those who became involved by appointment; "criminal lawyers," whose practice involved a good deal of criminal litigation (who became involved by referral, previous client, and friendship ties with the client or his acquaintances); and finally a few lawyers who became involved through their associations with institutions or groups.

Most of those who served by appointment were young lawyers, often with large and prestigious law firms, whose basic practice involved matters other than criminal law and whose career expectations did not lead them to anticipate much further contact with this kind of litigation. Many of them had equivocal legal ideologies.[8] Many large firms encourage their junior associates to become involved in criminal cases by court appointment, both to gain trial experience and to fulfill the public service obligations of the firm. These lawyers, as suggested above, tended to assume the Advocate clientele in large part because of their lack of experience and the consequent salience of the harshness of the penalties their clients faced. Because their career expectations did not include much future involvement with criminal law (once they ceased being associates,

8. Many were Theoreticians and were associates with large corporate firms. See note 15, Chapter 3.

participation in almost any criminal case—except perhaps for some "white collar" crimes—would be rare indeed), they were inclined not to view their cases as involving issues with which they would continue to be confronted. This is not to imply that all of these lawyers were necessarily indifferent to or opposed to the kinds of reforms in criminal justice administration that have occurred in recent years (though some were) but simply that their attitudes, the context of their involvement, and their legal experience and career expectations led them to focus upon the specifics of their cases, not upon broader legal or social issues.[9]

The other group comprised the "real" criminal lawyers, attorneys whose practice involved a good deal of criminal litigation. Twelve of the 16 lawyers interviewed who became involved by some means other than appointment reported that they practiced a substantial amount of criminal law, most of them practicing on their own or in small firms. By way of contrast, of the 12 interviewed who became involved by appointment, 10 reported that they never practiced criminal law *except* by appointment. As with those who became involved by appointment, few of these criminal lawyers had the legal ideology generally associated with "civil liberties" lawyers; i.e., most were Traditionalists. As suggested in the preceding section, some of these criminal lawyers did act as Civil Libertarians, as their experience and expectations broadened their horizons, but many simply acted as Advocates. Perhaps the traditional nature of criminal litigation—with its stress upon conflict resolution and upon reaching "truth" and a decision about a specific act[10]—tended to draw this type of lawyer into criminal practice. Relatedly, the traditional treatment by the Supreme Court of criminal appeals —deciding them on a kind of *ad hoc* basis (e.g., special circum-

9. For some, their cases were an educational experience, opening their eyes to a branch of the law they had not known before. Though none of those interviewed intended as a result to change jobs, a number expressed a desire to continue to participate in criminal litigation, though they planned to remain members of their firms.

10. At least manifestly. See Thurman Arnold, *The Symbols of Government* (New Haven, Conn.: Yale University Press, 1935), Chs. 6–7, for a stimulating discussion of some of the possible latent functions of the criminal trial.

stances, totality of circumstances)—tended to induce lawyers with extensive experience in criminal law to act as Advocates.

In any event, the recruitment pattern in criminal justice cases that came before the Supreme Court seems to account in large measure for the high incidence of attorneys with rather limited goals. Most of the cases were argued by "casuals" who moved into this area of law for only one or two cases, or by lawyers who practiced a good bit in the area but whose attitudes toward their function as lawyers tended to focus their attention upon the case as a discrete event.

The third group of lawyers—albeit a very small one—comprised those who became involved via their affiliations with various institutions or interest groups. These lawyers are important because, first, they tended to be Civil Libertarians, and second, their means of involvement—via groups that to one extent or another function as advocates for criminal defendants—suggests a trend that may be developing. If this is the case, there may be a "new breed" of criminal lawyers who will argue these many criminal cases in the future.

In any event, the bulk of the lawyers who argued criminal justice cases in the 1957–66 period were in fact Advocates. They were not drawn from the population of lawyers we generally conceive of when we think of "civil liberties" lawyers. Rather, they were recruited from a portion of the bar that rarely becomes involved in civil liberties cases (those appointed) or from the criminal bar itself, which has characteristically been interested in the limited goal of winning rather than in broader issues.

ADVOCATES AND JUDICIAL POLICY-MAKING

A number of different conceptions of what a policy-making process is, and how the judicial system fits or does not fit such definitions, have been advanced by students of the legal process. The notion of judicial decision-making can be conceived of as a synoptic, rational process or as an incremental system.[11] Joel Grossman has suggested, for example, that the notion of judicial

11. For a discussion of these two views, see Martin Shapiro, "Stability and Change in Judicial Decision-Making: Incrementalism or *Stare Decisis*," *Law in Transition Quarterly* 2 (1965): 134–57.

policy-making not be restricted simply to the discussion of the particular goals of participants but, rather, be viewed as a complex *process* in which many participants are active, pursuing a variety of goals.[12] Of particular interest here is Herbert Jacob's distinction between the role of courts in norm enforcement (involving essentially private disputes with little of obvious public concern at stake) and policy-making (in which important public issues are clearly at stake).[13]

How do the activities of the lawyers we have called Advocates fit into and illuminate a notion of judicial policy-making? Two characteristics immediately come to mind. First, Advocates themselves have little concern with "policy"; their concern is essentially with getting their clients off, regardless of the presence or absence in the consequent decision of matters of broad social or political policy. On the other hand, we have dwelt at some length on the fact that in the area of litigation in which Advocates have primarily been involved—cases involving issues of criminal justice—a great deal of broad policy has emerged.

But, and this is the important implication of the high incidence of Advocates in this particular area of litigation, the resulting policy has not been the product of the conscious goals of the lawyers (and, by inference, of the litigants themselves). To use Jacob's concepts, one might suggest that in most of the criminal justice cases the lawyers have primarily been concerned with norm enforcement, with getting their clients off, with settlement of the specific disputes, either with fitting their clients' cases under existing law or perhaps with incremental changes in the law. Majorities on the Court, on the other hand, have treated many of the cases as occasions for policy-making, not simply norm enforcement, as vehicles by which important kinds of normative and behavioral guides could be provided to large segments of the legal system.

In this area of law—and it is quite different and distinguish-

12. Joel B. Grossman, "A Model for Judicial Policy Analysis: The Supreme Court and the Sit-In Cases," in Joel B. Grossman and Joseph Tanenhaus, eds., *Frontiers of Judicial Research* (New York: John Wiley and Sons, 1969), pp. 405–60.

13. Herbert Jacob, *Justice in America* (Boston: Little, Brown, 1965), Chs. 2–3.

able from others to be discussed—there is not a nice fit between the goals and expectations of the lawyers and the outcomes in the Court. Neither the impetus for the suits in the first place, nor the kind of support they received, nor the expectations of the lawyers who argued them were consciously designed to produce the kinds of policy that resulted. Important reforms have come in the area of criminal law, but they appear to have been to a large extent unintended by-products of the activities of the lawyers. Nathan Hakman suggests a similar conclusion: "A closer look at the process itself, however, shows that most party litigants in noncommercial cases—especially cases involving serious social offenders (criminal cases)—are individuals pursuing or defending their own exclusively private claims and interests."[14]

In terms of a model of policy-making that attempts to relate the outcomes to the goals of various participants, the data presented here suggest that one cannot usefully conceive of the outcomes of many of the criminal cases in which Advocates were involved as being the product of the conscious activity of the lawyers. When the other two types of lawyers—Group Advocates and Civil Libertarians—are discussed in succeeding chapters, it will become apparent that the outcomes in their suits were often much more closely related to their activities. But in the criminal cases a model which views litigation as a conscious strategy to secure a certain type of policy from the courts does not appear to fit much of the litigation. The Supreme Court itself appears to have used cases—available as vehicles for policy development because Advocates brought them up with somewhat different goals in mind—to enunciate important social and legal guides.

TRENDS IN CRIMINAL CASES BEFORE THE COURT

Much of the criminal justice litigation that came before the Court during the 1957–66 period—including many cases in

14. Nathan Hakman, "The Supreme Court's Political Environment: The Processing of Noncommercial Litigation," in Grossman and Tanenhaus, eds., *Frontiers of Judicial Research*, p. 245.

which important policy about criminal administration was made[15]—was argued by lawyers whose interest was not in policy but simply in winning. Thus much of the policy that resulted was an unintended by-product of the activities of these lawyers. It seems possible that we are now in the midst of a trend toward change in the kinds of lawyers who argue criminal justice cases. To use the terminology developed in this study, it seems possible that lawyers acting as Advocates will become less frequent in litigation before the Supreme Court involving issues of criminal justice. In their place the bar arguing criminal justice cases may in the future be comprised of lawyers more like our image of the "civil liberties" lawyer—Group Advocates and Civil Libertarians, lawyers using their particular cases as vehicles to confront broader issues.

This section suggests some of the reasons why this trend may be developing and some of the possible consequences that will result from it. Before doing so, some caveats should be noted. One should bear in mind that the discussion which follows is in fact speculative. As with many exploratory studies, the material that is in a sense the most interesting is the most speculative, most removed from concrete data, and most based upon inference and extrapolation from material that is itself rather tentative.

The first caveat is perhaps the most obvious and the most important. It simply notes that the data gathered here deal with lawyers who argued cases at the highest appellate level. To draw inferences about other lawyers—especially those dealing with litigation at the pretrial and trial stages—obviously involves something of a leap. Both in making the leap and in evaluating the landing site, caution must be exercised.

Another caveat is again quite simple, yet important. This discussion deals with the future, and such observations are always subject to suspicion. This is perhaps especially true when talking about the Supreme Court in the year 1972. The Warren Court

15. The requirement of anonymity precludes a more specific statement indicating the cases referred to.

is finally dead. A new chief justice and three new associates have assumed office, and they are not likely to be sympathetic to much of the work of the Warren Court. To predict what the Supreme Court will be like in the future, always a hazardous endeavor, is especially so today. Since the trend toward using cases as vehicles for confronting larger policy issues is primarily a product of the receptivity of the Court, the recent changes in Court personnel are of particular relevance.

Finally, the trend suggested in criminal justice litigation depends to an important extent upon the institutional form that representation of indigent defendants will take. It is particularly important whether such representation takes the form of expanded systems of court appointment or the form of the development of institutions (like public defender offices) whose employees work full-time on criminal litigation. The trend in recruitment of different types of lawyers in criminal cases suggested here assumes a growth in public defender organizations. Thus, though it is suggested that we will see a change in the kinds of lawyers involved in criminal litigation, particularly at the appeals level, and this trend may have important consequences for the legal process, the argument must take account of the many uncertainties that surround it.

Why will more and more lawyers treat their criminal justice cases as involving more than the fate of their clients? Why will more Group Advocates and Civil Libertarians become involved in this area of litigation? Three related factors suggest these trends. First, we are moving toward the development of a group of lawyers who will become specialists in criminal litigation and who will work in institutions committed to the task of acting as legal lobbyists for the social offender. Related to the development of such institutions, the kinds of lawyers going into the area of criminal litigation may change, with more Reformers— lawyers with legal ideologies that focus their attention in specific litigation upon broader issues—becoming active in criminal justice cases as a means for policy development, and this will encourage continued use of cases for this purpose.

We are currently witnessing the development of the kinds of institutions alluded to above—public defender offices, expansion of legal aid programs, the development of legal services programs under the aegis of the Poverty Program. In large part in response to Supreme Court decisions dealing with the provision of counsel to indigent defendants, more defendants have lawyers. To the extent that lawyers are provided in this particular form—as members of *institutions* whose participants work to a large extent full-time on this area of litigation—then it seems probable that more and more of them will be likely to develop broader perspectives on their litigation, to want to use cases as vehicles for dealing with broader issues in criminal administration. Recall the discussion above of some of the lawyers in criminal cases who were Civil Libertarians: criminal lawyers with broad experience and expectations about future involvement were more likely to act not as Advocates but as Civil Libertarians.

Note, though, the importance for the trend suggested here of the method by which counsel is recruited for criminal justice litigation. If the method chosen is that of court appointment— bringing into criminal cases a large number of "casuals" for just a few cases—then the trend will not emerge so strongly, for it is the casual who often is most prone to be an Advocate, to be unaware of or unconcerned with the broader implications of his litigation. If, however, many states and localities conclude (as many already have—New York, Chicago, Los Angeles) that the most efficient way to provide representation to indigent defendants is through institutions like public defender offices, we may well see the development of an appeal bar that perceives its function as legal lobbyists for the social offender.[16] This is particularly true if such institutions develop specialized appeal sections.

A related development is the increasing activity in the area of criminal justice of litigating interest groups like the ACLU and the NAACP-LDF that have previously been primarily active in

16. Though, as discussed below, at the pretrial and trial levels cooperation and plea bargaining will no doubt continue. The trend discussed here seems more likely to occur at the appeals level and to have some indirect effects on trial lawyers as appeals counterparts press them to preserve issues for appeal.

other areas of civil liberties litigation. These groups tend to bring lawyers into cases in a particular context; the case is brought to the attorney as an example of some kind of broader issue, not as a discrete event. Thus, through public, quasi-public, or private means, an institutionalization of the defense of social offenders is likely to produce lawyers who will act as Civil Libertarians or Group Advocates, not as Advocates.

Relatedly, as institutionalization and specialization develop, perhaps more lawyers with the legal ideology of the "civil liberties" lawyer (the Reformer) will become attracted to this area of litigation. It may become easier to make a living in the defense of criminals,[17] and hence this area will become viable for reform-minded young lawyers. And as appeals litigation becomes more and more "politicized"—as more and more of it involves test cases—lawyers concerned with this use of litigation will be attracted. To some extent the increasing activity of litigating interest groups alluded to above is an example of this phenomenon. The ACLU and the LDF certainly did not run out of issues in the areas with which they were traditionally concerned. An increasing recognition of the fact that the administration of criminal justice impinged upon the issue areas they were traditionally associated with, plus a recognition that test litigation *could* be effective in this area, seems to account in part for their increased activity. The Supreme Court itself was to some extent responsible for this latter development, for it made its receptivity known by its conversion of apparently routine cases into milestones.

This is the third factor. The Supreme Court, by its willingness to abjure its traditional *ad hoc* approach to issues of criminal justice, will further encourage lawyers to begin to treat their litigation differently. Not only will lawyers become sensitized to

17. More important, to make a living without the economic scrambling that has often characterized criminal practice. See Abraham Blumberg, *Criminal Justice* (Chicago: Quadrangle Books, 1967), and Jerome Carlin, *Lawyers on Their Own* (New Brunswick, N.J.: Rutgers University Press, 1962), for descriptions of the often precarious existence of the criminal practitioner. For every Melvin Belli, Percy Foreman, F. Lee Bailey, or Edward Bennett Williams, there are hundreds or thousands of marginal practitioners in the area of criminal law.

the presence of issues in litigation that simply comes to them, but they will become aware of the problems that are ripe for attack and will begin, as in other areas of civil liberties, to look around for cases to use as tests. Notice here, again, the importance of institutions in this process. The lawyer who casually encounters a few criminal cases in a sense doesn't have a broad enough "menu" from which to select issues he might wish to bring to the appeals courts for resolution. It is the lawyer with a substantial volume of cases involving many different issues who is in a position to map out a strategy to attack a certain problem. And it is in the institutional setting suggested above—of specialists in that area—that such opportunities arise.

For all of these reasons, we are likely in the future to see criminal cases (especially on appeal) treated differently, to see the growth of a bar devoted to the use of litigation as a tool for policy development. As argued above, this has not been the case in the past. Such a development will be to a large extent the creation of the Supreme Court itself, both by its decisions relating to right to counsel and by its new approaches to criminal justice litigation. These developments have been the product not of the activities of the lawyers who argued the cases but of Court decisions.

This is a very important point. It suggests that the long-term impacts of the Supreme Court decisions in the area of criminal justice during the 1957–66 era lie not simply in reforms in the behavior of participants in the legal system or in protection of the rights of criminal defendants. The long-term importance of decisions like *Gideon, Mapp, Miranda,* and others may also involve the creation of a new type of lawyer, with a different and more "political" perspective on his litigation. These decisions may turn what was in the past a defensive area of litigation into a more offensive one. Cases may more and more become vehicles for policy development. Lawyers looking to use their professional expertise for social reform may become more prevalent in this area. This may be one of the more important consequences of Supreme Court litigation in the area of criminal justice in the period under consideration here.

CONSEQUENCES

If the trend suggested above does in fact occur, what might be the consequences of it? What difference will it make if there are fewer Advocates arguing cases before the Supreme Court and more Group Advocates and Civil Libertarians, especially in the area of criminal justice? The data presented here—based upon interviews with lawyers who argued cases before the Supreme Court—certainly do not tell us that one kind of lawyer rather than another will be more likely to reach the Supreme Court; by definition, all the lawyers interviewed did in fact reach the Court. And it cannot tell us who will win and who will lose; the numbers interviewed simply are too small, and the intricacies of the judicial decision-making process are too little understood. Since we haven't any data about the lawyers who fell by the wayside— who didn't for one reason or another get to the Supreme Court— we really can't say anything concrete about them either. But some speculative hypotheses can be advanced. Given what we know and suspect about the ways in which Advocates and Civil Libertarians view their litigation and their function as lawyers, what might be the consequences of the participation of more Group Advocates and Civil Libertarians in criminal justice litigation?

First of all, what of the behavior of the lawyer at the trial level? One fact, by now well known to students of the legal process but still startling to many, may be our starting point. About 90 percent of all criminal convictions in this country never reach the trial stage; they are settled by guilty pleas by the defendants. Though perhaps many defendants simply plead guilty because they are in fact guilty and are willing to "take their medicine," the evidence available suggests that many of them do so as a result of bargains reached between the defendant, his lawyer, and the prosecuting attorney.[18] After a plea bargain has been agreed upon, many of the formal legal proceedings—appearance before a judge, tendering of the guilty plea, acceptance

18. For discussions of plea bargaining, see Blumberg, *Criminal Justice*, and Donald J. Newman, *Conviction: The Determination of Guilt or Innocence without Trial* (Boston: Little, Brown, 1966).

of the plea by the judge, and eventual sentencing—are ritual ceremonies legitimating the bargain already struck. Such informal resolution of criminal proceedings, taking place not in the tense atmosphere of the courtroom familiar to fans of Perry Mason but in the jail cell and the prosecutor's office, is at the heart of the administration of criminal justice in this country. With the court system already overloaded handling the small percentage of cases that go to trial, the informal plea-bargaining process is essential if the legal system is not to collapse under the weight of its work load.

Plea bargaining—like other types of bargaining—takes place because the participants all have somewhat different but not totally unreconcilable goals and have resources that make some kind of compromise desirable. For the defendant, the plea bargain may result in the dropping of most counts in an indictment in return for a guilty plea to one or two; may help him avoid the publicity and possible trauma of a public trial with its attendant press coverage (in exchange for the relatively quiet anonymity of the cop-out ceremony); and, finally, may result in a sentence less severe than might be attendant upon conviction if he made the state go to the time and trouble of a trial.

For the prosecution, a plea bargain also has its advantages. Perhaps most important, it saves the time of a trial, a not inconsequential element given the crowding of court dockets and the low level of resources available to judges and prosecutors. It is also, relatedly, a speedy way of turning over cases, and with new ones arising every day, speed is important. The police, though they sometimes resent the bargain,[19] often view it as advantageous: it saves them the time and tedium of appearing in court and waiting around to do so. It also enables them to clear many cases off the books (e.g., when a defendant admits committing a number of crimes in return for a bargain not to be prosecuted for them), and clearance rates are an important measure and symbol of police efficiency. For both the police and the prose-

---

19. See Jerome Skolnick, *Justice without Trial* (New York: John Wiley and Sons, 1966), for a discussion of police attitudes toward plea bargaining.

cutor, the plea bargain has an added advantage: it frees them from the possibility that the defendant, when he goes to trial, will raise sticky legal issues dealing with the means by which he was apprehended—search and seizure, availability of counsel, station-house interrogation. Not only may such challenges require a fight in court, but they may result in exclusion of evidence and possibly an acquittal.

The defendant's lawyer is perhaps the key actor in the plea-bargaining process.[20] He is the mediator between the prosecution and the defense, acting often not as representative of the defendant but as what Abraham Blumberg calls a "double agent." Some evidence suggests that, more than any other participant, the defense attorney is most influential both in initially suggesting the guilty plea to the defendant and in convincing him that it is the wisest course to follow. The defense attorney may urge the cop-out for a variety of reasons. He may see a plea bargain as simply the most advantageous course of action for the defendant, resulting in the minimum sanction against him. Or, if the lawyer depends upon prosecutors and judges for their good will and must maintain good relations if he is to continue to obtain and settle cases, a guilty plea may appear advantageous to him personally. Thus plea bargaining occurs, as perhaps it inevitably must, and defense attorneys are vital participants in the process. And, as noted, they may be pursuing quite a variety of goals, some of which have directly to do with the interests of their clients, some with their own financial and career interests.

Though obviously any generalization must be guarded, it seems plausible to venture that an Advocate might behave somewhat differently from a Civil Libertarian or Group Advocate in plea bargaining. In general, an Advocate might be a good deal more amenable to the plea-bargaining process than a Group Advocate or Civil Libertarian would be. The Advocate views his case as primarily involving only the interests of his client; the Civil Libertarian and Group Advocate are much more interested

20. See Blumberg, *Criminal Justice*, Ch. 5, and Jonathan D. Casper, "Did You Have a Lawyer When You Went to Court?" *Yale Review of Law and Social Action* 1 (1971): 4–9.

in issues. The heart of the plea-bargaining process is the desire to most expeditiously (and advantageously for the client, one hopes) handle a particular case. The Civil Libertarian or Group Advocate tends to see cases in a larger perspective and may be less amenable to plea bargaining, both because he may be more "principled" and because the process by its very nature suppresses legal issues. Perhaps, then, the participation of more Civil Libertarians and Group Advocates would to some extent reduce the incidence of the plea-bargaining process.

Clearly, it is not so simple as suggested above. Various other factors may operate to influence the behavior of lawyers, beyond a change in views toward their litigation discussed here. A tremendous volume of cases, combined with understaffing, may force those in legal defense institutions to take the shortcuts offered by plea bargaining. The development of bureaucratic relationships between defense and prosecutors, relationships that are recurrent and that transcend the relatively ephemeral relationship between the attorney and any individual client, will also facilitate cooperation between defense and prosecution.[21]

These factors suggest the continuation of plea bargaining as usual, even in the face of the development of institutions providing counsel to indigent defendants.[22] But the presence of more Group Advocates and Civil Libertarians in criminal justice defender institutions may have some subtle effects upon plea bargaining. The development of specialized appeals sections may be of importance, for these appeals lawyers—assuming they view themselves as Group Advocates or Civil Libertarians—may put subtle pressure upon their trial colleagues to be more concerned with preserving issues for appeal. Whether these speculations

21. One link that is removed, though, in public defender systems is the dependence of the defense attorney upon the prosecution for quick disposition in order to turn over cases and generate fees (though work loads may make quick disposition quite desirable for the public defender as well). The public defender on salary does not make his living from bulk volume in the same way that many private criminal lawyers in lower courts do.

22. A recent ABA study concluded that plea bargaining will continue in the future to be an important element in settling criminal cases. See American Bar Association, *A.B.A. Project on Minimal Standards of Criminal Justice: Standards Relating to Pleas of Guilty* (Chicago, 1967).

will come true is thus very much a debatable question. But it is an issue that is worth further study.[23]

Suppose this kind of change does occur. Is it good or bad? Obviously the answer depends upon a specification of "for whom," and even then the response might well be mixed.

Is it to the defendant's advantage to be represented by an Advocate rather than a Group Advocate or Civil Libertarian? Obviously, if the defendant is represented by a Civil Libertarian or Group Advocate who is interested not in him but simply in the case as a means to raise issues, the defendant could be severely disadvantaged. In the most extreme case, if the attorney refused to raise technical issues that might get the defendant off because the lawyer would rather lose than win on a technicality, the defendant probably wouldn't want such an attorney. Though this appears implausible, a couple of the Civil Libertarians interviewed expressed ideas almost approximating this view. For example, one lawyer in a criminal case asserted, "I owed no loyalty to Mr. 'Smith' [his client]. Never met him in point of fact. I corresponded with him as infrequently as I could get away with. He had nothing to contribute to the issues. Unlike Justice Fortas who thought, I guess probably correctly, that Gideon did have something to do with the issues. . . . But neither the [appeal to the circuit court] nor the appeal to the Supreme Court had anything to do with a desire to spring Mr. Smith—I couldn't care less" [64]. If you or I were "Smith," we might have qualms about having this particular gentleman as our lawyer. The Civil Libertarian who took his position literally—as the above respondent at least appears to do—might not be the ideal lawyer for the defendant whose primary interest was in getting out of jail.

Another characteristic of the Civil Libertarian and Group Advocate might give pause to the defendant. The Civil Libertarian

23. There is some evidence, though it is very tentative, that a public defender is more likely than assigned counsel to plead his client guilty. But the nature of the data used and the admittedly very tentative quality of these conclusions seem to render the point still highly debatable. See Lee Silverstein, *Defense of the Poor in Criminal Cases in American State Courts* (Chicago: American Bar Foundation, 1965), Ch. 4, and Marvin R. Summers, "Defending the Poor: The Assigned Counsel System in Milwaukee County," *Wisconsin Law Review* 1969: 525–39.

or Group Advocate in an institutional setting that provides him with a broad menu of cases from which to select (and it is this very institutional setting that tends to produce Civil Libertarians and Group Advocates) may well be inclined to emphasize and invest most of his resources in those cases that appear to have the characteristics of "good" test cases. Cases clouded by technical issues that provide means for a court to avoid the major issues may not be particularly attractive. If cases (particularly on appeal) are viewed as vehicles for raising issues, then those that are better vehicles may receive more attention than those that are not. Though any decent lawyer will pursue a case handed to him to the best of his ability, it appears quite plausible that the serious Civil Libertarian or Group Advocate might tend to emphasize the "good" vehicles more than those with technical defects, those in which the issues are clouded by "extraneous" factors.

Thus, if we look at the consequences of an influx of Civil Libertarians and Group Advocates into criminal cases from the perspective of the defendant, it might well appear that it is not a particularly salubrious development. If the traditional image of the lawyer-client relationship is to be taken seriously, if the lawyer is expected to be the "mouthpiece" for his client, dedicating himself wholeheartedly to the single goal of maximizing the interests of his client, the rather different interests of the Civil Libertarian and Group Advocate appear to contradict this model. The Advocate, after all, is much like the lawyer in our paradigm of the traditional lawyer-client relationship.[24] But there is another side to the coin. We should look at this development not only from the perspective of the individual defendant but in terms of its impact upon the legal process and society at large.

Though from the viewpoint of a defendant an Advocate appears to be a desirable type of lawyer, from the viewpoint of the protection of civil liberties in our society Group Advocates and

24. Though the evidence dealing with plea bargaining suggests that many lawyers in criminal cases are pursuing goals—making money, protecting access to prosecutors, preserving friendships—that have little to do with the traditional notions of serving only the interest of the client.

Civil Libertarians are important as well. After all, the Supreme Court is essentially a passive institution, and if it is to resolve issues, it must be presented with occasions upon which to enunciate policy; it must be presented with cases. In succeeding chapters dealing with Group Advocates and Civil Libertarians, we will discuss in some detail the importance of litigation and of the court system as an access point for minorities who have difficulty gaining access in other political arenas. Here we can merely point out that it may be of great utility, from the standpoint of the system as a whole, to have lawyers continually looking for cases to use as vehicles for the development of new social, legal, and political policy.

A major part of the policy-development process by the legal system is the provision of occasions for policy development.[25] And perhaps the Civil Libertarian and the Group Advocate are most likely to provide such occasions. Though continually pressing the courts for reforms in protection of civil liberties and rights may not be a sufficient condition for new policy departures, it probably is a necessary one. Developing test cases, looking out for broader issues, and presenting them may be important for demonstrating to the courts that interest in and support for these issues do exist. In addition, organized groups willing to expend resources in support of civil liberties and rights may be important bulwarks when these rights come under attack.

Thus there is a societal dimension to the prevalence of Civil Libertarians and Group Advocates that cuts to some extent against the personalized desires of the individual client. Perhaps somewhat perversely, the lawyer whom you or I might choose if we happened to be arrested might not be the same kind of lawyer we would like others to have. In any event, there may well be emerging a trend toward the politicization of litigation in criminal justice, with some decline in the activity of Advocates. It has ramifications for the relationship between lawyer and client, for the kinds of issues that are likely to be raised in the legal

25. This point is discussed in Richard S. Wells and Joel B. Grossman, "The Concept of Judicial Policy-Making: A Critique," *Journal of Public Law* 15 (1966): 286–310.

arena, and for the general role of the legal arena vis-à-vis other political institutions. In this chapter we have made a first foray into some of these issues; we will return to them again in succeeding chapters.

SUMMARY

The Advocate is more interested in winning his case than in developing a new legal and social policy. For many Advocates, legal ideology tends to focus their perspective upon this limited goal. For many Advocates with equivocal legal ideologies, the lack of experience with the kind of litigation and the lack of expectation of future involvement, combined with the apparently high stakes of their clients, produced this view of litigation. The recruitment pattern for the litigation is thus crucial to the kinds of clienteles that are prevalent in criminal justice cases.

In terms of policy development the criminal justice cases are somewhat different from other areas of litigation to be discussed. The changes in policy have been significant but were not directly related to the goals of the lawyers who argued the cases. Though in other areas (e.g., the later sit-in cases, discussed in the next chapter) the policy outcomes were not what the lawyers were trying to accomplish, and though lawyers obviously often lose their cases or win them on grounds they don't prefer, many of the criminal cases were argued by lawyers for whom the issue of policy development simply was not salient. Whether they were unaware of the policy issues implicit in their litigation (probably rare) or were consciously unconcerned because of strong role conception, policy simply was not their concern.

Though this is what characterized the litigation in the past, it seems possible that the future will be different. As a result of both Supreme Court decisions relating to right to counsel and the Court's willingness to approach cases involving criminal justice differently, future litigation may, like other areas of civil liberties and rights, come to be dominated by lawyers with broader clienteles. This has important implications for the operation of the criminal justice system, for the lawyer-client relationship, and for the protection of civil liberties and rights in our society. In this chapter we began to speculate upon some of these implications. In succeeding chapters we will return to these questions for another look.

This, then, is the Advocate. If the trend in litigation suggested here does materialize, he may be a vanishing breed in civil liberties litigation, at least before the Supreme Court. He is, though, the attorney that probably comes to mind when most of us think about a criminal lawyer.[26] Perhaps on the trial level he will always predominate. If he is being replaced at the appeal level, some may mourn him; others may feel that his successors are a sign of progress. But two things about the Advocate do stand out. First, he participated in some of the most socially and legally significant litigation of the Warren Court. Second, his passing, if it comes, is both an integral part and a reflection of changes in the judicial system, changes in the process by which civil liberties and rights are affected and protected by litigation.

26. Though even the pop-culture images of lawyers seem to be changing. Contrast, for example, "Perry Mason" with "Judd for the Defense" and "The Storefront Lawyers," all television programs dealing with attorneys. Mason was simply interested in the innocence of his client, and other social or political issues did not play a part in his activities as an attorney. The more recent television dramas often suggest that the attorney's case, even when it is a criminal prosecution, may involve broader social, political, or economic issues.

5. *The Group Advocate*

We now turn to another group of lawyers who argued cases before the Supreme Court during the 1957–66 period. These lawyers, called Group Advocates, were the most common among those interviewed. They are much closer to our intuitive image of what a "civil liberties" lawyer is than are the Advocates, for Group Advocates are interested in using their litigation to protect and develop civil liberties and rights generally, not simply in winning cases. But one of the purposes of this study is to suggest that the kind of undifferentiated image of the "civil liberties" lawyer does not adequately encompass the complexity and diversity of lawyers who argue these kinds of cases. And the discussion of Group Advocates and Civil Libertarians is designed to suggest that even among those lawyers who fit our traditional image of the "civil liberties" lawyer—the lawyers who participate actively in a good deal of civil liberties litigation, who are concerned with more than simply winning, who are members of the litigating interest groups so important in recent civil liberties litigation—different styles of lawyering, different clienteles, and different goals appear.

The first task of this chapter will be to identify more precisely what characteristics distinguish the Group Advocate from other lawyers. A particular perspective on his litigation—a kind of "we-they" perspective in which the "we" includes a group to which the lawyer feels he has long-term commitments—is the key to the Group Advocate. This discussion of the Group Advocate requires attention to one of the major conceptual problems of this work: explicating the difference between the Group Advocate and the Civil Libertarian. Since they are so much more alike than either is like the Advocate, their differences tend to be obscured in contrast to their similarities.

After a discussion of what makes up a Group Advocate, we will turn to the question of the kinds of litigation in which they participated. They were the most prevalent group of lawyers, and they participated in three of the four areas of litigation discussed in this study—loyalty-security, reapportionment, and civil rights. Only in the area of criminal justice were Group Advocates almost completely absent. Thus, as the preceding chapter was not only about Advocates but also about criminal justice litigation, this chapter is not only about Group Advocates but also about the areas of litigation enumerated above. Patterns of recruitment into litigation are discussed in some detail, for they are important in suggesting why Group Advocates become involved. Friendship ties or social contact between lawyer and client leading to involvement in litigation were particularly important in two areas of litigation, loyalty-security and reapportionment. These ties explain not only why the lawyer became involved but to some extent why he perceived his clientele as he did, why he was a Group Advocate.

We will then take up another of the questions that this study repeatedly deals with, why a lawyer assumes his clientele. Group Advocates and Civil Libertarians have similar legal ideologies, so this variable—important in distinguishing Advocates from the rest of the lawyers—cannot be the key to distinguishing Group Advocates and Civil Libertarians. Other factors, including the personal and ideological ties of lawyer to client, the context surrounding the lawyer's involvement (e.g., did the case come from the ACLU and hence come as a "civil liberties" case?), and the lawyer's experience in the field of litigation, are all discussed.

The discussion will then turn to the implications of the activities of this group of lawyers for various models of the judicial process. Group Advocates are in fact just that—lawyers using their litigation (often having participated in the initiation of the cases in the first place) for the purpose of vindicating the goals and interests of groups to whom they are tied. Unlike the Advocates, their participation can be directly tied to an image of the legal process as an arena for the conscious development of legal, political, and social policy. Moreover, the group-process approach to the legal system, much in vogue in recent years, is closely related to the participation of this type of lawyer. In addition, the argument introduced in the preceding chapter—dealing with the importance of institutions in the process by which Group Advocates and Civil Libertarians are produced—will be explored in more detail.

WHAT IS A GROUP ADVOCATE?

A Group Advocate views his clientele in litigation as a particular group in society. The group is typically one to whom the lawyer perceives he has long-term commitments and with whose fortunes he identifies. Thus a Group Advocate is not simply a lawyer retained by a group to represent it in litigation; such a lawyer might be a Group Advocate, but he might also be an Advocate or a Civil Libertarian. Moreover, the group itself may not even be a party to the litigation. Group Advocates who feel their clientele to be blacks in America, a political faction in a state, or political radicals have been active in litigation in which no formally constituted group participated. Thus the Group Advocate views his litigation in a kind of "we-they" focus in which the "we" is some group, identifiable sometimes by formal membership but more likely by some demographic, political, or ideological characteristic and by shared attitudes.

Before going further, the problem of differentiating the Group Advocate from the Civil Libertarian requires some discussion. Both of them, contrary to the Advocate, are typically concerned in their litigation with more than simply winning for their client. Each often has distinct grounds for decision in mind when he considers why his case is important and how he would like it decided. It is important to recall here the distinction between a lawyer's goals (which often are intimately tied with the grounds of decision in a case) and his clientele. For clientele deals with the social domain of a lawyer's goals, *for whom* he is trying to accomplish a goal. And it is the degree of circumscription of the social domain—the difference between attempting to vindicate a legal principle for all of society and to do so for a particular group—that is the key to the distinction between the Group Advocate and the Civil Libertarian. Both kinds of lawyers may become involved in quite similar litigation, but they have different clienteles.

A couple of examples may make the distinction clearer. In two reapportionment cases, for example, the lawyers might have the same goal—reapportioning their state legislatures—but their clienteles might be different. One lawyer might value reapportionment mainly because of its utility for a particular political faction to which he perceives his interests as tied. The other might be completely unconnected with a political faction, indifferent to who stands to gain and who stands to lose by reapportionment. His interest might be simply in the vindication of a principle—equality, for example—that he felt to be important to the maintenance of a democratic political system. The first would be a Group Advocate, the second a Civil Libertarian. The difference lies in the social domain of their goals. To take another example, in two cases dealing with an issue of freedom of religion, one lawyer might be basically concerned with the abstract principle of separation of church and state, another with the harassment of a particular religious sect. Both might have the same goal—for example, the declaring of a certain law unconstitutional—but the difference lies in their perception of for whom this particular outcome is important.

Thus two lawyers with rather similar goals may have distinguishable clienteles. Though there is often an empirical connection between a lawyer's goals and his clientele that appears to differentiate Group Advocates from Civil Libertarians, it is not this variable that conceptually differentiates them.

The Group Advocate's commitment to his group may have a

variety of forms. It may be a kind of *personal* commitment, derived from social or friendship ties between lawyer and client. Thus, for example, in many of the reapportionment cases the attorney behaved as a Group Advocate for a political club or party faction in which the lawyer himself was active, whose members he knew intimately, and to whose fortunes he felt his own political ambitions were tied. By the same token, many of the lawyers who argued loyalty-security cases had long-standing personal ties with the individuals who became involved in loyalty-security difficulties. The cases came to them as those of friends in trouble, and the personal ties of the lawyers were crucial both to their initial involvement and to their perceptions of what kinds of issues the cases involved.

Closely related to this kind of personal commitment is a kind of *ideological* tie among lawyer, client, and the group in which the lawyer and the client are members. In the reapportionment cases it was not only personal ties with a political faction that shaped the lawyer's perspective on his litigation but political or ideological ties as well. The political fortunes of the faction—and the kinds of policies it might promote if it gained political power—were of concern to the lawyer. In the loyalty-security cases, again, agreement about programs for social and political change between client and lawyer tended to focus the lawyer's attention upon the group of political dissenters and radicals under attack by the government. Many civil rights lawyers also felt this ideological tie (though the friendship motive was often absent because so many of the cases on appeal were argued by specialized appeals lawyers who did not even meet their clients). Some of the lawyers were themselves black, and the tie between lawyer and client, and between lawyer and the group for whom he perceived the case as important, was intuitively obvious. For the white civil rights lawyers, who acted as Group Advocates for the black minority, the tie was somewhat less clear. Their identification with the interests of blacks, to be explored in more detail shortly, probably emerged from an initial sympathy with blacks and was nurtured and matured because of their organizational positions within litigating interest groups and their continued exposure to cases involving the rights of blacks.

This leads us to another kind of tie between the lawyer and the group he feels he is representing. This is a kind of *institutional* tie, often occurring when the lawyer is operating within an organization that is devoted to lobbying for the interest of a particular minority. Here the lawyer may become immersed in litigation of a single kind of issue content, involving the affairs of a particular group.[1]

To summarize, the key to the Group Advocate is his affiliation with a group and his identification of his case with the interests of that group. His tie to the client (and the group which he feels the case involves) is complex and can involve personal, ideological, and organizational dimensions.

GROUP ADVOCATES: LITIGATION AND GOALS

The Group Advocates were active in three areas of litigation, dominating civil rights and reapportionment and playing an important role in early loyalty-security litigation. Chapter 2 provided a brief overview of the litigation that occurred in these fields during the 1957–66 period, indicating what kinds of decisions came out of the Court. This section will focus upon the goals the Group Advocates were trying to achieve and how their goals were related both to their being Group Advocates and to the kinds of decisional outcomes that emerged from litigation before the Supreme Court.

Loyalty-Security Litigation

As suggested in Chapter 2, the loyalty-security cases during the 1957–66 period can be divided into two groups. The first group, occurring during the first half of the period, grew directly out of McCarthyism and involved the application of various kinds of

1. As was suggested in the preceding chapter, this type of tie may come to be more important in criminal justice appeals, as more lawyers operate out of institutions like public defender offices or legal services offices.

loyalty-security programs (e.g., Smith and McCarran acts, legislative investigations of alleged subversives, screening of government employees). These cases were essentially defensive in character, the litigation having been initiated by the government and the appeal being an attempt to defend against this government activity. These cases were most often argued by a particular group of lawyers—called here the *Radical Bar*—who participated in many of them and who provided the bulk of representation (at the Supreme Court level, at least) for those in loyalty-security difficulties. The members of the Radical Bar were Group Advocates for the political Left in this country, having personal and sometimes ideological ties with their clients and the kinds of political viewpoints they represented.

The second group of lawyers—to be called *ACLU lawyers*[2]—were active in the later cases, which were of a different character. They arose after the height of the McCarthy period, and many involved attacks upon state and municipal loyalty oaths.[3] These suits were initiated by private parties rather than at the behest of the government, and they represented an offensive attempt to mobilize opposition toward such programs. The lawyers in these cases had little or no personal or ideological commitment to their clients (who themselves often had no doctrinaire ideological positions but simply didn't like oaths) and acted as Civil Libertarians. This group of lawyers is discussed in detail in the following chapter.

In discussing the Radical Bar lawyers, we consider the questions of how they became involved in their litigation, why they are classified as Group Advocates, and what kinds of goals they were pursuing. First we will look at their career patterns, for this

2. The term "ACLU lawyer" is a euphemism used here to describe the typical lawyer who handles occasional cases for the ACLU but whose basic practice involves other matters and who does not depend upon civil liberties litigation for his livelihood. Many Radical Bar lawyers were members of the ACLU but do not fall into the category "ACLU lawyer."

3. As suggested in Chapter 2, there were a number of cases dealing with municipal and state loyalty oaths before the period discussed here. But these previous suits were primarily defensive in character, e.g., following a dismissal. The loyalty-oath cases in the latter part of the 1957–66 period were often offensive suits aimed at enjoining loyalty-oath programs.

was a crucial factor in both their involvement and their clientele in the litigation they eventually argued before the Supreme Court.

The typical member of the Radical Bar came from a family that was moderately active in radical politics. The lawyer reported that he had no particular reason for choosing his profession: being a professional was desirable in a vague and diffuse way, and scholarships to law school were more easily obtainable than those to medical school. Thus, though he came from a liberal or radical political background, the typical member of the Radical Bar did not choose the legal profession for the purpose of working for social change. Many members graduated from law school during the depth of the Depression. The New Deal and the emergence of the Congress of Industrial Organizations caught their interest, and most went into labor law, working either for industrial unions or the newly formed National Labor Relations Board. Most in the government left when Roosevelt died. The Depression was an extremely important influence in their lives, for it deeply impressed upon them the social and political ills of American society. The New Deal swept them up in the search for new programs and policies to cure these ills. As a result of their work with the emerging industrial labor unions, they came into personal contact with many political radicals, including members of the American Communist party and other left-wing factions. Whether or not the typical lawyer accepted their ideology, he came into contact with radicals, shared with them their concern about social conditions in America, and often became friends with them.

When the Cold War and the McCarthy period brought government action against the left wing, many of those in trouble turned to lawyers they knew and from whom they could expect a sympathetic response. Thus the typical member of the Radical Bar became involved in a few loyalty-security cases in the middle and late 1940s. Since many lawyers would not handle these cases, those who did became inundated with clients. One lawyer reports how he became active in loyalty-security litigation:

. . . We left the government—I had been a trial examiner for the NLRB; my partner had been working for [another government agency]. We were interested in practicing law and generally interested in things. Let me say this—I don't think that if the McCarthyite period hadn't come and people hadn't come to us—I don't think we would have . . . I mean, it's not our personality—it's almost that these cases just came. And we didn't feel in good conscience that we could turn them down, 'cause they were important cases. I don't mean we struggled over it—we thought they were good cases and we were glad to do them. But the kind of thing happens—more so in those days than today—this business, if you take one or two of these cases you find you're not handling any other [kinds of cases]. I mean, it's not your choice—it seems to be other people's choice. [78]

Some members of the Radical Bar also stressed the importance to their careers of their exposure to Marxism:

I went to college to be a minister. I had a debate scholarship from "Hometown." The women there—we were the only Negro family there—they raised the money to send me to college. And they sent me to be a minister. It is a Methodist college and my folks were Methodists. But in my sophomore year I met a boy from Russia, and I was arguing with him on all these things. He was a Marxist and he really knew his stuff and he gradually drew me in during my sophomore year. I told my professor of Bible that I didn't think I could—I didn't believe in God in the sense that he believed in it, and I didn't think that I could be a minister. And he said, "I think you're right." So I switched over to political science and by that time I was so involved with my political beliefs on Marxism that I decided . . . that my best prospects would be in law. [34]

The Radical Bar lawyer was ideologically receptive to the kinds of reforms advocated by the political radicals. His personal ties with radicals first led him into their cases, and the social and political climate of the time insured that he would continue to represent them. In addition, there was probably some selection by the client, for the radical might well have wished to be represented by a lawyer of similar political persuasion.[4]

4. For example, two black members of the Radical Bar suggested that they were sometimes called into cases in part because of their race. One reported, "He

One of the most striking aspects of involvement by the Radical Bar in litigation was the importance of friendship ties between lawyer and client. Ten of the 21 interview respondents who argued loyalty-security cases reported some friendship tie or social contact with their clients previous to involvement in their litigation. All ten were members of the Radical Bar. Some Radical Bar lawyers also became involved in litigation when members of unions they represented had loyalty-security difficulties. Finally, Radical Bar lawyers became involved as a result of their reputations. A lawyer quickly developed a reputation for willingness to become involved in loyalty-security cases; this led to the snowball effect alluded to above—one case led to another and then more. In this way a Radical Bar—a group of lawyers specializing in loyalty-security litigation—developed.

Involvement in any particular loyalty-security case was by no means a discrete event for a member of the Radical Bar. During the 1950s he was likely to be representing a number of individuals who had been caught in the loyalty-security net. A good part of his practice would involve counseling clients and representing them before loyalty-security review boards, legislative committees, and finally in court proceedings. The atmosphere of such proceedings was often one of fear and hostility. Since the lawyer was often personally acquainted with his client and held political beliefs sympathetic to his social and political goals, it was natural for the lawyer to empathize with his client.

The Radical Bar lawyers usually perceived their litigation in a "we-they" perspective. They identified with their clients both because of some similarity in views and because others lumped them together. Each case was to some extent viewed as a contest between the government (and society generally) and the

---

[the lawyer for the defendants in a case involving members of the Communist party] called from 'Eastport' to tell me that they were looking for another lawyer and that he suggested me. It was a little more specific than that. It was just inconceivable that the defendants would go to trial with a battery of say three or four lawyers and not have a Negro among them. It would be a reflection on them and everything that they advocated" [55]. On the other hand, some radicals might have preferred to be represented by more "respectable" lawyers but were unable to secure such representation and thus turned to those lawyers who were willing to handle their cases.

group of radicals under attack. The performance of many Radical Bar lawyers at legislative hearings tends to confirm the notion that they perceived the proceedings as personalized contests. The hearings were often highly acrimonious, and the lawyers for the witnesses often displayed scorn for the committees' members and purposes (and vice versa).[5] Relatedly, in his study of the provision of counsel to political radicals, Milnor Alexander cites as one of the major reasons for the difficulty the radicals had in obtaining counsel the fact that many lawyers feel that they must believe in the cause of their clients if they are to provide effective representation. Since many lawyers did not hold such sympathies for political radicals, the politically unpopular often had difficulty in obtaining representation.[6]

In calling them Group Advocates, it is not suggested that these lawyers were unsympathetic to the broad principles involved in their cases or to the application of these principles to individuals with whom they would disagree. Rather, the Radical Bar lawyers simply became so involved in the affairs and claims of the political radicals that they tended to view the litigation as primarily a contest between the government and the kinds of people they were representing. In the same way a civil rights lawyer may become immersed in the claims of black people and may perceive his litigation as primarily concerning their affairs, without in any way being unsympathetic to similar claims by other minority groups.

The Radical Bar lawyers were ambivalent about the specific grounds for decision in their cases. They were concerned with broad and principled decisions because such decisions would be the most effective way of curtailing their adversaries. Since a lawyer often felt that the activities of his clients were important in fighting for social reform, a narrow victory was useful

5. The flavor of many of the HUAC hearings is nicely evoked in Walter Goodman, *The Committee* (New York: Farrar, Straus & Giroux, 1968).

6. Milnor Alexander, "The Right to Counsel for the Politically Unpopular," *Law in Transition Quarterly* 22 (1962): 19–45. Another study, dealing with law students, indicates that fear of public reaction was a major factor making attorneys reluctant to become involved with political offenders. See Jack H. Olender, "Let Us Admit Impediments," *University of Pittsburgh Law Review* 20 (1959): 749–53.

because it kept the client in circulation. Any victory was felt to be important, both because it was a rebuff to a hostile government and because it placed one more obstacle in the path of continued government harassment. The lawyer's goals were sometimes affected by the interest of the client, for many clients in loyalty-security cases were themselves concerned with the broad civil liberties issues involved in their cases. On occasion a client would urge his lawyer not to raise technical issues because he preferred going to jail to getting off on a technicality:

I've known some clients who felt that way [wanted to stress only the broader issues]. And particularly in this area where Committee witnesses . . . I've tried to tell people that that's a very unreal question because while they may have the feeling that they only want to have the broad issues, I try to tell them that it doesn't really make much difference what their feeling is. The Court's going to pick out something which even if you don't present it, they think is *de minimus*. And it's not really your choice. For example, [another member of the Radical Bar] once told me about one of his cases—a [client] absolutely forbid him to raise any other questions. I think he succeeded in dissuading him, but the Court didn't take the case. It's not that I disagree with the client's point of view. I can understand these people who say, "Why should I go through all this trouble just to get off and not raise the principle?" [78]

In summary, members of the Radical Bar acted in litigation as Group Advocates for the political Left. Their interest in the grounds for decision varied. The case often came to the lawyer in the context of an acquaintance in trouble, and the lawyer often felt a close personal identification with his client.

Reapportionment

The reapportionment cases were the most politically partisan of those falling under the rubric of civil liberties and rights. The issues involved in the litigation affected directly the fortunes of political parties, and the suits were largely partisan in their initiation and motivation. Individuals already involved in party politics or with personal political ambitions often served as plaintiffs in the suits (e.g., in the Alabama, Colorado, and Virginia cases). The goals of the suits, as set forth by the lawyers who argued them, were overtly political: "reforming the politics of [my state]" or "shaking up [our society]."

The political character of these suits was reflected in the involvement and clienteles of the lawyers. The lawyers interviewed who argued reapportionment suits tended to be active in the politics of their states, and this political activity was directly related to their involvement in the litigation. Table 7,

TABLE 7. POLITICAL PARTY ACTIVITY: REAPPORTIONMENT LAWYERS VERSUS ALL OTHERS.[a]

Activity	Reapportionment Lawyers	Other Respondents
None	0	25
Contribute money to party	1	39
Active in election campaigns	2	19
Delegate to party nominating conventions	0	5
Party official	4	4
Been candidate for office	5	23
Total	12	115

[a] The items form a Guttman Scale. Respondents are placed at the highest level of activity reported.

though the small numbers make it only suggestive, indicates that the reapportionment lawyers were indeed highly active in partisan politics. Approximately 75 percent of the reapportionment lawyers fall into the two highest categories of political party activity, while 55 percent of other respondents fall within the two lowest categories. Nine of the 12 reapportionment lawyers reported affiliation with the Democratic party, with the remaining three being Republicans.

The relevance of political activity was reflected in the ways in which the reapportionment lawyers became involved in the litigation. Of the eight interviewed, the means of involvement were as follows: "previous client," one; "group," three; "friendship," four. The lawyer who became involved through "previous client" was on retainer to the client who filed the reapportionment suit. The three who became involved by virtue of their association with a group were all members of local political clubs which decided to file suit attacking apportionments they felt were disadvantageous to the political or social interests they represented (two of the clubs were nonpartisan groups whose members were primarily city or suburban dwellers; the third was a Democratic party club). Finally, four became involved through their friendship ties with politicians, developed as a result of the lawyers' participation in party affairs. As one lawyer put it, ". . . and that's how I came to be the attorney—by being politically associated and being friendly" [26].

None of the attorneys interviewed (with the exception of the lawyer who was acting in behalf of a retainer client) received fees for their participation in the cases. This is another indication that the lawyers felt some personal or ideological interest in the outcome of the suits. Although it is by no means implied that the attorneys were not in part motivated by a sense of public duty or that reapportionment was seen simply as a means of personal aggrandizement, many of the attorneys perceived that their interests and those of the groups with which they were associated were tied to reapportionment.

In the Colorado and Virginia suits the plaintiffs were themselves political officeholders. In some of the other suits individuals who acted as plaintiffs later held public or party office. Many of the plaintiffs and their lawyers perceived litigation as a potential means of defeating their political opponents. One of the rationales provided by the Court for entering the political thicket was the fact that the "normal" channels for change via the political process were foreclosed (since apportionment was usually the prerogative of malapportioned legislatures whose members had little to gain and much power to lose by reapportioning themselves). The relevance of this rationale is demonstrated by the kinds of individuals who acted as plaintiffs and attorneys in the reapportionment litigation—they tended to represent the political forces which had the most to gain from reapportionment.

Thus most of the lawyers interviewed who argued reapportionment cases were lawyer-politicians, pursuing two careers at once. Their law practices provided them with a steady income, and celebrated cases sometimes gave them a kind of free publicity.[7] For many of them, though, their real interest and ambition lay in politics, either elective or party office. They were drawn into reapportionment litigation (or helped to initiate it) as a result of their close ties with political clubs or factions that were disadvantaged by malapportionment. The litigation offered them an opportunity to combine their interests, to use their professional expertise in support of partisan political goals they desired.

The reapportionment lawyers interviewed were acting as Group Advocates in behalf of their political factions. Though the lawyers tended, in varying degrees, to be concerned with the significance of the litigation not only for the political groups with which they were allied but also for the maintenance of a democratic political system, their primary focus in the suits was upon the fortunes of their groups.

Their clienteles were related to their goals in the cases, to the kind of doctrinal outcome they sought. As suggested in Chapter 2, members of the majority of the Court took essentially two different positions in the reapportionment decisions. One group, led by Chief Justice Warren, attacked the problem with a kind of blanket principle: equal population apportionment (within somewhat ill-defined parameters of divergence) for both houses. The other position, advanced by Clark and Stewart, would have decided the cases on a more *ad hoc* basis, looking at each state's apportionment and judging whether it was "arbitrary," "discriminated invidiously," or was a "crazy quilt" without rational basis. The latter approach not only did not guarantee population apportionment of *both* houses but, as applied, allowed more deviation from equal population apportionment.

As noted above, the lawyers interviewed saw their clienteles

7. The common wisdom suggests that lawyers are active in politics in order to further their legal careers: make contacts, gain publicity, etc. For these lawyers, though, it also worked the other way around; their litigation was a means of aiding their political careers. For a useful discussion of the relationship between legal and political careers, see Heinz Eulau and John D. Sprague, *Lawyers in Politics* (New York: Bobbs-Merrill, 1964).

as political factions and their litigation as a clash between policies rather than principles. When asked about the grounds for
decision they preferred in their cases, most expressed a preference for the one man–one vote formula. But their reasons for
such a preference were not couched in rhetoric stressing the
importance for democratic systems of maximizing equality.
Rather, their preference (and this was intimately tied to their
clienteles) was justified in more pragmatic terms, since they felt
the "principled" approach would be a more effective method of
promoting rapid reapportionment. The remarks of two respondents give the flavor of this view:

We were interested in knowing what it [malapportionment] was and
in having everybody else know what it was. But we were not as interested in establishing a great constitutional principle for the United
States of America as we were in shaking [our state] up a little bit.
Or a lot. But we didn't want it in murky words or murky language, or
anything talking about "egregious discrimination" or "crazy quilts"
or that sort of thing, like they wound up *Baker v. Carr* with. [44]

We liked the broad simple principle of one-man–one-vote. The simplicity of the formula made it so easy to quickly change the legislatures. . . . So the simplicity of the formula avoided sophisticated
evasive schemes of trying to circumvent the principle of equal representation based upon the number of people to be represented. [26]

Another respondent suggested the same point, that the lawyers were primarily interested in changing the locus of political
power in their states, not in abstract principles. After he had ex-
plained that although at first the suit had simply attacked malapportionment in one house, the argument eventually shifted to
the population formula for both houses, he was asked the following question:

*A hypothetical question. Do you think you would have been satisfied
if you had won the case by using the Clark-Stewart grounds rather
than the simple equal protection formula?*

I think I would have to answer that in point of time. Certainly at the
outset our goals were more modest, and, you know, had there been a
ruling as to one House, I think that would have been enough to get

some movement in the situation which had been at a dead standstill since the turn of the century in this state. As the climate of thinking changed and as there were other decisions which came down, we became more ambitious. [81]

Notice the interest not in vindicating principles for their own sake but in getting "some movement in the situation."

To recapitulate, the reapportionment cases were argued by Group Advocates acting in behalf of political factions. They viewed their clienteles not as some hypothetical construct of the American people (compare some of the comments by Civil Libertarians in Chapter 6) but as particularly circumscribed political groups with whom the lawyers felt themselves tied. The suits were designed and pursued to "shake things up," to allow the "outs" to get in, to provide entry to a political arena that had previously been closed.[8]

Civil Rights

Litigating interest groups[9] have been vitally important in civil rights litigation, as have been a number of courageous unaffiliated lawyers from southern communities who were willing to handle civil rights cases. The Legal Defense Fund (LDF) has both local cooperating attorneys and a staff in New York. In many of the important civil rights cases the cooperating attorney handled the case through the state supreme court, and the appeal to the Supreme Court of the United States was then handled by an attorney from the New York office. Thus there has to some extent been a specialized appeal bar active in civil rights litigation at the Supreme Court level.[10]

8. This was essentially the rationale adopted by the Court for its entrance into the political thicket. As suggested in Chapter 2, though, there is some evidence that reapportionment may not have the impact upon party competition and public policy that many of its proponents (and the lawyers) anticipated.

9. The major groups include the Legal Defense Fund of the NAACP, the ACLU, the Lawyers' Constitutional Defense Committee (affiliated with the ACLU), the Congress of Racial Equality, the Southern Conference Educational Fund (affiliated with CORE), the National Lawyers' Guild, and the Southern Christian Leadership Conference.

10. This discussion of civil rights litigation before the Supreme Court deals with rather broad and strategic concerns. Much of the excitement and drama attached to civil rights activity and litigation on the local level in the South is

Since litigating interest groups were so important both in the recruitment process and in shaping the clienteles of the lawyers who argued civil rights cases before the Court, a very brief description of the activities of the most important of these groups, the Legal Defense Fund, may serve as a preface to our discussion of the lawyers.[11]

The Legal Defense Fund grew out of the NAACP and was founded in 1939 by members of the NAACP national board. It is, however, an independent organization and not tied directly to the parent group. The LDF has provided legal representation to members of all the major civil rights groups, not simply those associated with the NAACP. As the civil rights movement gained momentum, attorneys affiliated with the LDF bore a large share of the burden of defense of civil rights demonstrators. The organization consists of a national headquarters in New York, with a staff of full-time lawyers, and a group of volunteer cooperating attorneys throughout the nation.

The extent of the activity of the LDF can be seen from Table 8.[12] In a typical case handled by the LDF, a local cooperating

TABLE 8. LEGAL DEFENSE FUND ACTIVITIES, 1963–68.

	1963	1964	1965	1966	1967	1968
Individuals defended by LDF	4,200	10,400	17,000	14,000	13,000	unavailable
Groups of cases listed in LDF docket	107	145	225	375	420	593
Lawyers on staff, including interns	9	12	17	17	28	25
Cooperating attorneys on local level	71	102	121	187	250	288

missed. For an account of the experiences of one lawyer active in the South, see William Kunstler, *Deep in My Heart* (New York: William Morrow, 1966).

11. The information about the Legal Defense Fund comes primarily from interviews with attorneys associated with it. In addition, valuable information about the nature of the organization and the strategies it has pursued in litigation is found in Clement E. Vose, *Caucasians Only* (Berkeley and Los Angeles: University of California Press, 1959).

12. The data come from NAACP Legal Defense and Educational Fund, *Report 66* (New York, 1967) and *The Quiet Revolution* (New York, 1969).

attorney handles the litigation at the trial and the first appeal. He is in contact with the headquarters staff, receiving guidance, research assistance, and sometimes financial aid. If the case is important enough, the national office might send down a staff attorney to work with the local cooperating attorney. After the case completes all appeals below the Supreme Court of the United States, the national office sometimes assumes full responsibility for it, with a staff attorney preparing the petition for *certiorari* and the brief and arguing the case. A lawyer with the national office indicated some of the factors affecting the selection of an attorney to argue before the Supreme Court:

> Well, a variety of things determine that. One would be the general importance of the issue. For example, if it were a jury discrimination case—that would involve settled issues in which no particular . . . no unusual degree of skill or experience would be useful—there would be a tendency for a local lawyer to argue it, or perhaps a junior member of the staff to argue it. Then, another factor that's taken into account is the ability or experience of the local lawyer. If you had a case in which you had a really able, well-experienced, well-trained cooperating lawyer, then it would be more likely that he would argue it than if he were someone just out of law school or his talents didn't run in that direction. That is further compounded by the fact that . . . in a sit-in case where you had six or eight cases argued together . . . it's easier to let the local lawyer have a role in that because you can get the benefit of his local flavor and knowledge of the situation. And though you lose some capacity to deal with the constitutional issues and experience in dealing with them and so on, that can be compensated by someone on this staff who has that—taking part in the case. . . . So we try to put together a legal team . . . that can deal with the issues with various different types of talents. [75]

The LDF is a rather hierarchical organization. Two major institutional factors produce this hierarchical structure. The national office has a good deal of control over funds expended by the local cooperating attorneys, which insures that the local lawyers will keep in close touch with the national office and be amenable to its suggestions. In addition, the national office is equipped with a large and well-trained legal staff, which enables it to keep track of and supervise the efforts of the cooperating attorneys as well as offer them research aid and advice on strategy.

This control is important to the organization. Since many of the cases handled by the LDF involve issues which will eventually be decided by the Supreme Court, it is vital that a good record be made and that the issues be properly framed and preserved for appeal. In addition, since a single issue is often raised in litigation from many localities, appeals must be coordinated. Thus an attorney affiliated with the LDF who becomes involved in a civil rights case is by no means on his own. From the national organization he receives not only extensive support but also a good measure of direction and control.

Most of the lawyers interviewed (11 of 14) who argued civil rights cases became involved in the litigation as a result of their association with civil rights organizations. The remaining three became involved by referral or through a previous client, and all had reputations for willingness to handle civil rights cases. Among those interviewed, ten came from a locality where discrimination was practiced and where the case arose. The other four came from the New York City area, and all were associated with the NAACP and LDF. Three of the four from the NAACP and LDF national offices became involved at the Supreme Court level, with the other handling the case from the initial trial stage. The lawyers from the New York area typically handled a number of cases before the Supreme Court (two handled two each during the 1957–66 period; the other two handled six each). The lawyers from other communities typically argued only one case before the Court during the period.

Of the 14 lawyers interviewed who argued civil rights cases, three were in solo practice, five were associated with law firms, three were employees of litigating interest groups, one was a law school professor, one worked for a legal services office, and one was a federal government employee. The typical pattern by which a lawyer became involved in a case was either direct contact by a client because of the lawyer's affiliation with a civil rights group or referral by the organization of a client to the lawyer. Thus it was in the context of affiliation with an interest group that most lawyers came to the cases that they eventually argued before the Supreme Court. Their affiliation with these organizations produced their group-oriented clienteles.

Another factor relevant to the clienteles and goals of lawyers in civil rights cases is the general context of the civil rights movement. The activities that led to litigation were intimately tied to the lawyers' views of what they were trying to achieve, whom they were representing.

Much of the activity of the civil rights movement out of which litigation during the 1957–66 period grew—particularly sit-ins and other public demonstrations—had mixed purposes. In the sit-in cases, for example, the demonstrators wished to call public attention to the denial of their rights and to mobilize the conscience of the nation. They were also attempting to bring direct pressure—by publicity and economic sanctions—upon those who discriminated and thereby induce them to modify their discriminatory behavior. Finally, in addition to these symbolic and pragmatic considerations, the demonstrators were testing the constitutionality of the laws under which they were being discriminated against. In some cases there were ordinances forbidding integration; in others local informal practice was buttressed by actions of the governmental power structure. Demonstrations thus involved not only tests of will and force but also constitutional issues. The goals of the demonstrations were varied, and litigation was but one concern.[13]

In some of the earlier civil rights litigation, dealing with school segregation and restrictive covenants, for example, the attack on discrimination was in effect run by lawyers; they shaped the goals and the techniques by which the goals were to be achieved. Offensive litigation was the strategy chosen, and it met with significant success. In the protest demonstration aspect of the civil rights movement the lawyer entered the process at a later stage. The basic strategy—direct-action protests and violation of

13. For an analysis of the black protest movement using game-theoretic concepts, see James Q. Wilson, "The Strategy of Protest: Problems of Negro Civic Action," *Journal of Conflict Resolution* 5 (1961): 291–303.

discriminatory laws—had been chosen by the leaders of civil rights groups or simply by spontaneous action of black citizens. Such direct action often led the protesters into court, and at this stage the lawyer became important. But the basic act had already taken place, and the lawyer was confronted with a situation and had to deal with it.

The lawyers who became involved in the civil rights demonstration litigation had a number of goals. First, most wanted to win the cases, for sometimes the punishment meted out to demonstrators was harsh. Others were primarily interested in using the litigation to outlaw discrimination generally. Some of the lawyers from the South hoped to use the litigation to teach their communities object lessons in tolerance, using the courts as a vehicle to impress upon their fellow citizens the illegitimacy and immorality of racial discrimination. Some wished to use the courts as a lever to influence action by Congress, hoping to have the courts push Congress toward passage of civil rights legislation. The common factor in all the lawyers' goals was concern with racial discrimination and with black people as a group. The LDF lawyers and other individuals who participated in this litigation were paradigms of the Group Advocate.

The sit-in cases present a fascinating study in the relationship between the goals of lawyers and the decisions of the Supreme Court.[14] The cases affected many people: it has been estimated that at least 3,600 people were arrested in sit-in demonstrations in the South and that 70,000 people participated in such activities.[15] A total of 61 sit-in cases were granted *certiorari* by the Court between 1957 and 1967, and all but four were decided in favor of the demonstrators (many without opinion). The cases were handled by LDF lawyers, by attorneys from other litigating interest groups, and by a few unattached lawyers.

14. For a detailed discussion of the sit-in cases, see Joel B. Grossman, "A Model for Judicial Policy Analysis: The Supreme Court and the Sit-In Cases," in Joel B. Grossman and Joseph Tanenhaus, eds., *Frontiers of Judicial Research* (New York: John Wiley and Sons, 1969), pp. 405–60.

15. This estimate comes from Southern Regional Council, "The Student Protest Movement: A Recapitulation," Report 21 (1961). The actual figures are probably higher, since this estimate covers only activities through 1961.

The LDF attempted to coordinate the briefs and arguments in the sit-in cases. It brought its attorneys and other lawyers involved together for seminars to discuss the issues, and it held moot courts at the Howard University Law School prior to a number of oral arguments before the Court. When coordinating the arguments and selecting attorneys, the LDF "tried to put together a legal team that could deal with the issues with various different types of talents" [75]. One LDF lawyer characterized their participation in the sit-in cases:

We took up every single sit-in case there was. We didn't differentiate. In some we varied our arguments, and we tried to demonstrate there was state action in some of them where perhaps on the surface there might not have been. . . . We came at the thing six and eight ways. "Sure the man had a property right, but his property right merely consisted of the right to discriminate"—that didn't get anywhere. Then we came up . . . we had all the foreign law—we had maybe twenty countries and showed that only in America, you know. . . . But we never tried to put the Court in . . . to present to the Court an issue it had to say yes or no to. We gave it a variety of avenues to decision— and in fact that's what it did. We gave it all kinds of grounds. But end results of the case was that sit-inners always won. [75]

But at least some of the lawyers who argued sit-in cases before the Court did not share this view. Some felt that they had cases which would *require* the Court to reach the question of discrimination in a public accommodation in the absence of any overt state action. They argued this point and were disappointed when the Court managed to dispose of their cases on relatively narrow state-action grounds:

We thought we had the case where the Supreme Court had to rule that segregation by private restaurateurs would amount to significant state action and violated the 14th Amendment. That in this case there would be no way for the Court to avoid or evade the issues—we thought this was the case. We were also worried that the case was too good, that they'd rule against us. This was the case. The other cases decided that day went off on trespass grounds, void for vagueness, or some other clear state interference. Well, those cases were decided on the basis of constitutional principles that had been established in other cases. None of them involved the *Shelley v. Kraemer*[16] notion. And we felt we had it. The record we felt was perfect on this point. [21]

In this and other sit-in cases the Court decided in favor of the demonstrators, but upon some narrower ground than the lawyers wished. One important factor in these cases appears to have been the part played by the U.S. Solicitor General, Archibald Cox, who entered many of these cases as *amicus curiae* (often at the invitation of the Court). He consistently urged the Court to find in favor of the claims of the demonstrators, but usually on fairly narrow grounds. He may have been concerned with protecting the integrity of the Court from outside attack, or he may have philosophically believed that the broad question should not be decided by the Court. Surely in the later stages of the litigation he was concerned with the effect of the litigation on efforts to pass the Civil Rights Act of 1964, which included a public accommodations section.

In any event, some of the lawyers tended to resent the position of the Solicitor General. This was especially true when a lawyer was bent upon having the Court decide the broad issue:

The [federal] government's position at this time was interesting. One of the things I want to mention was the terrible brawl that I had with Archie Cox at the time. Obviously, I never thought he'd take the last point. That was too extreme to ask the government to take, but there was no reason why Cox shouldn't have taken the second point, that where a private man discriminates and he calls the cops to throw some guy out, that's state action and that's bad. Cox wouldn't even go *that* far. He said *Shelley v. Kraemer* did *not* support going that

16. Shelley v. Kraemer, 334 U.S. 1 (1948), the major restrictive-covenant case, held that private agreements not to sell or rent property to blacks did not violate the equal-protection clause of the Fourteenth Amendment because of the absence in the simple agreement of any state action. But the Court went on to hold that such agreements could not be enforced in court, for such enforcement would be unconstitutional state action in favor of discrimination. If Shelley could be taken to stand for the proposition that some normally unexceptionable legal practices and laws (e.g., enforcing contracts) were unconstitutional when applied to support racial discrimination, the sit-in lawyers argued that the same was true for trespass, breach-of-peace, and other laws used to prevent racial integration of public accommodations.

far, and therefore as you of course know, in most of the sit-in cases they've had to reverse them on the most technical grounds.

I'm not satisfied with the outcome of *any* of the sit-in cases, not just [my case], because here I blame Cox. I believe that the principle that a policeman can't go into Woolworth's counter and arrest a man there trying to get a hamburger should have been established, but Cox wouldn't take it—he tried to argue each case on some technical ground he found and I think that was a mistake. [The brief filed as *amicus* in my case] was one of the most pusillanimous documents I have ever read, in the sense that he didn't come to grips with any of this. [58]

Thus some of the lawyers did hope to have the Court reach the broad issue, but none was successful. The Court has at its disposal so many options in any case that it can, if it wishes, usually avoid important issues. As one respondent said about the sit-in cases, and about the lawyers who felt that they had the Court boxed in, "Well, that's just fatuous. I've seen all these lawyers saying 'I've got the Court trapped and the Court has to do such and such.' Well, the Court doesn't *have* to do a damned thing. The Court does what it chooses. . . . They do what they god-damned well please. You just don't tell the Supreme Court what to do. And if worse comes to worse, they can just decide not to decide the case, which they did in other demonstration cases—dismissed as improvidently granted" [75].

The idea of a kind of tacit bargaining with the Court was mentioned by another lawyer who argued another type of civil rights case for the LDF:

So, though we talked about the whole scale of [mentions a broad issue which was partly touched by this particular case], we had no expectation really of getting a judicial response that went that far. But, as a tactical matter it was terribly useful to be able to argue to the Supreme Court [the broad issue]. Essentially for bartering purposes, so that they would come as a compromise position that that limited position which was adequate for us to win our case. And winning our case, this was important to our clients. Also, losing the case would have been very bad. But winning it even on a half-way basis, we were persuaded, was, you know, would be a real accomplishment. From that point of view, it seemed to make great tactical sense to be

able to argue that case as broadly as possible. . . . [An official of the
LDF] and I talked about whether we were asking . . . whether bringing that case was loading up the Supreme Court more heavily with
difficult problems than was helpful to them. . . . And I don't think this
was really megalomaniac to the extent that, one in his [the LDF official's] position regards the Court as a co-working institution. He has
an obligation to worry about whether he is asking the judges to do
more than they should be doing effectively at a given time, or you
know, what are the limits of their institutional capacity in terms of
timing and the scope of problems and whatnot. [7]

Three important points about the civil rights litigation emerge
from this quotation. First is the notion that the lawyer bargains
with the Court, bringing in the "big issue" so that the Court is
in a position to decide the case in his favor on the basis of a more
narrow one.[17] Second, it suggests the importance of the choice of
cases to take to the Supreme Court. It was important that the
civil rights movement not take too many "losers" to the Court,
for this would reflect upon the legitimacy of civil rights protests
generally. Finally, this lawyer indicates that some active civil
rights lawyers were concerned with the Court itself, taking into
consideration in their calculations about what cases to take up
to the Court not only the chances for victory but also the burdens
being placed upon the Court (though of course these considerations were related).

In the sit-in cases, though, the lawyers were not so selective.
This relative lack of selectivity was primarily a result of the
spontaneous development of much of the litigation. Unlike the

17. This point was stressed by many of the lawyers who argued sit-in cases.
By urging the Court to decide the broad constitutional issue, they suggested, they
made it "easier" and more likely for the Court to decide the cases in favor of their
clients on narrower grounds.

The sit-in cases also involved a kind of "bargaining" with Congress. Some of
the lawyers suggested that by pressing the Court to provide a judicial and constitutional solution to the problem of racial discrimination in public accommodations, they placed pressure upon Congress to speed legislation. Legislation provided leeway for the exceptions (e.g., Mrs. Murphy boarding houses) that were
important to many congressmen, a flexibility that might have been denied had
the Court settled the issue with a blanket constitutional prohibition upon discrimination in public accommodations. By the same token, the reluctance of the
Court and the Solicitor General to face the basic issue probably reflected a desire
to defer to Congress and avoid the confrontation implicit in a judicial solution.

school segregation, restrictive-covenant, poll-tax, or miscegenation cases, for example, many of the lawyers did not participate in the mapping of a litigation strategy before the legal proceedings were begun. The lawyers were faced with the problem of trying to develop winning strategies within the context of specific cases rather than in the abstract. They tended to take all the cases to the Supreme Court, altering their arguments as they went along.

Thus most of the civil rights cases were argued by lawyers, operating often in the context of litigating interest groups, who perceived their clienteles as a particular minority in our society, blacks. In some cases the lawyer participated in the mapping of the legal and political strategy that eventually resulted in litigation before the Supreme Court. The sit-in cases, on the other hand, were a more spontaneous development in which the lawyer entered the litigation after the case had been initiated (usually by the application of some criminal sanction to the demonstrators). The obvious questions, why these lawyers were Group Advocates and why they became involved with the civil rights movement, are discussed in the next section.

We have now covered the three major areas of litigation in which Group Advocates were involved. Though the lawyers discussed here were all Group Advocates, representing in their litigation clienteles comprising fairly defined groups in society, the groups were of different character, and the lawyers' interest in particular doctrinal outcomes varied a good deal.

Notice that the groups they represented—though they varied greatly in the degree of interaction their members had (ranging from a group like "black people," basically defined by demographic characteristics, to the political factions for the reapportionment lawyers to the ideological faction of the Radical Bar lawyers)—all were to some extent "interest groups." All were characterized by interaction and shared attitudes, and the lawyers were themselves members of the groups. In a sense this is a crucial difference between the criminal justice litigation and the other areas; criminals are not a "group" in the sense the others are. Though they have one characteristic in common—the application of legal sanctions against them—their degree of shared attitudes and interaction seems much less salient.

WHAT MAKES A GROUP ADVOCATE?

In discussing the Advocate, some suggestions were offered about why a lawyer is likely to become an Advocate. Legal ideology seemed an important explanatory variable, though other factors operated at the margin. Legal ideology is also the basic determinant of the Group Advocate, but again other variables are important.

The legal ideology of the Group Advocate is the opposite of the Advocate's. Most Group Advocates are Reformers: they believe in the law as a mechanism for social change and democracy and in the legal profession as an active force for the application of the law for purposes of social change. More specifically, of the 34 lawyers interviewed who were Group Advocates, 25 were Reformers, 7 were Traditionalists, and 2 had equivocal legal ideologies.

Legal ideology is crucial in several ways to the clientele of the Group Advocate. First, the legal ideology of the Reformer provides him a consistent frame of reference that guides his approach to specific litigation. His views about the role that law and litigation can play emphasize the broader aspects of particular cases, attune him to the notion that individual cases may have broad implications. Just as the Traditionalist's view of the law predisposes him to look at cases as discrete matters for resolution, the Reformer's view suggests to him that cases are important for their social and political ramifications.

Legal ideology is important in a more indirect way as well, for it can be quite important in determining a lawyer's general career pattern. A lawyer who takes his ideas about the role of the law and the legal profession seriously, if he is a Reformer, will not likely be attracted by a practice that is greatly removed from the uses of the law that his ideology suggests are important. In addition, a lawyer who takes seriously his notions about the role that the profession ought to play—notions for the Reformer of

active intervention in and sometimes initiation of socially significant litigation—again may not be attracted by either the large
corporate firm or the economic scrambling of the marginal solo
practitioner doing personal injury and real estate work. Thus the
lawyer with a set of reformist policy preferences and a commitment to using his expertise in support of these preferences may
well move either toward a position with a litigating interest
group or at least toward activity in interest groups (even if he
does not depend upon them for his livelihood) that are likely to
involve him in litigation dealing with broader social issues.

Thus legal ideology may affect a lawyer's career pattern and
perhaps thereby the kinds of litigation in which he becomes involved. This was important, as suggested in preceding sections,
for the lawyers who eventually became members of the Radical
Bar and argued loyalty-security cases. It also appears to have
been quite important for many of the lawyers who ended up
specializing in civil rights litigation, though the evidence for this
view is admittedly highly speculative. The Radical Bar lawyers'
eventual involvement in loyalty-security cases can be traced
back to their activities in labor litigation during the 1930s. It is
argued in the next chapter that many of the lawyers recently
active in loyalty-security cases differed in several respects (including their clienteles), and this difference was perhaps in
large part attributable to their age. This age difference may have
been important for civil rights lawyers as well. The civil rights
lawyers interviewed were about 15 years younger than the Radical Bar lawyers (mean ages, 59 versus 45). Many civil rights
lawyers thus began their practices around 1950. At this time
tensions of the Cold War had built up, and fear of Communists was gripping the nation. Many lawyers with an interest
in social reform who began to practice law at this time may
have been wary of getting involved in the type of "civil liberties" litigation that was prominent, for much of it involved
alleged Communists.[18]

18. For example, three lawyers interviewed who eventually became active in
civil rights and civil liberties litigation indicated that they had been asked, while
in law school in the late 1940s, to join the National Lawyers' Guild. They indi-

As a result, it seems possible that many lawyers with the legal ideology that might have led them into the general area of civil liberties litigation chose different paths. A number went into general practice, surfacing in civil liberties litigation after the end of the McCarthy period as members of the ACLU. Others chose civil rights, another area of social and political reform into which to throw their professional expertise and energy. This area, too, had its very real dangers, particularly if one attempted to practice in the South. But in a more general career sense, civil rights did not have the dangers of taint and perhaps professional ruin that might have appeared to be associated with defense of loyalty-security cases. Thus a combination of a Reformer's legal ideology, a natural empathy for the plight of those subjected to racial discrimination, and a social and political climate which made civil rights law to some extent less dangerous produced a number of lawyers who became vital in litigating interest groups dealing with civil rights. After the initial commitment, continued involvement and immersion in the affairs of what became quickly "their" group were crucial to their becoming Group Advocates.

Finally, legal ideology was important because it tended to affect the kinds of group memberships that the lawyers developed. For Radical Bar lawyers, particularly, involvement in their own professional organization, the National Lawyers' Guild—a bar association formed by lawyers who felt that their views about the law and the function of their profession were not represented by the ABA—was significant for their involvement in loyalty-security litigation. By the same token, many of the civil rights lawyers, especially those not working full-time in litigating interest-group institutions, came to their cases through their part-time work with organizations like the NAACP, ACLU, and CORE.

Clearly legal ideology is the primary determinant of the clientele of the Group Advocate, both directly after he becomes in-

---

cated that though they had been in sympathy with many of the aims of the organization, they had refused to join because they feared that membership in an organization accused of Communist domination might adversely affect their careers.

volved in a particular case and indirectly through its effects upon his career choices and organization memberships. But it is equally clear that legal ideology is not an unambiguous determinant of clientele. Two things stand out: nine Group Advocates were not Reformers (seven Traditionalists and two with equivocal legal ideologies), and a substantial number of Reformers were not Group Advocates but were Civil Libertarians.[19]

First, let us discuss the Group Advocates who were not Reformers. They fall into two major groups. The first group includes two lawyers who argued reapportionment cases. Both of these lawyers were Traditionalists, the legal ideology associated with the Advocate. Both practiced in small firms whose major business dealt with personal injury, real estate, and commercial law. Their practices did not include much exposure to typical civil liberties cases. It was through their interest and activity in politics that they became involved in the reapportionment cases. Thus, though their legal ideologies did not make them particularly sensitive to the broader ramifications, their personal and ideological ties with their clients—with the political factions that stood to gain from victory—appear to have been influential in their assumption of the Group Advocate clientele.

The other major group includes a number of black lawyers who argued civil rights cases.[20] The black lawyers interviewed, especially those who practiced in the South, were among the most conservative on the dimension of legal ideology. In large part as a result of their legal training, they had highly conservative views of what the role of the law was, stressing it as a conflict-resolving mechanism. In addition, they were among the most vehement in denouncing initiatives by attorneys in the development of litigation.[21] These lawyers adhered to their views in the face of both the most striking example of the use of litigation for social reform—the civil rights litigation—and their own partici-

19. Of the 42 Reformers interviewed, 4 were Advocates, 13 were Civil Libertarians, and 25 were Group Advocates.

20. Five of the remaining seven lawyers who were Group Advocates but not Reformers.

21. This negative view of initiative is probably largely a result of the lawyers' realization that a hostile community and bar might well seize upon any infraction of the Canons of Ethics as grounds for disbarment.

pation in it. This seems to indicate the enduring nature of legal ideology; it is not a kind of ephemeral attitudinal structure deriving from participation in a particular case. Though they were Traditionalists, their identification with blacks—a matter of necessity—seems to help explain the adoption of the Group Advocate clientele.

But what of the other side of the coin, of the Reformers who were not Group Advocates but were Civil Libertarians? We will discuss the Civil Libertarians in detail in the next chapter. But the discussion in this chapter may suggest factors that determine whether a lawyer with the Reformer legal ideology will be a Group Advocate or a Civil Libertarian.

Whether the lawyer has personal ties with his client is of great importance. The personal ties of the Radical Bar lawyers with their clients were largely responsible for their being Group Advocates rather than Civil Libertarians. The lawyers active in later loyalty-security cases—Civil Libertarians—lacked these ties. Cases did not come to them in the context of a friend in trouble. The same personal ties helped determine the Group Advocate clientele of the reapportionment lawyers.

Ideological ties are also important. For the Radical Bar and reapportionment lawyers there was a connection between the policy preferences espoused by the client and those valued by the lawyer. This, too, contributed to the perception of the case as involving a group rather than a principle. Again, to foreshadow a little, the later loyalty-security lawyers—who were Civil Libertarians—did not have this ideological nexus with their clients. Cases came as "civil liberties" cases involving principles, not clients either personally or ideologically identified with the lawyer.

Finally, the context surrounding involvement is important. Especially for the civil rights lawyers, the fact that the cases came to them because of their association with interest groups whose *raison d'être* was the promotion of the interest of blacks was crucial. Though the civil rights lawyers were by no means indifferent or hostile to the application of the principles inherent in their cases to other minority groups (Indians, poor people, etc.), their immersion in the affairs of one particular group tended to focus their attention upon the application of these principles to their group.

GROUP ADVOCATES AND JUDICIAL POLICY-MAKING

We have discussed what a Group Advocate is, how he tends to view his litigation, and what tends to produce Group Advocates in litigation before the Supreme Court. Now we will turn to the question of how the activities of Group Advocates relate to the judicial policy-making process.

When talking about Advocates in the preceding chapter, we noted the discontinuity between the kinds of outcomes of interest to the lawyers and those which emerged from the decisions of the Supreme Court. The outcomes were to a large extent unintended consequences of the activities of the attorneys. This discontinuity involved not only the lawyers' failure to get what they wanted (e.g., losing when they wanted to win) but also a fundamental difference in perspective on the litigation. The Advocate was primarily interested in the result; the Supreme Court's treatment of many of the cases suggested an interest in general policy that was enunciated in the context of deciding the case.

For many of the Group Advocates this gap was narrowed to a great extent. Though the eventual impact of the litigation (in terms of behavior in the society) was by no means always what the lawyer desired, the litigation was at least often treated by the Supreme Court in terms of policy issues affecting broad groups in the society, and these were equally the concern of the lawyer. The lawyers had consciously pursued the litigation for the purpose of obtaining certain kinds of policy outcomes. Sometimes the lawyers were highly successful, as in the reapportionment, loyalty-oath, and some of the civil rights cases. They were "successful" in the sense that the kinds of policies for which they were working—as representatives of groups that would benefit from such policies—did in fact emerge from the litigation in which they were involved.

In other cases they were less successful in this sense. In the sit-in cases and in most of the loyalty-security cases involving attacks upon legislative investigating committees, the Supreme Court decided on grounds a good deal more narrow than the lawyers wished. Though the cases were very frequently won, the decisions went on grounds of established law or upon relatively technical or idiosyncratic points. To some extent these cases exhibited a kind of mirror image of those in which many Advocates in criminal justice litigation were involved. In the former, Group Advocates interested in policy affecting their groups obtained narrow victories; in the latter, Advocates seeking narrow victories achieved broad outcomes affecting large classes of people. We return to these characteristics of judicial policy-making in the concluding chapter.

Our discussion also indicates that the so-called "group process" approach to the legal process is quite apt for a range of the civil liberties and civil rights litigation argued before the Supreme Court during the 1957–66 period. Clement Vose characterizes the activities of interest groups in litigation as follows:

There is a logical relationship of organizational interest in litigation and the importance of courts in forming public policy. Although courts act only in cases between parties with concrete interests at stake, organizations concerned with the impact of the outcome may become quite active participants. Organizations may do this by sponsoring a "test case" brought in the name of a private party, they may aid the government attorney in a case, or they may file a brief as an *amicus curiae*. Considering the importance of the issues resolved by American courts, the entrance of these organizations into cases in these ways seems in order.[22]

Interest groups are important in civil liberties and civil rights litigation in two related ways. In much of the litigation, organized interest groups figured both in the process by which lawyers were recruited and in mobilizing resources in support of the suits. The groups were in varying degrees institutionalized—ranging from highly structured organizations like the LDF to

22. Clement E. Vose, "Litigation as a Form of Pressure Group Activity," *Annals of the American Academy of Political and Social Science* 319 (1958): 31.

more amorphous "organizations" like the political party factions supporting the reapportionment suits to the even less institutionalized left wing and its Radical Bar—but they were crucial to the process by which a lawyer became involved in the litigation and to his perceptions of his role in it.

The group-process approach also illuminates the perceptions of the lawyers. For litigation is a "group" phenomenon not only in the overt participation of organized interest groups but also in terms of what the lawyer is trying to achieve. Thus litigation can be "lobbying"—an attempt to use litigation as a means to produce desired policy outcomes—not only when organized groups participate actively. Litigation also becomes a form of lobbying, or perhaps a better term is "politicized," when a case is more than a discrete dispute but is pursued for purposes of policy development or the representation of broad group interests.[23]

This politicization of litigation is certainly not a phenomenon unique to recent times.[24] Though it is perhaps a fruitless endeavor to attempt to define the notion of "politics," under any of the reasonable possibilities that have been suggested—"who gets what, when, and how," "the authoritative allocation of values,"

23. Nathan Hakman, in his analysis of civil liberties and civil rights litigation, concludes that groups have not been so important as group-process theorists like Vose and Peltason have suggested. Hakman bases his argument upon the overt participation of groups in providing attorneys, financing cases, intervening as *amicus curiae*, and so on. But, as he himself admits, cases can be an important form of group lobbying even if no one group overtly participates. Hakman's approach is very useful, for without tying the notion of group interest to some concrete form of activity, the notion of the group interest becomes an almost metaphysical concept. But I think that the activities of Group Advocates—whether or not they were overtly supported by interest groups—suggests that many of the lawyers in fact did perceive their litigation as a form of lobbying or group activity. Thus I think that his major conclusion—"In terms of litigation strategy, it was found that Supreme Court non-commercial cases, like most other litigation, are carried to the Supreme Court primarily to resolve immediate disputes among private adversaries"—is to some extent mistaken. See Nathan Hakman, "The Supreme Court's Political Environment: The Processing of Noncommercial Litigation," in Grossman and Tanenhaus, eds., *Frontiers of Judicial Research*, p. 246.

24. For case studies of "politicized" litigation earlier in this century, see Benjamin R. Twiss, *Lawyers and the Constitution* (Princeton, N.J.: Princeton University Press, 1942), a study of the fight to preserve laissez-faire economic policy, and Vose, *Caucasians Only*, a study of the NAACP and the restrictive-covenant cases.

"who gets his way in collective decisions"—it is clear that the decisions of courts (the outcomes of litigation) fit the rubric. Since organized interest groups play important roles in other political forums—legislatures, bureaucracies, executives—it is hardly startling to note that they also participate in the legal forum, given the important nature of the issues fought out there.

Groups and their representatives, the Group Advocates, participate in litigation not only to gain desired outcomes in court decisions. Though this is often the motivation—stemming from the fact that access is difficult in other political forums (as in the reapportionment and early civil rights cases)—the courts can also be used as a kind of leverage point to influence the activities of other institutions. Thus the sit-in cases were pursued not only to attempt to end racial discrimination in public accommodations but also to put pressure on Congress. In part, it was hoped that by attempting to induce the Supreme Court to decide the question, pressure might be placed upon Congress to step in and decide it, thus creating a flexibility they would lose if they left it up to the Court.

Relatedly, litigation can be important and "political" simply as a means of raising issues, of making latent conflict manifest. Jack Peltason discusses this point: "To win judicial support is a strategically important step for any interest. It brings the prestige of the judges, their opinions, and their sanction to enforce a desired policy. Many illustrations could be cited which indicate the importance of having the judges on your side, but the judges' side does not always win. A judicial decision is but one phase in the never-ending group conflict, a single facet of the political process."[25] Though many have questioned the utility of the extreme emphasis upon the activities of groups that sometimes seems to characterize some of the "group theorists," the point is an important one. Litigation has been used to bring into the open in our political system a range of issues that have before been to some extent latent, smoldering beneath the surface.

This view is an apt description of the civil rights litigation dur-

25. Jack Peltason, *Federal Courts in the Political Process* (New York: Random House, 1955), p. 64.

ing this century, of the reapportionment litigation, and to some extent of the criminal justice cases.[26] These cases were important not only for the policy that emerged from Court decisions but for the interaction between the Court and other political institutions. Courts cannot determine political outcomes in issue areas like racial segregation, reapportionment, or the rights of criminals, but they can, by their decisions, take steps that make it essential for other institutions—legislatures and executives—to participate in the process of collective decision.

Thus in the area of civil rights a particular constellation of forces in Congress made real movement toward the end of racial discrimination in the South difficult if not impossible. The Court, by stepping in, obviously was not able to end discrimination. But what it did accomplish was to make a start, to bring the issue to the surface, to lend its legitimacy to one side on the question, and thus to make it imperative that other institutions begin to address themselves more directly to the question. This is the key to the "politicization" of litigation in the area of civil liberties and rights. The Court functions as a kind of access point and agenda-setter, not a final decision-maker.

So we can see that litigation has been crucial in making latent conflict manifest, placing covert political conflict on the agenda for other political institutions. Those who decry an activist Court, one that meddles in the affairs of other branches, are typically the forces of the status quo, not necessarily proponents of any particular policy position.[27] It is in disturbing the status quo, in forcing the confrontation of issues, that the Court has performed its most significant political function.

Since the politicization of litigation depends to some extent upon the development of new legal institutions, and since there are indications that these institutions are becoming more wide-

26. Though, as suggested above, the criminal cases differed in that there was not the conscious intent on the part of the lawyers that characterized the civil rights and reapportionment litigation.

27. For example, there are striking parallels in the rhetoric of the liberals of the thirties and the conservatives of the fifties and sixties attacking the Court. What these critics had in common was not so much philosophies about the proper role of the Court in the political system as it was the fact that their respective oxes had been gored.

spread, some interesting questions arise about the future. Again, it must be noted that we are very much in a transitional period in the history of the Court, so the most that can be done is to speculate.

First, as is implicit in the previous discussion, Group Advocates —especially operating in the context of litigating interest groups —present a much different aspect of the relationship between lawyer and client than we are accustomed to thinking about. The Group Advocate is not simply performing a service for his client, and often his services are not available to all who desire legal representation. He is often himself a partisan, sometimes even an ideologue, who views his professional activities as intimately tied to a political struggle. His client (sometimes hardly known to the lawyer, sometimes his close friend, sometimes the lawyer himself) and his client's interest are in a sense a means, not an end. The client and his case serve as a means to get into court; the end is to obtain some desired policy outcome. Since the Group Advocate is usually in the service of a member of his group, conflicts are not frequent.[28] Yet this role of the lawyer in society is distinctly different from that usually envisioned on television programs, in Law Day speeches, and in the Canons of Legal Ethics.

The proliferation of Group Advocates and the institutions that produce them have implications for the legal process as well. It can be reasonably argued that, in part as a result of the successes that disadvantaged groups have had in recent years in court, the notion of "going to court" is becoming in our society a much more salient technique of getting one's way. Examples abound today: the drive for equal time for those who wish to stress the danger in cigarette smoking or automobile pollution; attacks on abortion laws, drug abuse laws, and capital punishment; attempts to reform the welfare system; currently developing efforts at promoting conservation via lawsuits. Obviously, all of these activities involve issues with a "legal" dimension. But the dimension was always there. What is to some extent new is the fact that those

---

28. The conflicts are much more salient for Civil Libertarians, discussed in the following chapter.

with intense preferences have begun in increasing numbers to use the legal process as a means to try to get their way. There also seems to be a trend toward going to court earlier, a trend toward the notion that when one is dissatisfied with the outcomes in the political arena, "going to court" occurs not as a last resort after all other "traditional" political activities have been exhausted but as a primary strategy.

In part this may be a consequence of the fact that others have had success, as in the civil rights, reapportionment, and criminal justice cases. A legal system open to some minority groups invites other minorities and disaffected groups to try the same thing. But in an important sense in the issue areas suggested above—conservation, welfare, drug control—the minorities are of a different character. They have not been institutionally oppressed, denied access to other arenas, in the way that blacks were. Rather, these issues involve partisans with intense preferences who feel they cannot win in other arenas. In addition to receptivity, another factor fostering this trend is the proliferation of litigating institutions (interest-group and quasi-public institutions like legal services offices) that attract lawyers and make it possible for them to make a living in the practice of law for social reform. The two factors are obviously related, for the creation of these institutions partially depends upon the notion that a "legal" strategy is likely to meet with some success.

Obviously there is in the American political system—and has been for a long time—a tension between the Court and other institutions of government. Many have argued that there is a kind of cycle at work in which the Court strikes out in a new direction, eventually meets opposition from other institutions, and then is forced to either retreat or turn to other areas of concern: a cycle of activist and passivist courts.[29] The argument implicitly notes the limits upon the ability of the legal system to shape national policy. The events in the decade and a half following the 1954 *Brown* decision are a poignant reminder of the

29. This argument is very persuasively advanced in Robert G. McCloskey, *The American Supreme Court* (Chicago: University of Chicago Press, 1960).

kind of interaction that occurs between the Court and other institutions.

But the discussion above suggests that forces at work in the American legal system may exacerbate the tensions inherent in the so-called activist Court model. The legal system may be experiencing the institutionalization of a segment of the bar that will act as advocates for minority groups, that will continually press the courts to delve into a widening variety of "political" issues. As epitomized by the Group Advocates, the legal profession may be developing more structures and institutions devoted to pressing upon the courts issues they may wish to duck. We will return to this question after discussing the third group of lawyers, the Civil Libertarians. At this point it is worth suggesting that the Group Advocates we have been discussing may be the wave of the future in the legal profession dealing with civil liberties and civil rights at the appellate level.

What the response of the courts will be to this wave is, of course, problematical. The control over agenda exercised by the courts, especially the Supreme Court, makes it possible for them to duck many issues that they are called upon to decide. But the development discussed here will at least make such "ducking" more difficult. For the justice interested in reaching out to decide these kinds of issues, the job will be perhaps easier, for the cases will be there. For those with a more restricted role in mind, the cases will be there, and ducking may be more difficult.

SUMMARY

A large proportion of the lawyers who argued civil liberties and civil rights cases before the Supreme Court during the 1957–66 period were acting as representatives of groups to whom they felt long-term commitments. In some instances, organized litigating interest groups participated in the process by which the lawyer was recruited; in others, the "group" with whom the lawyer was tied was not a formal party to the litigation.

These Group Advocates perceived their litigation (and their

role in it) as involving issues wider than the simple interest of their formal clients. Rather, they viewed the cases as involving policy issues in which large segments of society had an interest, and the cases were a means to the end of advancing the interest of those segments. Thus they were acting as representatives of groups in the legal arena in much the same way that other political participants act as representatives of their groups in other political arenas.

Lawyers become Group Advocates for a variety of reasons. Their legal ideology—that of the Reformer—provides them with an attitudinal underpinning for participation in litigation with social significance and for their perception of the broader issues implicit in their litigation. A Group Advocate's ties to his client, both ideological and personal, also serve to influence him to identify his litigation with the interests of the group of which the client (and the lawyer) is a member. Participation in institutions that are committed to acting as advocates in the legal arena for the interests of particular groups (e.g., the LDF) is also important in the process by which some lawyers come to act as Group Advocates.

There may be a trend in the legal system toward the development of more lawyers who will act as Group Advocates. To put it another way, there may be a trend toward the institutionalization of the defense of civil liberties and rights in the legal system. The future may well bring more institutions devoted to the protection, through litigation, of the interests of particular minority groups. Relatedly, there seems to be movement in the American political system toward more frequent use of the legal arena as a forum in which groups attempt to get their way in collective decisions. What was in the past a last resort may be becoming an early line of attack or defense by political groups desiring change in social and political policy. The Group Advocate, then, not only is the most prevalent type of lawyer among those interviewed but may become increasingly important in litigation involving issues of civil liberties and rights.

6. *The Civil Libertarian*

Civil Libertarians comprise the third group of lawyers who argued civil liberties and civil rights cases before the Supreme Court during the 1957–66 period. They have been discussed in some detail in the chapters dealing with Advocates and Group Advocates, so their characteristics are already somewhat familiar. In this chapter, as in those that preceded it, we will first sketch out the approach to litigation that characterizes this type of lawyer and that differentiates him from the others. The distinctive feature of the Civil Libertarian is that his clientele is not limited to an individual or group but, rather, encompasses all of society.

After a discussion of the characteristics of Civil Libertarians, we turn to the types of litigation in which they participated. Civil Libertarians were involved in criminal justice, loyalty-security, and a smattering of miscellaneous cases involving First Amendment freedoms of speech, press, and religion. The discussion of the litigation in which Civil Libertarians were involved leads to the next recurring question: what tends to produce in litigation a lawyer with the clientele of the Civil Libertarian? Legal ideology is important, but it is combined with other characteristics, especially cues provided by the Court and the context in which the lawyer becomes involved. Finally, we discuss the implications for the legal process and for the develop-

ment and protection of civil liberties of the activities of Civil
Libertarians.

WHAT IS A CIVIL LIBERTARIAN?

Perhaps the most salient characteristic of the Civil Libertarians
is the impersonality with which many of them viewed their
litigation. Recall the remarks made by the Civil Libertarian
quoted in Chapter 4 who had argued a criminal justice case: "I
owed no loyalty to Mr. 'Smith' [his client]. Never met him in
point of fact. . . . He had nothing to contribute to the issues."

Or, consider the remarks of a lawyer who argued a state
loyalty-oath case:

If I'm proud of anything in the whole case, it was that I was able
to keep us from winning it. [I.e., the lawyer was careful not to win
the case on a narrow ground in a lower court because he wanted to
get the case to the Supreme Court and have the broader issue resolved. The case was ultimately won.]

We didn't go up for some sect. We didn't fight the case for school
teachers alone. It was not a matter of dramatic hyperbole to say that
we were there because of the garbage collector. Because this legislation was binding on every type of employee of [the state] or of any
city . . . and our real client was the illiterate apolitical garbage collector in the city. Someone would come and say to him, "Hey, Joe,
sign this." And he would say, "What is it?" and they would say, "Ah,
don't worry about it, sign it." We felt that would be the most egregious character of this whole law, from a moral point of view. And we
designed the case for the garbage collector. And he was our client.
And we tried to maintain the case for him, all the way through.

And the funny part of it was, there is a garbage collector. It wasn't
quite a garbage collector, but he's a municipal employee in [town]
who none of us knew anything about, who didn't sign, and who lost
his job. He read [the oath] and he'd been with the city 14 years, and
had a fairly good-sized family. And he refused to sign it because he
said, "I'm a free man and I couldn't understand what they wanted
me to sign. I read it and it didn't make any sense to me." And it seems
to me, when one worries about democracy, and worries about human
beings, that here is a testimony to the basic dogma of democracy, the
basic belief in individual man. Some five, six years later, that man

who said, "I don't know what it is and therefore I won't sign it"—that the Supreme Court of the United States basically said, in very simple words, took the same position: "When you read it you really don't know what you're reading, and therefore it's no good." So that's why we fought it and this is why we attempted to keep from winning it. [42]

Or, recall the remarks of another Civil Libertarian who argued a criminal case: "So this is the kind of principle that we're fighting for in these cases, and 90% of the time, the individual that's in the case, whether he be Cahan or he be Dorado, or Escobedo —they're pretty scurvy little creatures, and what *they* are doesn't matter a whole hell of a lot. It's the principle that we're going to be able to use these people for that's important" [2].

Though these remarks are among the most extreme, they do serve to point up the distinctive character of the Civil Libertarian. His clientele is certainly not his client, nor is it the group that the client might represent. His clientele is all of society, and what is important in the case is the principle implicit in it. Moreover, and this is the key to the distinction between the Civil Libertarian and the Group Advocate, the Civil Libertarian is not especially concerned with the application of the principle to any particular group with whom he feels a personal or ideological tie. It is the principle in its general application (to some extent the principle for its own sake rather than for the sake of a particular group) that concerns him.

This concern is related to the impersonality of the Civil Libertarian's perception of his litigation. As respondent 42 noted quite explicitly, his client was not the individual who was party to the suit but, rather, some hypothetical construct of Everyman existing in his imagination. Perhaps even more than the Group Advocate, the Civil Libertarian views his case as a kind of excuse to get into court and to raise issues that concern him. According to the lawyer quoted above, winning in a lower court would have been quite a blow, since it would have interfered with his desire to get a broader issue to the Supreme Court!

There is an obvious potential for conflict if a lawyer is a serious Civil Libertarian. This does not mean that the typical Civil

Libertarian is such an intense ideologue that he smugly watches his client go to the gas chamber rather than muddy up the case with mere legal technicalities. But to have a serious Civil Libertarian as an attorney may be a luxury that many defendants simply cannot afford. As suggested in Chapter 4, there may be conflicts between the concerns of a Group Advocate or Civil Libertarian and the client's interest.

Reference-group theory suggests this conflict: "There are also instances where multiple reference groups impinge simultaneously on the same sphere of comparison or the same realm of attitude, and then they may either reinforce the same outcome or produce conflicting consequences for the individual."[1] As noted, clientele reference group or individual are essentially identical concepts, and both of the consequences suggested above occur for the Civil Libertarian.

The dilemma posed—between concern with principles and concern with clients—may be resolved (or fail to occur in the first place) if the client himself is concerned with principles. In many loyalty-oath cases and other First Amendment cases in which Civil Libertarians participated, this was indeed true. The client himself was concerned not with getting off on technicalities but with vindicating principles, and hence there was no conflict between his and his lawyer's interests. Thus the kind of reinforcement suggested in Herbert Hyman's remarks does occur.

In the criminal justice cases, though, principled clients were (understandably) not so common. How the lawyers who argued criminal justice cases resolved this dilemma varied a good deal. Obviously, no lawyer is going to admit (either to an interviewer or probably even to himself) that he sold out his client in an attempt to vindicate a principle. His problem may be simplified if he can come to believe that he has no choice but to raise the broad principled issue, that a broad ground is his only hope for victory. To some extent the provision of cues by the Supreme Court can promote this view, for if the Court indicates that it

1. Herbert Hyman, "Reference Groups," *International Encyclopedia of the Social Sciences* (New York: Macmillan and the Free Press, 1968), 13: 356.

wants to treat the case in terms of a broader issue, the burden is taken off the lawyer. For some lawyers whose interest from the outset was in the broader principles, this outlet insured that the tensions did not become too great. The following remark by a lawyer who argued a recent and celebrated criminal case points out the dilemma: "I think all of us in the 'Jones' cases had a big period of soul-searching—at least some of [the other lawyers] so indicated to me—as to whether we were asking the Court to go too far. In other words, balancing representation of our client against the broader public interest. . . . We all resolved it, all decided we weren't, but obviously it was a big step and that was something of a problem" [51].

Others, in cases in which cues were not so readily apparent (the above case was one in which several cases were combined for argument), may fix simply upon the fact that the Supreme Court granted *certiorari* as a kind of license to stress broader issues. Thus the Civil Libertarian's relatively impersonal view of his litigation may create a kind of dissonance, and efforts to resolve it may be important to his being "comfortable" with the litigation.

The Civil Libertarian's general interest in principles may lead him to attempt to initiate litigation in which they can be vindicated. For example, respondent 42, who argued a loyalty-security case, reported that he had become involved in his litigation in the following manner: "I became convinced that our school teachers in this state are such a bunch of little ninnies anyway, and so afraid of opening their mouths, that any further legislation that would in any way restrict them would have catastrophic results on academic freedom. So I personally made up my mind that I was going to fight it, and I was going to find a client someplace."

Others took up their cases with somewhat less enthusiasm: "I was the only lawyer in town who was connected with the ACLU for about four or five years. I was on vacation when [the incident that led to litigation took place] and he gave a statement to the press that he wanted the ACLU to represent him, and he asked specifically for me, by name." Why did he ask for the ACLU?

"I think probably by general reputation. He's a cultured, educated man, and he told me that he was afraid that no other lawyer, private lawyer . . . they might fear, they might be afraid to represent him. And so he came to me—on that basis. And I was scared to represent him, but I'd been talking about free speech and the Constitution for 25 years and I either had to take his case or leave town—one of the two. So I took it. I wasn't really happy about it—I was excited about it . . . but hell, I had to take it" [7].

Thus the Civil Libertarians came to their litigation with varying degrees of enthusiasm, but the bulk of them had one thing in common—an affiliation with the ACLU. This affiliation and the context it provided the lawyer were crucial to the clientele he felt he was serving.

CIVIL LIBERTARIANS: LITIGATION AND GOALS

Following the pattern of the preceding chapters, we will now discuss the litigation in which Civil Libertarians were involved. Here we will find the clues for the later discussion of why some lawyers turn out to be Civil Libertarians.

Loyalty-Security

We have already discussed the loyalty-security litigation in some detail, for a good part of it was argued by Group Advocates. Many of the early cases (involving issues arising out of the government loyalty-security programs of the 1950s) were argued primarily by Radical Bar lawyers, who had personal and ideological ties to their clients, who acted as Group Advocates for the political Left in this country. The cases were primarily defensive, having been initiated at the behest of the government in its attempts at fighting alleged internal subversion.

The later loyalty-security cases, many of which involved attacks upon state loyalty oaths, arose after the height of the anti-Communist fear and were to a large degree offensive suits aimed at enjoining vestiges of government loyalty-security programs. The clients in these cases were more often not political radicals or ideologues but, instead, a variety of citizens who objected to these programs. These cases were more frequently argued by ACLU lawyers, attorneys who became involved via their affiliation with the ACLU and who acted as Civil Libertarians.

In Chapter 5 the involvement of members of the Radical Bar in loyalty-security cases (as Group Advocates) was related to a coherent pattern of policy preferences, socio-economic background, group memberships, and a career experience that brought them into contact with radicals who eventually got into loyalty-security difficulties. The ACLU lawyers' involvement in the later loyalty-security cases calls for some explanation, but it is not as neat and is somewhat more speculative. The difference in career patterns of the ACLU and Radical Bar lawyers is to a great extent a matter of difference in ages. Like the lawyers who came to specialize in civil rights litigation, many of the ACLU lawyers began the practice of law around 1950.

The social and political climate faced by the ACLU lawyer starting out his practice was much different from that which had faced the Radical Bar lawyer in the 1930s. The struggle over union organization was waning, and the fervor of the New Deal had to a large extent worn off. The pressures of the Cold War and McCarthyism were building, and tolerance for social activism and dissent was declining. The activist liberal bar association formed in the late 1930s—the National Lawyers' Guild—had been wracked by charges of Communist domination and torn by mass resignations.

In this climate many ACLU lawyers began their careers. It was not a time in which it appeared profitable or even safe to practice much civil liberties law. Not having as liberal political views as the Radical Bar, and facing a social and political climate in which the opportunities for the practice of law for social reform appeared bleak, the typical ACLU lawyer chose a more socially and politically acceptable general practice. But both his policy preferences and his attitudes toward the function of the law and the legal profession in society made complete non-involvement in civil liberties cases unattractive. Therefore, the ACLU lawyer joined the ACLU. Through his involvement he could satisfy his desire to participate in civil liberties litigation, while at the same time not make his career dependent upon such a practice.

The ACLU as an organization and its cooperating attorneys were apparently not so activist in seeking to defend political dissenters in the 1950s as they appear to be today.[2] The possibilities of the lawyer's being tarred with the brush used on clients were by no means imaginary.[3] The remarks of the ACLU lawyer quoted on p. 170 (respondent 7), who alluded to his fear of becoming involved in the litigation of an official of the Communist party (in 1965), suggests that vestiges of reticence about this kind of litigation existed long after the end of McCarthyism.

The ACLU lawyers surfaced when things cooled off to some extent. They became quite active in later loyalty-security litigation and are today highly active in the kind of latter-day loyalty-security cases involving student radicals and black militants. One should not place too much emphasis upon fear, for the ACLU lawyers have certainly been courageous. But the impression remains that the time at which the ACLU lawyers became members of the bar had a good deal to do with their choice of what kind of practice to pursue. In many respects, ideological and demographic, they were not much different from the Radical Bar lawyers. Had they been born a decade earlier, they might well have been members of the Radical Bar. But their entrance into the legal profession at a particular period in our history is important to an understanding of why they were not so active

2. This is not to say that no lawyers associated with the ACLU participated in loyalty-security litigation during the 1950s but, rather, that the organization reflected to some extent the general fear of involvement with communism that characterized the society. The ACLU attempted to purge its Communist members in the early 1950s by use of a disclaimer of Communist affiliations as a condition for membership. The characterization of the ACLU made here is based upon interviews with staff and cooperating attorneys. A similar view is suggested by Nathan Hakman, "The Supreme Court's Political Environment: The Processing of Noncommercial Litigation," in Joel B. Grossman and Joseph Tanenhaus, eds., *Frontiers of Judicial Research* (New York: John Wiley and Sons, 1969), pp. 226–27. It should be noted that this characterization of the ACLU would likely be challenged by some associated with the organization.

3. See, for example, U.S. Congress, House Un-American Activities Committee, *Communist Legal Subversion: The Role of the Communist Lawyer*, 86th Cong., 1st sess., 1959, H. Rept. 41.

in the earlier loyalty-security cases and have recently become so important in this area of litigation.

Criminal Justice

Most of the lawyers who argued criminal justice cases, if you recall, were Advocates.[4] Chapter 4 suggested briefly some characteristics that were important in producing the Civil Libertarians who argued criminal cases, especially the experience the lawyer had with this type of litigation and the cues provided by the Court.

The experienced criminal lawyer, who argues a number of criminal cases regularly and who expects to be continually confronted with these matters, is more likely to perceive the broader issues implicit in his case. Not so likely as the inexperienced lawyer to be struck by the severity of the penalty, the criminal lawyer, at least in the kinds of appeals cases discussed here, appears to have been more aware of the broader issues implicit in his litigation. Thus some of the Civil Libertarians in criminal cases (three of the seven) were lawyers with extensive criminal practices.

Cues affected the clientele perceptions of the other four. The Court may, by at least a couple of techniques, make it clear to a lawyer that it wants a case treated in a certain way, that certain issues should be his paramount concern. In the *Gideon* case, for example, the Court specified in its grant of *certiorari* that it wanted the case briefed and argued on the issue of overruling *Betts v. Brady.* The Court clearly indicated that the important issue would not be the provision or lack of provision of counsel to Gideon but would be the general issue of provision of counsel to all indigent defendants in state proceedings.

The Court may also communicate its interest to lawyers in a more indirect fashion. The most common cue of this sort is the grouping of a number of cases together for argument and decision. If the Court groups a number of cases, it indicates to the

4. Of the 28 lawyers interviewed who argued criminal justice cases, 20 were Advocates, 1 was a Group Advocate, and 7 were Civil Libertarians.

lawyers that the issue common to the cases will be considered. A good example of this practice in the field of criminal procedure was the much publicized group of cases decided under the title *Miranda v. Arizona*. The Court granted *certiorari* in four cases (from New York, Arizona, California, and a federal case out of the Ninth Circuit), all of which involved the question of the voluntariness of confessions and the right to counsel. The fact that all were lumped together indicated to the attorneys that the Court wanted to use these cases to deal further with the broad questions of provision of attorneys and coerced confessions raised in the *Escobedo* decision.

Thus either in the granting of *certiorari* itself or in the grouping of cases, the lawyer's perceptions of the issues may be affected. One lawyer recounted:

Initially we considered it just a case and we were going to do the best job for our client. This was our view almost 100% at the [state] Supreme Court, because we were arguing on the facts of this case. . . . I mean under the existing law. . . . But [the state supreme court] rejected the argument. And from that point on, you of course can't argue facts in the Supreme Court of the United States, and we just went on the full basis, and from this point on, we knew that the whole issue, the whole constitutional principle was involved. And that the client's interest should not be sacrificed, but we knew that we were up there because there is more at stake than just our client. If only your client's interests are at stake, they won't grant *cert*. And, from that point on, we were interested in the principle, basically. [46]

So the Court itself may affect a lawyer's perception of the issues in the case and of his clientele. Yet this does not always occur. As the above quote points out, the Supreme Court is supposed to hear only those cases in which there are broad issues at stake. Yet by no means do all lawyers experience a shift in their clienteles as their cases reach the Supreme Court; most retain the clienteles with which they began.

Other Civil Libertarians

There were nine remaining Civil Libertarians among the lawyers interviewed. One argued a civil rights case, and eight argued cases falling in the residual category of "other" litigation.

The Civil Libertarian who argued the civil rights case was the only southern white lawyer interviewed who had no attachments to litigating interest groups. His concern in his litigation was not primarily with using the case as a vehicle to attack the effects of discrimination upon blacks. Rather, he considered his case as important as a kind of educational device for his community and for the South generally. He was concerned with using the symbol of a white lawyer, not attached to any of the "outside" activist civil rights groups, defending the rights of a black man. His goal in the litigation was not primarily to advance the cause of the black man but, rather, to promote general adherence among both white and black to the principle of equality and thus to change the life style of his country.

The other Civil Libertarians argued a variety of cases, most of which involved First Amendment issues of freedom of speech, press, and religion (and none of which involved loyalty-security issues). Six of the eight were affiliated with the ACLU; some were full-time staff members, some of them took cases on a part-time basis. They were Civil Libertarians, for like the ACLU lawyers in loyalty-security cases, they viewed their clienteles as all of society and their cases as a vehicle for vindicating principles. Two of the eight cases were essentially offensive, i.e., injunctive suits; the other six were essentially defensive in character, having been instigated at the behest of the government.

WHAT PRODUCES CIVIL LIBERTARIANS?

Legal ideology appears to be the key to the Civil Libertarian, as it was for the Group Advocate and the Advocate. Of the 23 Civil Libertarians, 13 were Reformers, 4 were Traditionalists, and 6 had equivocal legal ideologies. The relationship between the Reformer legal ideology and the Civil Libertarian clientele has been suggested before. The view of the law as a mechanism for democracy and social change provides a perspective upon the litigation, and the preference for a bar active in promoting and intervening in litigation affecting broad social and political issues fits well with the kind of gadfly role that many Civil Libertarians play.

The obvious question that must be grappled with is, what determines whether a lawyer is a Group Advocate or a Civil Libertarian, given the fact that both possess similar legal ideologies? For many of the civil rights and Radical Bar lawyers already discussed, the lawyers' career patterns seemed important to their being Group Advocates, both because of their attachment to various groups and as a consequence of the political and social climate that they faced when they began their practices. As has been implicit in this discussion, the characteristic that most of the ACLU lawyers have in common is their affiliation with the ACLU. The relationship between ACLU membership and a lawyer's being a Civil Libertarian is complex, but there are two major facets.

First, when a lawyer receives his case by referral from the ACLU, it provides a very distinct context for the case. It comes to the lawyer as a "civil liberties case," for this is the criterion that is supposed to determine what kinds of cases the ACLU will support. Moreover, when the case comes by such a referral, the lawyer will typically not be personally connected with the client. As suggested in the preceding chapter, personal and ideological ties are crucial to the fact that members of the Radical Bar act as Group Advocates. For the ACLU lawyer, though, the case typically does not come as one involving a friend in trouble; rather, it comes as one in which an organization devoted to a certain class of principles has some interest. Thus the context surrounding the case—which stresses the principled aspects of the litigation rather than particular ideology or policy preferences—is particularly important in producing the Civil Libertarian characteristics of the ACLU lawyers.[5]

5. For some ACLU lawyers who entered loyalty-security litigation with trepidation, an impersonal view of the litigation was probably crucial to their willingness to participate. Stressing detachment from the clients' views and emphasizing the principled aspects of the cases helped allay their anxiety about the professional dangers implicit in such litigation. Otto Kirchheimer, in his discussion of lawyers in political trials, suggests a similar point: "Without identifying himself with the cause that is possibly detested by many members of the community, a lawyer might become associated with the political defense by pleading the case's

Relatedly, the ACLU itself acts as a general socializing institution beyond its impact upon specific litigation. The organization's credo stresses defense of principles in and of themselves, not their application to particular groups. It is a matter of great pride among ACLU lawyers that their organization has defended both blacks and members of the KKK, left-wing radicals and neofascists. The legal socialization of some of the lawyers interviewed was strongly tied to their affiliation with the ACLU; they became active in it early in their practices and had occasionally worked as full-time employees of the organization. For others, their less extensive affiliation still left its imprint. Thus not only does affiliation with the ACLU provide a context for specific litigation, but it also tends to shape the lawyers' general perspective toward what it is to be a lawyer. For some ACLU members, cross-cutting memberships (e.g., many Radical Bar members were also active in the ACLU; many LDF lawyers have likewise been active in the ACLU) affected their views of their litigation and produced Group Advocates. But for many, the ACLU is their major affiliation (at least in terms of involvement in civil liberties and civil rights litigation), and it tends to shape their approach to their litigation.

Thus a combination of factors, including the nature of a lawyer's general practice (which depended to some extent upon *when* he entered the legal profession), the kinds of group memberships he has, and the context surrounding his involvement, is important in the process by which some Reformers act as Group Advocates while others act as Civil Libertarians.

What of the Traditionalists who were Civil Libertarians? Three of them argued criminal cases, and, as noted before, cues by the Supreme Court and their experience in the litigation were important. In two of the cases the Supreme Court provided cues by grouping the cases, and the lawyers shifted their clien-

---

implications in terms of the constitutional order. Opinion might be rallied for the principle and symbol involved rather than, or even in spite of, the cause. This procedure will allow lawyers from a variety of walks of life . . . to come forward in the defense of some aspects of the activity of a foe of the existing regime." Otto Kirchheimer, *Political Justice* (Princeton, N.J.: Princeton University Press, 1961), p. 250.

teles from Advocate to Civil Libertarian as they came before the Supreme Court.

One of the lawyers specialized in criminal law, as well as being affiliated with the ACLU, and this accounts for his somewhat broader perspective. The fourth and final Traditionalist/Civil Libertarian was a lawyer whose general practice included business and corporate law. His involvement in a civil liberties case was in a sense accidental (he professed that he didn't like this type of litigation), the result of his involvement in a First Amendment freedom-of-the-press case of one of his retainer clients. He treated the case as the simple representation of a client at the state court level. But as the case moved toward the Supreme Court, he became more intensely interested in its broader constitutional aspects, in part because he felt this was the only way he might win and in part because as he delved into the matter, he became both indignant at the treatment of his client in lower courts and intrigued with the implications of his litigation for freedom of the press generally.

Finally, there is the group of six lawyers with equivocal legal ideologies. Two argued criminal cases, one of which involved cueing by the Court, and the other was a lawyer with extensive criminal practice. The other four argued a mixed bag of cases, with activity in the ACLU being characteristic of three of them.

The Civil Libertarians as a whole were often characterized by involvement with a particular organization (and a lack of cross-cutting memberships or friendship ties with clients), the ACLU, which produced in them their generalized concern with civil liberties. Their association with the ACLU provided them with a context surrounding their cases and helped to form their identifications not with groups their clients represented but with principles generally. For others, experience in a particular field of litigation or cues provided by the Supreme Court seemed to be crucial in making them Civil Libertarians.

This latter point raises an interesting question. The Civil Libertarians whose legal experience determined their clienteles argued criminal cases. Other lawyers discussed here have this characteristic experience in a field of law and the expectation that they will continue to be involved in it, yet many tended to be Group Advocates rather than Civil Libertarians. Why the difference? For the criminal lawyers who became Civil Libertarians, two factors seem important. First, in a sense they did not have the personal identification and empathy with their clients that characterized many civil rights, Radical Bar, and reapportionment lawyers. This is not to say that they were heartless or lacked sympathy for individuals who were driven to social offenses, but at the same time they tended to be somewhat more jaundiced and perhaps cynical about their clients. This is not particularly surprising, since criminals are perhaps hard to view as a kind of oppressed minority in the same way that blacks, political radicals, and underrepresented voters may be. The lack of personal empathy and ideological ties that characterized the relationship between many of the Group Advocates and their clients accounts in large part for the criminal lawyers being Civil Libertarians.

Relatedly, few of the criminal lawyers interviewed—even those whose practices included primarily criminal law—were working out of institutions devoted to lobbying for the rights of persons accused of crime. Most were private practitioners, either on their own or in small firms, who happened (for a variety of reasons, some by choice, some by accidents of career) to become specialists in criminal law. If the lawyers had been in institutions whose *raison d'être* was advocacy of the rights of accused persons, interacting with other lawyers doing the same thing and receiving salaries for such activity, then they would perhaps be more likely to behave as Group Advocates than as Civil Libertarians. If the trend suggested in Chapter 4 occurs—the development of more institutions devoted to the defense of individuals accused of crime—more criminal lawyers may act as Group Advocates.

CIVIL LIBERTARIANS AND JUDICIAL POLICY-MAKING

The discussion at the end of the preceding section raises an important question. We have differentiated two similar styles of lawyering, the Group Advocate and the Civil Libertarian. So what? What difference might it make if in the future civil liberties and civil rights litigation tended to fall in the hands of lawyers with one type of clientele rather than the other? As usual, this most important and interesting question is one which requires us to move away from the data. But some speculation may be worthwhile.

For purposes of this discussion, let us differentiate two types of social and political climates in which lawyers might be pursuing civil liberties and civil rights litigation. In one period, which might be characterized as "expansionist," the litigation would be generally directed at the expansion of the rights guaranteed by the Constitution and their extension to minority groups previously denied them. This seems to have been characteristic of much of the 1960s. The other type of period is the kind of crisis that this country has periodically seen, in which particular minority groups have come under special attack, by both governmental and private forces. The Red scare of the 1920s and the McCarthyism of the late 1940s and 1950s immediately come to mind.[6] During such periods the bulk of civil liberties litigation is directed at defense against incursions, and the degree of public and governmental hostility may make the securing of legal representation by those under attack somewhat difficult.

One of the most striking things about a lawyer who is a serious Civil Libertarian is the fact that his services are available to all. His commitment to principles rather than to their application to particular groups makes him willing to defend a myriad of types of people whose rights might be abridged. This, indeed, is the source of a great deal of justified pride on the part of the ACLU, an organization that has produced the majority of Civil Libertarians in Supreme Court litigation in recent years. Again, this is not to imply that Group Advocates (or even Advocates) are opposed or even indifferent to the extensions of rights to minori-

6. The effects of antiwar activity, student protest, and black militancy and the reaction of government to these activities make the future hard to predict. Perhaps we are beginning another period of attack upon civil liberties and rights, but with a different set of "subversives."

ties other than those they represent. It is simply to suggest that the scope of their concern may be more limited because of the salience of the group which they perceive themselves as primarily representing.

It might also be plausibly argued that Civil Libertarians will be innovative in developing the protection through litigation of the rights of new minority groups. As has been repeatedly suggested, Group Advocates are typically the products of institutional or quasi-institutional settings, of participation in organizations created for and devoted to the protection of particular groups. Perhaps other minority groups—who do not as yet enjoy the fruits of such organizations and institutions—must first depend upon individuals to begin to explore the potentialities of litigation as a tool in their behalf. This argument, then, might suggest that the existence of a number of Civil Libertarians is important as a kind of force to break ground in the development of the use of the law and litigation in behalf of new minority groups. Once this innovation has begun, then perhaps litigating institutions will develop and take over the burden of continued activity. Thus in two recent areas, rights of accused criminals and of the poor, though we are in the midst of the development of institutions staffed with lawyers devoted to Group Advocacy, this is a recent, secondary development. Lawyers with a more generalized commitment to civil liberties—the Civil Libertarians —have been important in the process by which such institutions develop.[7]

Finally, Civil Libertarians may be quite important simply because of their commitment to principles rather than particular groups. One could well be comfortable with an extensive institutionalization of defense of civil liberties if one had confidence that all, or close to all, minority groups enjoyed the fruits of such organization. In the absence of such a proliferation of or-

7. Obviously, the process is terribly complex. The ability of the Supreme Court to make new departures on its own (as the criminal justice cases argued by Advocates suggest), the activities of other political institutions in developing the war on poverty and its Legal Service Program, the fact that organizations like the LDF are branching out into new areas of litigation—all of these suggest that the dynamics by which new civil liberties policy and institutions are created involves many participants interacting with each other.

ganizations and confidence that representation would be available, the openness and breadth of concern of the Civil Libertarian is perhaps crucial. For by his very willingness to defend almost anyone, the Civil Libertarian is a kind of generalist in behalf of civil liberties. Those individuals and groups without their specialist defenders are thus more likely to get an adequate defense.

There is the other side of the coin, though. The discussion above was couched mainly in terms of the extension of civil liberties and rights to new minority groups. What of the situations (of which we have had many in our history) in which particular groups come under attack, where individuals historically enjoying constitutional protection are subjected to attempts at its deprivation? It is in this context that Group Advocates, with their personal, ideological, and institutional ties to their clients, are crucial. To put it broadly and crudely, perhaps the Group Advocate can be better counted upon in periods of repression to remain in the battle to defend the rights of "his" group. For a variety of reasons, in a period of repression, victims may depend very heavily upon Group Advocates willing to stand up and provide representation. The reasons are both attitudinal and institutional.

The Group Advocate typically has close ties with his clients, both personal and ideological. When members of the group to which he is tied (blacks, political radicals, or whatever) are under attack, these ties may be crucial, for they will bring him into litigation into which others may fear to venture. The fact that many Group Advocates come out of institutions or groups is also important. These institutions do exist, and to one degree or another they are able to mobilize resources in support of the defense of those under attack. For the individual lawyer, this may mean that he can continue to defend people without fear of losing his practice, for it does not depend so much upon his general reputation as upon his organization's ability to provide him with a salary. Additionally, in a time (like the McCarthy period) in which lawyers defending a particular type of case may become alienated from the mainstream of their profession, interaction with other attorneys similarly situated may persuade them to remain members of the profession and offer their services.[8]

Again, it would be an overexaggeration to suggest that all Civil Libertarians are likely to be fair-weather friends, quickly dropping out of sight at the first sign of attack. At the same time, there seem to be reasons to believe that they will be under much greater pressure to withdraw. First, many of the ACLU lawyers/ Civil Libertarians depend for their livelihood not upon civil liberties cases but upon a general practice. If, in a period of repression, lawyers begin to be tarred with the brush used on their clients, the economic pressure to avoid certain types of cases can be great. In addition, the Civil Libertarian typically does not have a very close relationship with his client, either personal or ideological; perhaps for most of us, it is easier in a crisis to stand up for our friends than for abstract principles. Finally, since in a society such as ours civil liberties are in a sense always under attack or amenable to extension to new groups, the Civil Libertarian has a wide menu of issues from which to choose. If the rights of one particular minority are under attack, and the economic and social pressures to withdraw are great, the Civil Libertarian can turn his attention elsewhere, still retaining the notion (no doubt correctly) that he is acting in behalf of those general principles he cherishes.

Thus in periods of repression perhaps Group Advocates may be more willing than Civil Libertarians to represent the politically and socially unpopular. Not only is he a Group Advocate, but he operates out of a context that is more likely to produce adherence to his position when it comes under attack. Obviously if his organization is itself destroyed, the Group Advocate will

8. *Rights*—the newsletter of the Emergency Civil Liberties Committee, one of the few litigating interest groups active in mobilizing defense of political radicals during the McCarthy period—exhibited a continual hortatory tone, attempting to provide reinforcement for those active in loyalty-security litigation at a time when they appeared to have few friends. The periodical, published in New York, appeared first in 1953–54 (vol. 1) and thereafter was published irregularly. As suggested before, it appears that the National Lawyers' Guild was also vital in this regard, for it provided a professional association and a means for interaction among a group of somewhat isolated lawyers.

not be able to continue to function as easily. But in the legal process, as in the broader political process, organization and mobilization of resources are crucial to successful participation. And the institutional settings that produce Group Advocates are most likely to continue to provide counsel in periods of attempted repression.

In this fashion, it might well make a difference whether the bulk of civil liberties litigation was handled by Civil Libertarians or Group Advocates. In a sense, the arguments above suggest that we need both types of lawyers. But they also suggest that under different political, social, and legal conditions the two types of lawyers might behave differently.

SUMMARY

We have now concluded our discussion of the third of the major clientele types that are the subject of this study. The Civil Libertarian is a lawyer who views his clientele as all of society and his case as a vehicle for vindicating a general principle for its own sake, or for the sake of the nation, not for the sake of a particular group.

The Civil Libertarians were active in some criminal litigation, in the later loyalty-security cases, and in a number of other First Amendment cases not involving loyalty-security issues. They were lawyers generally characterized by the legal ideology of the Reformer and by association with the ACLU. This affiliation was significant both because it provided them with a context for the specific litigation in which they became involved and because of its general socializing effects in shaping their view of their function as lawyers.

Many of the areas of law pioneered by Civil Libertarians are now being populated by Group Advocates, the products of institutions that have been developing to protect the rights of a variety of minority groups previously lacking such institutionalized defense. In terms of judicial policy-making and the protection through litigation of civil liberties and rights, the Civil Libertarians seem to play a particularly important role. At the same time, the institutionalization that in a sense succeeds their activities may provide a stronger bulwark against attempts at infringement should they arise.

7. Conclusions

The judicial policy-making process involves large numbers of individuals often pursuing different and perhaps unrelated or conflicting goals. We have discussed one group of participants, attorneys in private practice who argued civil liberties and civil rights cases before the Supreme Court. The discussion has pointed up differences in the ways in which these lawyers were recruited into their litigation and the goals they were pursuing in their cases.

The organizing concept for this discussion has been clientele. Lawyers with different clienteles dominated different areas of litigation. We have explored the determinants of a lawyer's clientele and suggested that a lawyer's clientele in a particular case is not simply the product of the case itself. Rather, it is to a large extent the product of an enduring attitudinal structure—his legal ideology—that affects his general approach to being a lawyer. Other factors are also important, including the context surrounding his recruitment into the litigation, the nature of his legal experience in the past and expectations about his future practice, and cues provided by the Court itself. The concept of clientele—and the patterns in incidence of clientele types in various areas of litigation—are of importance in understanding the process of judicial policy-making.

CLIENTELES AND THE GROUP-PROCESS APPROACH

Scholars using this approach have long talked about litigation as being representative of "interests" in society. Peltason has urged, for example, "It is necessary to see the distinction between the formal parties to a legal controversy and the interests they represent. A litigant represents and is part of an interest, but should never be confused with the whole interest. A decision has consequences for others—sometimes thousands of others—not immediately before the court. Thus, the action of litigants is but one small segment of all the activity which makes up the interest represented."[1]

Taken literally, of course, this statement is true. The mere existence of class actions suggests that individual suits can affect broad groups of people. The use by the Court of individual cases in the area of criminal justice as means to enunciate broad policy affecting the whole legal system is another example of this phenomenon. Relatedly, the activities of litigating interest groups in initiating suits, recruiting attorneys, and pursuing litigation also indicate that individual cases can represent the interests of wide segments of the polity. The use of the concept of "interest" by the group-process theorists often has a kind of metaphysical quality about it, for it appears to be an undefined term, not operationalized but simply apparently sitting out there in society. The clientele of a lawyer in a sense deals with this notion of interest. Though it is restricted to one participant in litigation —the lawyer—it attempts to tap his notions about the nature of the "interest" he is representing. In a sense the approach taken in Peltason's remarks above would suggest that some of these lawyers, particularly the Advocates, sometimes failed to "see the distinction" between formal parties and interests represented. But the concept of clientele attempts to focus the notion of "interest." Instead of having to talk about an interest apparently identifiable only by an outside observer, clientele suggests that the parties themselves may differ in terms of their perception of

1. Jack Peltason, *Federal Courts in the Political Process* (New York: Random House, 1955), p. 44.

the interest they represent. Thus a focus upon interests and groups can be refined, dealing not only with overt group activity and metaphysical "interests" but with the perceptions of actual participants.

CLIENTELES AND FOUR PATTERNS IN JUDICIAL POLICY-MAKING

We have at various points spoken about the notion of judicial policy-making. Though the legal process can be viewed primarily as a conflict-resolving process[2]—a collective process by which disputes among individuals, groups, and institutions are resolved in a legitimate and authoritative fashion—by necessity the legal system also makes important collective decisions, makes social and political policy for our society. Grossman has formulated this notion of judicial policy-making as follows: ". . . policy-making is defined . . . as a problem-solving endeavor or enterprise in which the actors (adjudicators, litigators, enforcers, administrators, or the public) make conscious or unconscious choices regarding the removal or change of conditions which form an identifiable problem. . . ."[3] The differentiations in clienteles suggested here seem to be of some utility in analyzing the process of policy-making. Note especially Grossman's suggestion that the actors in the process may make "conscious or unconscious" choices that affect both their behavior and the kinds of policy outcomes that occur as a result of their activities.

Clearly the policy that emerges from litigation does not simply result from the preferences or values of the judges alone. Other actors also play important roles in the judicial policy-making

2. An example of this view: "The function of the law is the orderly resolution of conflicts. As this implies, 'the law' (the clearest model of which I shall take to be the court system) is brought into operation after there has been a conflict. Someone claims that his interests have been violated by someone else. The court's task is to render a decision that will prevent the conflict—and all potential conflicts like it—from disrupting productive cooperation." Harry C. Bredmeier, "Law as an Integrative Mechanism," in William M. Evan, ed., *Law and Sociology* (Glencoe, Ill.: Free Press, 1962), p. 74.

3. Joel B. Grossman, "A Model for Judicial Policy Analysis: The Supreme Court and the Sit-In Cases," in Joel B. Grossman and Joseph Tanenhaus, eds., *Frontiers of Judicial Research* (New York: John Wiley and Sons, 1969), p. 408.

process. The participants of interest here—the private attorneys —were differentiable in terms of their goals and clienteles. Though, by definition, all of the lawyers studied did eventually reach the Supreme Court, they did so for very different reasons. Yet in many of the cases important decisions emerged, decisions enunciating policy that affected more than simply the parties to the cases.

We have alluded to discontinuities between the outcomes that occurred in litigation and the preferences and goals of the attorneys. For many of the Advocates, decisions dealing with issues far beyond their interest (and sometimes even their awareness) emerged from their litigation. For some of the Group Advocates and Civil Libertarians, decisions dealing with rather technical issues the lawyer hoped to avoid emerged from their litigation. For some of the lawyers, finally, there were not such discontinuities; the kinds of goals and motivations that led to the initiation of the suit and the lawyer's involvement were vindicated by court decisions.

Though it is, of course, dangerous to impute motives or intentions to the Supreme Court, because it is not an individual but a collectivity,[4] we have seen essentially four patterns in a policy-making model involving lawyers and the Court (see Table 9).[5] If we simplify the model by introducing a dichotomy, we can characterize the goals of the two sets of participants as involving either "result" or "policy." These terms, admittedly crude and somewhat ambiguous, reflect the previous discussion's emphasis upon a decision as affecting either the individual clients or broad groups in the society.

Though the patterns are admittedly simplified, they do suggest the complexity of the judicial policy-making process. Two of them are "pure"—types I and III—for there is congruence between the goals of the participants. They also correspond most closely to our intuitive images of the judicial policy-making process: type I is the paradigm of litigation as a mechanism for

4. The imputation of motives to attorneys, though complicated by the fact that many have complex and sometimes conflicting goals, is done with more confidence, for it is based upon interview material.

5. Here we refer to the majority of the Court and its institutional opinion.

TABLE 9. FOUR PATTERNS IN JUDICIAL POLICY-MAKING.

Participant's Concern with Outcome		Example
Lawyer	Supreme Court	
I Result (Client)	Result (Client)	Early criminal justice cases argued by Advocates (e.g., "special circumstances," etc.)
II Result (Client)	Policy (Group)	Later criminal justice cases argued by Advocates
III Policy (Group)	Policy (Group)	Civil rights, reapportionment, and loyalty-oath cases argued by Group Advocates and Civil Libertarians
IV Policy (Group)	Result (Client)	Sit-in cases and early attacks on legislative investigations argued by Group Advocates

resolution of disputes between particular parties; type III is the paradigm of "political" litigation designed for and successful in producing political or social reform. The other two types are not "pure," for they exhibit discontinuities between the goals of the participants. Type II—including the criminal justice cases argued by Advocates that resulted in important shifts in constitutional policy—suggest that the Supreme Court is able to convert run-of-the-mill cases into important occasions for policy. Type IV indicates "political" litigation that did not succeed in its broader goals.[6] Thus neither of the "pure" and intuitively plausible images of litigation adequately accounts for all of the judicial policy-making in the area of civil liberties and rights in recent years.

To understand the judicial policy-making process in detail requires exploration of the activities of all of the participants in the process—from the cop on the beat to the Supreme Court justices—for all play a part. What we have discussed here is obviously much more limited in scope, for we have examined but one group of participants in a limited area of litigation. But this discussion does suggest that not only may we differentiate the

6. Though the cases were often "won" in the sense that the petitioners' convictions were reversed.

preferences of judges—as judicial behavior research has done in recent years—but that we can do the same for other participants. Only when we have looked at them all will we begin to understand the process more fully. It is crucial that we continue to examine the activities of various participants, for it is only then that patterns in judicial policy-making are likely to emerge.

CLIENTELES AND THE RAISING OF POLITICAL ISSUES

One of the crucial functions performed by attorneys is to provide what Wells and Grossman have called "occasions for decision."[7] Unlike other political institutions, courts are less able to place items on their agenda; their "passive virtues" make them, more than other institutions, reactive. We have seen in this study that the Court's control over its docket and its freedom in choosing grounds for decisions does give it a good deal of flexibility. It can and has taken relatively narrow disputes and turned them into vehicles for enunciation of broad policy; on the other side of the coin, the Court has often been able to duck broad policy questions and to resolve cases on the basis of relatively narrow and well-established points of law. But the Court cannot do either unless a case is before it; it cannot decide or refuse to decide issues unless some concrete dispute is presented for resolution.

One can simply dismiss this issue with the statement that any important political or social issue in the society will, by some ill-defined process, eventually make its way to the Court. In a sense this statement is simply true, for there are few important political issues in our society that the Court has not at least had the opportunity to deal with. But to take this approach—to focus simply upon the Court and the choices it makes (or refuses to make)—is to ignore a good deal of important political activity in our system.

Relatedly, the type of lawyer active in an area of litigation may have an impact upon the menu of cases that faces the Court. If two of the types discussed here—Group Advocate and Civil

7. Richard S. Wells and Joel B. Grossman, "The Concept of Judicial Policy-Making: A Critique," *Journal of Public Law* 15 (1966): 286–310.

Libertarian—predominate in an area of litigation, the Court is likely to be provided with occasions for decisions in ways that it might not be if the bar were composed exclusively of Advocates. The Advocate, the traditional lawyer, does not actively seek out litigation; he waits for cases to come to him. He is not attuned to the broad policy issues that may be implicit in his litigation; he sees the case as basically a contest to be won. Though after an Advocate becomes involved in a case, he may produce arguments in his client's favor that do involve important policy innovations, he is not likely to begin with an interest in policy and to seek out a dispute with which to get into court. In addition, he may well settle for a compromise in an earlier proceeding rather than press for a resolution of the broader policy issue implicit in his case.

Group Advocates and Civil Libertarians might be expected to behave differently. They are often looking for cases raising issues in which they have an interest. As noted earlier, they may in fact take a role in initiating litigation. When cases come to them, they are interested in their social and political ramifications, are attuned to picking them up quickly. They may be less likely to accept a compromise at a lower level and will attempt to preserve issues for appeals. When operating out of institutional contexts that provide them with a wide menu of cases, they will likely select those that most nicely frame issues with which they are concerned. Thus it might be argued that in a field of litigation, if the legal counsel who are active (on the appeals level, at least) are Group Advocates or Civil Libertarians, the Court is likely to be presented more often with occasions for decision dealing with important policy issues. As noted above, this is not to say that the Court will necessarily take advantage of the occasions. But such cases—especially those in which issues have been preserved and framed—are a necessary condition for judicial policy-making if not a sufficient one.

The growth of so-called public interest law firms, the emphasis upon permitting younger members of large firms to do *pro bono publico* work in addition to their general activities as associates with their firms, and the legal services programs developed under the auspices of the Office of Economic Opportunity indicate that the trend toward more Group Advocates and Civil Libertarians at the appellate level may be reflected in changes in the practice of law generally. No doubt most lawyers will continue to be Advocates, but there may be a larger group interested in and willing to perform the functions of Group Advocates and Civil Libertarians.

In addition to providing the Court with occasions for decision, the lawyer—particularly the Group Advocate and the Civil Libertarian—performs an important promotional and lobbying function. By urging the Court to use cases to establish certain kinds of policy and by adducing the data supporting these changes, the lawyer may affect the willingness of the Court to move in certain directions. The importance of litigation in the process by which the law is changed and adapted to social and political conditions has been suggested:

One of the ways in which pressure to change may be exerted upon the law is through the courts, by the frequent occurrence of litigation. . . . To the extent that such disputes are brought before the courts, judges are exposed in various ways to the views of segments of opinion within the community on those issues, a process which presumably facilitates continuous modification of the law to conform with such expressions of opinion. When such opportunities for contact with views held by various groups in the community are infrequent, it is to be expected that the law will be less sensitive to changes in the views of the community.[8]

The bar may not only provide occasions for decision but may indicate the breadth of the interests in society supporting various changes, may help keep the courts in touch with social and political forces at work. A proliferation of lawyers pursuing litigation to promote social and political change—with the marshaling of evidence to support such change—may be crucial to the process by which courts are induced to engage in such policymaking. Lawyers and their clients and the groups that support

8. Julius Cohen, Reginald A. H. Robson, and Alan Bates, *Parental Authority: The Community and the Law* (New Brunswick, N.J.: Rutgers University Press, 1958), p. 196.

them may be important "constituencies" for courts, not only in producing occasions for and evidence supporting change but also in providing a reference group to support an activist Court. The justices are themselves trained as lawyers and are members of the legal community. Recent history does not suggest that the opposition of influential segments of the bar necessarily prevents an activist Court. Yet the existence of support within the bar for certain courses of action may provide vital reinforcement for some members of the Court.

CLIENTELES AND THE LAWYER-CLIENT RELATIONSHIP

At various points we have alluded to the implications of some of our findings for the relationship between lawyer and client. The traditional image of the lawyer as the free-lance specialist offering his services to anyone who is able to pay his fee is quite obviously not apposite to all of the lawyers discussed here. The "traditional image" may in fact by now be a straw man, something no sophisticated individual would take seriously. Since lawyers are humans, not automatons, the fact that they may be motivated by their own preferences, moral values, or notions of good public policy should not be startling.

The lawyers discussed here did not all function in litigation as the mouthpieces for the interests of their formal clients. Many were political partisans and perhaps ideologues who viewed their particular cases as an excuse to get into court to vindicate preferred principles or policies. Many of the lawyers were not conflict mediators, providing the professional service of mediating and helping to resolve disputes between their clients. Rather, many were conflict generators, using their litigation as a means to raise important political and social issues rather than to resolve particular disputes. Relatedly, for some of the attorneys discussed here, it cannot be said that their services were available to all. Their own preferences, views of their function, and institutional affiliations precluded their being involved in certain kinds of cases; their services were available exclusively or primarily to litigants with particular kinds of causes to plead.

As suggested in the preceding chapter, the characteristics of the lawyers discussed here may have an impact upon what classes of citizens are able easily to secure legal representation. In the discussion of the loyalty-security cases the career patterns and preferences of the Radical Bar lawyers were important to the process by which a group of particularly unpopular clients was provided with legal representation during a period in which substantial segments of the bar didn't want to get involved. Relatedly, we have also suggested that the trends in representation of social offenders may affect the future course of criminal justice litigation.

The material presented here seems also to have important implications for the kinds of expectations a client may reasonably entertain toward his attorney. Lawyers interested in using cases as vehicles may react differently toward the informal compromise procedures that characterize so much of our criminal justice system. In many kinds of cases—especially civil injunctive actions—lawyer and client may have quite similar views about the goals of the litigation, and the client may not stand to lose a great deal personally by defeat. In other cases a lawyer whose mind is "cluttered" by concern with broad issues may not be what a client wants. The implications are not necessarily so crude. The difficulties are not likely to take the form of the high-minded Civil Libertarian standing by shrugging as his client goes to the gas chamber because the lawyer refused to muddy up his test case with a lot of technicalities.

The problems may be a good deal more subtle. What of the lawyer in a public defender appeals section, for example? Overworked, interested in policy, lacking personal contact with his clients, he is presented with hundreds of cases that may be potentially appealed. His resources are scarce and must be allocated. Which cases get his maximum attention and which are processed in a *pro forma* or perfunctory manner? Those that frame important legal issues nicely, that look like they will be accepted for appeal? Or those that raise rather technical issues whose impact will travel no further than the individual client? Obviously, the answer to this question is a matter for further empirical research. But the data presented here suggest that the question is by no means an academic one, that the proliferation of a crop of Group Advocates in criminal justice cases operating out of public defender organizations may make the answer of some consequence.[9]

The Supreme Court itself has begun to recognize changes in the role of the legal profession and of lawyers vis-à-vis clients.[10] If the bar becomes more characterized by interest-group activity and group practice, by lawyers who are partisans rather than mouthpieces, then these issues are going to become more and more salient.

LITIGATION AS A POLITICAL PHENOMENON

Related to this development in the characteristics of the bar involved in civil liberties and civil rights litigation is what might be called the "politicization" of litigation. Use of the legal system and litigation as the means of attaining goals also sought in the legislative and executive arenas is by no means a recent phenomenon. The activities of the NAACP over the years and the fight through litigation to preserve a laissez-faire economic policy are but two earlier examples of the integration of the legal and political systems in America.

Though the relationship between litigation and attempts to influence public policy in other arenas is not new, there are indications that the politicization of litigation is perhaps on the increase. Courts have become more important institutions for those who wish to secure certain ends in public policy. Not only in "traditional" areas of civil liberties and rights but in new issue areas, people are "going to court." Recent litigation dealing with repeal of capital punishment, liberalization of abortion laws, reform of the welfare system, changes in drug control laws, protection of natural resources, and control of campus unrest

9. Obviously, no more satisfactory is the absence of any counsel that so long characterized our criminal justice system, or the incompetent and inadequate representation that is still all too prevalent.

10. E.g., NAACP v. Button, 371 U.S. 415 (1963), and Brotherhood of R. Trainmen v. Virginia, 377 U.S. 1 (1964).

seems to indicate that more and more issues of public policy are being at least in part fought out in the courts. Not only are issues traditionally not the subject of litigation being brought to court, but the notion of going to court occurs sooner to those desiring to get their way. Litigation, once in a sense a last resort, now is one of the first steps in the strategies of those who wish to change public policy. Thus we may be seeing not only an institutionalization of the defense of the civil liberties and rights of "traditional" minority groups (blacks, poor people, political dissenters), but new minorities and issues are resorting to litigation. And, more important, these new groups and the issues with which they are concerned are not so much institutionally oppressed—denied access to other political arenas—but are simply those who have either already lost in these other arenas or have expectations that they would do so if they tried to get their way there. The fact that more and more lawyers are coming out of law schools to operate in institutional contexts like litigating interest groups, leading them to view litigation as an essentially "political" activity, is contributing to this trend.

If one accepts the many plausible theories about a kind of cyclical pattern in the activities of the Court, one might anticipate that this proliferation of activity by the Warren Court might be followed by a drawing back, a consolidation of gains rather than continued activism. Recent changes in personnel certainly suggest that the current Court may be less activist than its predecessor. But if the trends in styles of lawyering suggested here materialize, the withdrawal may be more difficult. For the decisions of the Warren Court not only affected social and political policy in the areas they touched but also contributed to the development of a segment of the bar much more attuned to and concerned with the use of litigation for "activist" and "political" goals. Though the Court's control of its docket will obviously enable it to duck issues it doesn't want to treat, and to decide cases upon narrow grounds, it may be under considerable pressure to do otherwise. More Group Advocates and Civil Libertarians are now practicing law, their appetites have been whetted, and they will continue to press their demands upon the

Court, not only in the established issue areas but in new ones as well.

In a sense these speculations move far from the actual data that have been presented. Yet the analysis of the activities of the lawyers discussed may augur for the future of Supreme Court litigation dealing with civil liberties and rights. The data presented here suggest the complexity of the motivations which move lawyers to become involved in civil liberties and civil rights litigation, their perceptions about why their cases are important, and their reasons for pursuing the cases up the appeals ladder. Different areas of litigation have been characterized by lawyers with different characteristics and motivations. But there is perhaps a trend developing. Defense of civil liberties and rights—at the appeals level, at least—is becoming more and more institutionalized. Not only are organized groups participating in the litigation and legal specialists coming to play an increased role, but also the lawyers themselves see their function as representing broader issues, not simply clients. What this trend will mean in the long run—for the role of courts in our society, for the development and protection of political and civil rights, for the relationship of lawyer to client—poses many open questions. But the importance of the bar in this process and the potentialities for examining its behavior that have been suggested here seem worthy of continued scrutiny.

Glossary

Clientele: The set of persons (ranging from the individual client to all of society) whom a lawyer perceives as being primarily affected by the outcome of a case in which he is involved. The lawyer's most salient reference individual or group.

A. Advocate: A lawyer whose clientele is his client. An Advocate is concerned primarily with the effect of the case upon his client, not with the broader legal, political, or social ramifications of the case. Advocates argued most criminal justice cases.

B. Group Advocate: A lawyer whose clientele is a particular group (racial, ethnic, ideological) rather than his formal client. The Group Advocate typically has long-term commitments to the the group he feels he is representing. Group Advocates were active in the civil rights, reapportionment, and early loyalty-security litigation.

C. Civil Libertarian: A lawyer whose clientele is all of society. The Civil Libertarian views his case as a vehicle by which general democratic principles may be vindicated, not primarily in the interest of his client or a particular group but for the benefit of society at large. Civil Libertarians were active in some criminal justice cases and the loyalty-oath litigation.

Legal ideology: A lawyer's attitudes toward the function of the law and the role of the legal profession.

A. Traditionalist: A lawyer whose legal ideology is comprised of a view of the law as essentially a conflict-resolving mechanism and a preference for a passive bar. Many Advocates are Traditionalists.

B. Reformer: A lawyer whose legal ideology is comprised of a view of the law as a mechanism for social change or protection of basic liberties and a preference for an active legal profession (i.e., one in which it is permissible for lawyers to assist in the initiation of litigation to promote social justice or democratic principles). Most Group Advocates and Civil Libertarians are Reformers.

Radical Bar lawyer: A member of the group of lawyers most active in loyalty-security litigation during the 1950s. Radical Bar lawyers had personal and ideological ties to their clients and served as Group Advocates for the political Left in their litigation before the Supreme Court.

ACLU lawyer: A lawyer who handles occasional civil liberties cases (often by referral from the ACLU) but whose basic practice involves other legal matters. ACLU lawyers were active in the later loyalty-security litigation and were Civil Libertarians.

Appendix: Research Instruments

INTERVIEW SCHEDULE

1. Could you tell me something about how you became involved in the
   _____ case?
   [Probe]: At what stage did you become involved?
2. Did you consider the case primarily important for your client or for
   broader social considerations?
   [Probe]: Did your interest change over the course of your involvement?
3. Were you interested in winning the case on any possible ground or in
   establishing a particular point of law?
   [Probe]: More specifically, you argued a number of grounds before
   the Court [specify the grounds]. Did you have any preference among
   them?
4. When deciding upon arguments to stress in your brief and in the oral
   argument, did you take account of the position of particular justices
   and try to use this in framing arguments you felt might be effective?
   [Probe]: Could you tell me more specifically what you did?
5. Now, I have a couple of questions about oral argument before the
   Court.
   (a) Some lawyers tell me they dislike this part of the case most.
   They find the questioning makes them tense, nervous, anxious, and
   that it frustrates them in what they want to say. Others tell me they
   think it is the high point of the case. How did you feel about it? [The
   two reactions suggested were alternated in different interviews, presenting one first and in the next interview the other first.]
   [Probe]: What did you enjoy [dislike] about it?
   (b) Did you get the feeling that oral argument is important in
   winning or losing the case?
   [If yes, Probe]: What can you do in oral argument that is decisive?

6. Were you satisfied with the results of this litigation?
   [Probe]: Why? [Why not?]
7. Now, I have some questions about the law and the legal profession. You're going to find some of them very general. This is purposeful, to see what different individuals volunteer in response to a general question. The first is perhaps the most general of all.
   What do you think should be the primary role of the law and the judicial process in American society today?
8. If you were a judge, what do you think would be more important in your decisions: developing the continuity of the law and following precedent, or doing justice in particular cases?
   [The order of the two alternatives was reversed in succeeding interviews.]
   [Probe]: Do you think these considerations often come into conflict for a judge?
9. Most people view the law as a profession, like medicine. In a recent study it was found that many lawyers in fact view themselves as not much different from businessmen, swapping their services and time for monetary compensation. Do you consider the law a profession? What does the concept of profession mean to you?
10. Do you think that a lawyer ought to attempt, in his everyday activities and in his litigation, to shape the law to respond to new social needs? Is this part of the function of the lawyer in society?
11. Do you think a lawyer ought to pick and choose among the cases that are presented to him so that he often gets involved in those with the broadest social significance?
12. Now I have a couple of questions. What I'm trying to get at is how much initiative you think it is proper for a lawyer to take in getting involved in a case. The first question is sort of two-pronged:
   Do you think a lawyer ought to seek (as least within the bounds of the Canons of Ethics) cases in order to become involved in those whose outcomes he considers especially important? Relatedly, do you think the Canons of Ethics are outmoded on the point of initiatives by attorneys?
   [Probe]: Some lawyers tell me they think the canons are not so much outmoded as inapplicable to litigation involving civil liberties and civil rights. That is, that in these cases initiatives are proper which would not be proper in a P.I. case or other commercial cases. Do you agree?
13. With reference to these currently developing programs of legal services to the poor under the Poverty Program, do you consider it proper or improper for such a legal service organization to advertise—that is, make it known to the indigent segment of the population that legal services are available free or at nominal cost—say, by handbills in a grocery store?
14. Again with reference to such a legal service organization, I'd like you to consider the following activity: A lawyer in a legal service office sees a problem in the community—say, a general problem involving

landlord-tenant relations or a credit problem—that he thinks needs resolution. He thinks it might be resolved by litigation, but he realizes that he needs a client. He goes to another arm of the Poverty Program —say, the Community Action Project workers—and tells them he'd like to have someone who would be willing to litigate this problem. In this way an individual is referred to the lawyer, and he litigates the issue. Some say this is stirring up litigation, maintenance, etc., and hence improper. Others say this is what the offices are for and it's entirely proper. How would you feel about such activities?

15. Would you consider it proper or improper for a lawyer to go into a rural area of the South (assuming he had some independent means) and tell the Negroes there, "These are your rights and you're not enjoying them, but you might be able to if you would be willing to litigate. And I'll represent you for free"?

16. If you read in the newspaper about an individual whose rights you felt were being flagrantly violated, would you be likely to take any steps, either directly or through a third party or organization, to become involved in the case as an attorney?

17. Finally, I have a couple of questions about your career. Could you tell me something about why you became a lawyer in the first place? [Probe]: Did you have any idea what kind of practice you wanted to have?

18. [If respondent had returned a questionnaire]: You indicated on your questionnaire that you considered yourself a specialist in _____. How did you come to specialize in this area? [If respondent had not returned a questionnaire]: Do you consider yourself a specialist in any particular area of the law? How did you come to specialize?

19. Could you tell me something about your current practice? What kinds of cases do you handle? [Probe]: What percentage of your practice involves civil liberties or civil rights matters?

QUESTIONNAIRE

I. Public Policy Preferences

Below are a series of cases recently decided by the Supreme Court of the United States. Please indicate your agreement or disagreement with the decision of the Court by circling the appropriate number on the scale following each case. The scale should be interpreted as follows:

agree strongly	+3	+2	+1	0 neu- tral	−1	−2	−3	disagree strongly

1. Baker v. Carr (1962)	+3	+2	+1	0	−1	−2	−3
2. Mapp v. Ohio (1961)	+3	+2	+1	0	−1	−2	−3
3. Brown v. Board of Education (1954)	+3	+2	+1	0	−1	−2	−3

4. Reynolds v. Sims (1964)　　+3　+2　+1　0　−1　−2　−3
5. Gideon v. Wainwright
　　(1963)　　　　　　　　　+3　+2　+1　0　−1　−2　−3
6. Roth v. United States
　　(1957)　　　　　　　　　+3　+2　+1　0　−1　−2　−3
7. Dennis v. United States
　　(1951)　　　　　　　　　+3　+2　+1　0　−1　−2　−3
8. Escobedo v. Illinois (1964)　+3　+2　+1　0　−1　−2　−3
9. Beauharnais v. Illinois
　　(1952)　　　　　　　　　+3　+2　+1　0　−1　−2　−3
10. Ginzburg v. U.S. (1966)　　+3　+2　+1　0　−1　−2　−3
11. Miranda v. Arizona (1966)　+3　+2　+1　0　−1　−2　−3

Below are a series of statements concerning current issues of public policy. Please indicate your agreement or disagreement with each statement as you did above.

1. Given current housing patterns in northern cities, bus-
   sing is a valid remedy for
   racial imbalance in schools.　+3　+2　+1　0　−1　−2　−3
2. Fair housing legislation cov-
   ering owner-occupied dwell-
   ing units should not be
   enacted.　　　　　　　　　+3　+2　+1　0　−1　−2　−3
3. People in the United States
   should be free to advocate
   the violent overthrow of the
   government.　　　　　　　+3　+2　+1　0　−1　−2　−3
4. The registration provisions
   of the McCarran Act are
   sound policy.　　　　　　　+3　+2　+1　0　−1　−2　−3
5. Membership in the Com-
   munist party is proper
   grounds for dismissal of a
   high school teacher.　　　　+3　+2　+1　0　−1　−2　−3
6. There should be no cen-
   sorship of literature or
   movies.　　　　　　　　　+3　+2　+1　0　−1　−2　−3
7. Under no circumstances
   should speech be punished,
   even if it amounts to libel or
   slander.　　　　　　　　　+3　+2　+1　0　−1　−2　−3
8. Bible reading and prayer
   (with participation optional)
   should be permitted in public schools.　　　　　　　　+3　+2　+1　0　−1　−2　−3

9. Demonstrations involving violation of trespass laws are a proper form of protest against racial discrimination.

+3 +2 +1 0 −1 −2 −3

10. The burning of draft cards is a form of expression which should be protected under the First Amendment.

+3 +2 +1 0 −1 −2 −3

11. Peaceful disruption of rail and ship transport of supplies is a valid form of protest against U.S. policy in Viet Nam.

+3 +2 +1 0 −1 −2 −3

12. The recently enacted program of Medicare for the aged was needed and overdue.

+3 +2 +1 0 −1 −2 −3

13. We should further extend medical care services to provide similar coverage to all citizens.

+3 +2 +1 0 −1 −2 −3

14. Recent Supreme Court decisions dealing with criminal procedure have unduly sacrificed the interests of society to those of the individual.

+3 +2 +1 0 −1 −2 −3

15. We should further escalate our war effort in Viet Nam to attain victory.

+3 +2 +1 0 −1 −2 −3

16. We should begin immediate withdrawal of our troops from Viet Nam.

+3 +2 +1 0 −1 −2 −3

17. Communist China should not be admitted to the United Nations at this time.

+3 +2 +1 0 −1 −2 −3

18. We should move in the direction of more public ownership of utilities like water, electricity, and mass transit systems.

+3 +2 +1 0 −1 −2 −3

19. Nationalization of basic industries like steel and automobiles would not serve the interests of the American people.

+3 +2 +1 0 −1 −2 −3

II. Background Characteristics

Please indicate responses by filling in blanks or checking the appropriate item.

1. Date of birth:_____
2. Place of birth:_____
3. Your nationality background:_____
4. Approximate generation of your family in United States you represent (counting your first paternal ancestor born in America as first generation):

    __1 __2 __3 __4 __5 __6 __7 or above
5. Your political party affiliation: __Republican __Democratic __none __other (specify:_____)
6. Your religious affiliation: __Catholic __Protestant __Jewish __none __other (specify:_____)
7. College:
    a. Institution:_____
    b. Dates attended:_____
    c. Subject majored in:_____
    d. Approximate rank in class: __top $\frac{1}{10}$ __top $\frac{1}{4}$
      __top $\frac{1}{2}$ __top $\frac{3}{4}$
    e. Degree(s) received and year(s) granted:_____
8. Law school:
    a. Institution:_____
    b. Dates attended:_____
    c. Approximate rank in class: __top $\frac{1}{10}$ __top $\frac{1}{4}$
      __top $\frac{1}{2}$ __top $\frac{3}{4}$
    d. Were you on law review staff? __yes __no
    e. Degree(s) received and year(s) granted:_____
9. Graduate education:
    a. Institution:_____
    b. Dates attended:_____
    c. Subject of graduate study:_____
    d. Degree(s) received and year(s) granted:_____
10. Current position:
    a. Organization:_____
    b. If a law firm, size of firm: Number of partners:_____
      Number of associates:_____
    c. Your position in the organization:_____
    d. Number of years you have been associated with organization:_____
    e. Number of years you have held current position:_____
    f. Your approximate income per year: __under $10,000
      __10,000–15,000
      __16,000–20,000
      __21,000–30,000
      __31,000–40,000
      __41,000–50,000
      __above 50,000

11. Parents' education: *Father*   *Mother*
(please check   __some grade school   __some grade school
highest level   __completed grade school   __completed grade school
attained)   __some high school   __some high school
__completed high school   __completed high school
__some college   __some college
__completed college   __completed college
__some graduate work   __some graduate work
__graduate degree   __graduate degree
(specify:_____)   (specify:_____)

12. Father's principal occupation (if retired or deceased, please indicate major occupation during career):_____

13. Mother's principal occupation (if retired or deceased, please indicate major occupation during career):_____

14. Parents' religious
affiliation: *Father*   *Mother*
__Catholic   __Catholic
__Protestant   __Protestant
__Jewish   __Jewish
__none   __none
__other   __other
(specify:_____)   (specify:_____)

15. Parents' political
party affiliation: *Father*   *Mother*
__Democratic   __Democratic
__Republican   __Republican
__none   __none
__other   __other
(specify:_____)   (specify:_____)

III. Career Pattern

1. Have you been associated with any law firms? __yes __no
If yes, which firms? _____
_____
_____

2. Have you been in solo practice? __yes __no
If yes, in what cities? _____
_____
_____

3. Have you been employed as an attorney
by a government agency? __yes __no
If yes, which agencies?_____
_____
_____

4. Have you served as a clerk for a judge? __yes __no
If yes, which judges have you served?_____
_____
_____

5. Have you taught at a law school? __yes __no

If yes, which schools?_____

_____

6. Have you held elective office or an appointive position with a state or federal agency?   ___yes   ___no
    If yes, please specify position:_____

    _____

7. Do you consider yourself a specialist in any particular area(s) of the law?   ___yes   ___no
    If yes, which area(s)?_____

    _____

IV. Organizational Memberships
1. Are you a member of the ABA?   ___yes   ___no
2. Are you a member of your city bar association?   ___yes   ___no
3. Are you a member of your state bar association?   ___yes   ___no
4. Are you a member of other legal professional organizations? ___yes ___no
    If yes, please specify which ones:_____

    _____

    _____

5. Are you a member of any community or fraternal organizations (e.g., Rotary, Kiwanis, Moose)?   ___yes   ___no
    If yes, please specify which ones:_____

    _____

    _____

6. Are you a member of any groups interested in legislation (e.g., NAM, ACLU, American Legion)?   ___yes   ___no
    If yes, please indicate which ones:_____

    _____

    _____

7. Are you a member of any civil rights organizations (e.g., NAACP, Urban League, CORE)?   ___yes   ___no
    If yes, please indicate which ones:_____

    _____

    _____

8. If you are a member of a political party, how would you characterize your participation in party affairs? (check each appropriate item)
    ___contribute money to party
    ___active in election campaigns
    ___delegate to party nominating conventions
    ___are (have been) party official
    ___have been party candidate for office
            Name:_____
            Date:_____

Bibliography

BOOKS

Arnold, Thurman. *The Symbols of Government*. New Haven, Conn.: Yale University Press, 1935.
Bar Association of New York City, Special Committee on the Federal Loyalty-Security Program. *Report*. New York: Dodd, Mead, 1956.
Beaney, William M. *The Right to Counsel in American Courts*. Ann Arbor: University of Michigan Press, 1955.
Becker, Theodore L., ed. *The Impact of Supreme Court Decisions*. New York: Oxford University Press, 1969.
Bickel, Alexander. *The Supreme Court and the Idea of Progress*. New York: Harper & Row, 1970.
Blumberg, Abraham. *Criminal Justice*. Chicago: Quadrangle Books, 1967.
Bontecou, Eleanor. *The Federal Loyalty-Security Program*. Ithaca, N.Y.: Cornell University Press, 1953.
Buckley, William F., and L. Brent Bozell. *McCarthy and His Enemies*. New York: Henry Regnery, 1954.
Carlin, Jerome. *Lawyers' Ethics*. New York: Russell Sage Foundation, 1966.
———. *Lawyers on Their Own*. New Brunswick, N.J.: Rutgers University Press, 1962.
Carter, Dan. *Scottsboro*. Baton Rouge: Louisiana State University Press, 1969.
Chaffee, Zechariah, Jr. *Free Speech in the United States*. Cambridge, Mass.: Harvard University Press, 1941.
Cohen, Julius, Reginald A. H. Robson, and Alan Bates. *Parental Authority: The Community and the Law*. New Brunswick, N.J.: Rutgers University Press, 1958.
Cohn, Roy. *McCarthy: His Side of the Story*. New York: New American Library, 1968.

Dixon, Robert. *Democratic Representation.* New York: Oxford University Press, 1969.

Eulau, Heinz, and John D. Sprague. *Lawyers in Politics.* New York: Bobbs-Merrill, 1964.

Fellman, David. *The Defendant's Rights.* New York: Rinehart, 1958.

Fenno, Richard, Jr. *The Power of the Purse.* Boston: Little, Brown, 1966.

Goodman, Walter. *The Committee.* New York: Farrar, Straus & Giroux, 1968.

Gross, Neal, Ward Mason, and Alexander McEachern. *Explorations in Role Analysis.* New York: John Wiley and Sons, 1958.

Harrington, Michael. *The Other America.* New York: Macmillan, 1963.

Havard, William C., and Loren P. Beth. *The Politics of Mis-Representation.* Baton Rouge: Louisiana State University Press, 1962.

Inbau, Fred E., and John E. Reid. *Criminal Interrogation and Confessions.* Baltimore: Williams and Wilkins Co., 1962.

Jacob, Herbert. *Justice in America.* Boston: Little, Brown, 1965.

Jewell, Malcolm. *State Legislatures: Politics and Practice.* New York: Random House, 1962.

Kalven, Harry, Jr. *The Negro and the First Amendment.* Columbus: Ohio State University Press, 1965.

Kirchheimer, Otto. *Political Justice.* Princeton, N.J.: Princeton University Press, 1961.

Kunstler, William. *Deep in My Heart.* New York: William Morrow, 1966.

Kurland, Philip. *Politics, the Constitution and the Warren Court.* Chicago: University of Chicago Press, 1970.

Latham, Earl. *The Communist Controversy in Washington.* Cambridge, Mass.: Harvard University Press, 1966.

Lewis, Anthony. *Gideon's Trumpet.* New York: Random House, 1964.

McCloskey, Robert G. *The American Supreme Court.* Chicago: University of Chicago Press, 1960.

Merton, Robert. *Social Theory and Social Structure.* Glencoe, Ill.: Free Press, 1957.

Murphy, Walter. *Congress and the Court.* Chicago: University of Chicago Press, 1962.

Newman, Donald J. *Conviction: The Determination of Guilt or Innocence without Trial.* Boston: Little, Brown, 1966.

Packer, Herbert. *The Limits of the Criminal Sanction.* Stanford, Calif.: Stanford University Press, 1968.

Peltason, Jack. *Federal Courts in the Political Process.* New York: Random House, 1955.

———. *Fifty-eight Lonely Men.* New York: Harcourt, Brace & World, 1961.

Prettyman, Barrett, Jr. *Death and the Supreme Court.* New York: Harcourt, Brace & World, 1961.

Rovere, Richard H. *Senator Joseph McCarthy.* New York: Harcourt, Brace, 1959.

Sayler, Richard H., Barry G. Boyer, and Robert E. Gooding, Jr., eds. *The Warren Court: A Critical Analysis.* New York: Chelsea House, 1969.

Schubert, Glendon. *Judicial Policy-Making*. Glenview, Ill.: Scott, Foresman, 1965.

Silverstein, Lee. *Defense of the Poor in Criminal Cases in American State Courts*. Chicago: American Bar Foundation, 1965.

Skolnick, Jerome. *Justice without Trial*. New York: John Wiley and Sons, 1966.

Stouffer, Samuel A. *Communism, Conformity and Civil Liberties*. New York: Doubleday, 1955.

Truman, David. *The Governmental Process*. New York: Alfred A. Knopf, 1951.

Twiss, Benjamin R. *Lawyers and the Constitution*. Princeton, N.J.: Princeton University Press, 1942.

Vose, Clement E. *Caucasians Only*. Berkeley and Los Angeles: University of California Press, 1959.

Wasby, Stephen L. *The Impact of the United States Supreme Court: Some Perspectives*. Homewood, Ill.: Dorsey Press, 1970.

ARTICLES

Alexander, Milnor. "The Right to Counsel for the Politically Unpopular." *Law in Transition Quarterly* 22 (1962): 19–45.

Bishop, Joseph W., Jr. "The Reverend Mr. Coffin, Dr. Spock, and the ACLU." *Harper's* (May 1968), pp. 57–68.

Blumberg, Abraham. "The Practice of Law as a Confidence Game." *Law and Society Review* 1 (1967): 15–39.

Bonfield, Arthur E. "The Dirksen Amendment and the Article V Convention Process." *Michigan Law Review* 66 (1968): 949–1000.

Bredmeier, Harry C. "Law as an Integrative Mechanism." In William M. Evan, ed., *Law and Sociology*. Glencoe, Ill.: Free Press, 1962.

Cahn, Edgar S., and Jean Camper Cahn. "Power to the People or the Profession: The Public Interest in Public Law." *Yale Law Journal* 79 (1970): 1005–48.

Casper, Jonathan D. "Lawyers and Loyalty-Security Litigation." *Law and Society Review* 3 (1969): 575–96.

Crosskey, William. "Charles Fairman, 'Legislative History' and the Constitutional Limitations on State Authority." *Chicago Law Review* 22 (1954): 1–143.

Dolbeare, Kenneth M. "The Public Views the Supreme Court." In Herbert Jacob, ed., *Law, Politics, and the Federal Courts*. Boston: Little, Brown, 1967.

Dye, Thomas R. "Malapportionment and Public Policy in the States." *Journal of Politics* 27 (1965): 586–601.

Fairman, Charles. "A Reply to Professor Crosskey." *Chicago Law Review* 22 (1954): 144–56.

Friendly, Henry. "The Bill of Rights as a Code of Criminal Procedure." *California Law Review* 53 (1965): 929–58.

Grossman, Joel B. "A Model for Judicial Policy Analysis: The Supreme Court and the Sit-In Cases." In Joel B. Grossman and Joseph Tanenhaus, eds., *Frontiers of Judicial Research*. New York: John Wiley and Sons, 1969.

Hakman, Nathan. "The Supreme Court's Political Environment: The Processing of Noncommercial Litigation." In Joel B. Grossman and Joseph Tanenhaus, eds., *Frontiers of Judicial Research*. New York: John Wiley and Sons, 1969.

Hart, Henry M. "Foreword: The Time Chart of the Justices." *Harvard Law Review* 73 (1959): 84–125.

Hofferbert, Richard. "The Relation between Public Policy and Some Structural and Environmental Variables in the American States." *American Political Science Review* 60 (1966): 73–82.

Hogan, James E., and Joseph M. Snee. "The McNabb-Mallory Rule: Its Rise, Rationale and Rescue." *Georgetown Law Journal* 47 (1958): 1–46.

Hyman, Herbert. "Reference Groups." In *International Encyclopedia of the Social Sciences*, 13:353–61. New York: Macmillan and the Free Press, 1968.

"Interrogations in New Haven." *Yale Law Journal* 76 (1967): 1521–1648.

Kamisar, Yale. "A Dissent from the Miranda Dissents: Some Comments on the 'New' Fifth Amendment and the Old 'Voluntariness' Test." *Michigan Law Review* 65 (1966): 59–104.

————. "What Is an 'Involuntary' Confession? Some Comments on Inbau and Reid's *Criminal Interrogations and Confessions*." *Rutgers Law Review* 18 (1963): 728–59.

McKay, Robert. "Court, Congress and Reapportionment." *Michigan Law Review* 63 (1964): 255–78.

Medalie, Richard J., Leonard Zeitz, and Paul Alexander. "Custodial Police Interrogation in Our Nation's Capital." *Michigan Law Review* 66 (1968): 1347–1422.

Murphy, Walter F., and Joseph Tanenhaus. "Public Opinion and the United States Supreme Court." *Law and Society Review* 2 (1968): 357–84.

"The New Public Interest Lawyers." *Yale Law Journal* 79 (1970): 1069–1152.

Olender, Jack H. "Let Us Admit Impediments." *University of Pittsburgh Law Review* 20 (1959): 749–53.

Paulson, Monrad G. "The Sit-In Cases of 1964: 'But Answer There Came None.'" *Supreme Court Review* 1964: 137–70.

Pulsipher, Allan G., and James L. Weatherby, Jr. "Malapportionment, Party Competition, and the Functional Distribution of Governmental Expenditures." *American Political Science Review* 62 (1968): 1207–19.

Reiss, Albert, and Donald Black. "Interrogation and the Criminal Process." *Annals of the American Academy of Political and Social Science* 374 (1967): 47–57.

Shapiro, Martin. "Stability and Change in Judicial Decision-Making: Incrementalism or *Stare Decisis*." *Law in Transition Quarterly* 2 (1965): 134–57.

Steel, Lewis M. "Nine Men in Black Who Think White." *New York Times Magazine*, 13 October 1968, p. 56.

Summers, Marvin R. "Defending the Poor: The Assigned Counsel System in Milwaukee County." *Wisconsin Law Review* 1969: 525–39.

Tanenhaus, Joseph, et al. "The Supreme Court's Certiorari Jurisdiction: Cue Theory." In Glendon Schubert, ed., *Judicial Decision-Making.* Glencoe, Ill.: Free Press, 1963.

Vose, Clement E. "Litigation as a Form of Pressure Group Activity." *Annals of the American Academy of Political and Social Science* 319 (1958): 20–31.

Wells, Richard S., and Joel B. Grossman. "The Concept of Judicial Policy-Making: A Critique." *Journal of Public Law* 15 (1966): 286–310.

Wilson, James Q. "The Strategy of Protest: Problems of Negro Civic Action." *Journal of Conflict Resolution* 5 (1961): 291–303.

Wolf, Peter H. "A Survey of the Expanded Exclusionary Rule." *George Washington Law Review* 32 (1963): 193–242.

PAMPHLETS

American Bar Association. *A.B.A. Project on Minimal Standards of Criminal Justice: Standards Relating to Pleas of Guilty.* Chicago, 1967.

NAACP Legal Defense and Educational Fund. *The Quiet Revolution.* New York, 1969.

————. *Report 66.* New York, 1967.

Southern Regional Council. "The Student Protest Movement: A Recapitulation." Report 21, 1961.

U.S. Congress, House Un-American Activities Committee. *Communist Legal Subversion: The Role of the Communist Lawyer.* 86th Cong., 1st sess., 1959, H. Rept. 41.

Table of Cases

Index

Activists, 85n

Advocate, 6, 90–123; defined, 72–73, 92–93, 199; and legal ideology, 91, 98, 99–105; and criminal justice, 91, 96–97, 105–7; and judicial policy-making, 107–9; and plea bargaining, 117–18. *See also* Group Advocate

Alexander, Milnor, 134

American Civil Liberties Union, 8, 24, 74–75, 88, 96n, 112–13, 140n, 153, 169, 170, 180; lawyers, 130, 200; and McCarthyism, 171–72; and Civil Libertarians, 175, 176–77; lawyers and loyalty-security litigation, 176–77n

American Committee for the Foreign Born, 23n

Antiwar activity, 24n, 180n

Bailey, F. Lee, 113n

Belli, Melvin, 113n

Bentham, Jeremy, 13

Bible: in public schools, 68

Bill of Rights: and the states, 39–40

Black, Justice Hugo L.: and *Barenblatt*, 27; and due-process clause, 40; and *Betts*, 41n; and *Gideon*, 43; and *Wesberry*, 57

Black(s), 19; militants, 24n, 180n; attorneys, southern, 104n; as members of Radical Bar, 132–33n; lawyers in civil rights cases, 154

Blumberg, Abraham, 117

Brandeis, Justice Louis D., 94n

Bredmeier, Harry C., 188n

Brennan, Justice William J., 27

Burger Court: and *Miranda* rules, 12n; and criminal justice, 40n

Canons of Legal Ethics, 78, 83, 154n, 161

Censorship, 69

Chaffee, Zechariah, 86

Civil Libertarian, 6, 165–85; defined, 73–74, 199; and Group Advocate, distinction between, 74–75, 126–27; in criminal cases, and defendant, 119–20; characteristics of, 166–70, 178; and loyalty-security cases, 170–73; litigation and goals, 170–75; and criminal justice, 173–74; and civil rights cases, 174–75; and legal ideology, 175; what produces, 175–79; and judicial policy-